much love, from jamie

Jamie Barkes Pursley

Jamie Barkes Pursley

Copyright © 2017 Jamie Barkes Pursley

All rights reserved, including the right to reproduce this book or portions thereof in any form whatsoever without prior written permission.

ISBN: 1541080793

ISBN-13:978-1541080799

Cover by Scott Cuzzo Design at www.scottcuzzo.com

Hand lettering by RachelBee Designs at www.therachelmayo.com

DEDICATION

This book is dedicated to Aaron, Kayden, Dave, Kathy, Scott, Heather, and all of the Barkes and Pursley family and friends who loved Jamie.

The hand sketched words between the chapters are words her friends and family shared to describe Jamie and her journey.

Jamie's words are unedited, and a great reminder for all of us to live life fully with no regrets. Every day we have is a gift.

Enjoy Much Love, From Jamie.

~ Tammy Helfrich
Honored to be her friend

Jamie Barkes Pursley

CONTENTS

1 My Diagnosis
2 Deciding on Treatment
3 My First Chemo
4 The Dreaded Haircut
5 Shaving My Head
6 Birthday Girls...
7 Low counts = no chemo...
8 Christmas in Indiana
9 Starting the new year...
10 Good news...
11 Back to chemo finally..
12 Really feeling the chemo..
13 Genetic testing...
14 Chemo side effects..
15 Surgery new...
16 Moving to Kentucky
17 Surgery update...
18 Post surgery...
19 Moving on to radiation...

20 House hunting in KY..

21 Komen Race in Indy...

22 Our summer in a nutshell..

23 Happy 4th Anniversary to us...

24 October is Breast Cancer Awareness Month!

25 Happy Halloween!

26 Merry Christmas from the Pursleys!

27 Long time no blog...

28 Round Two..

29 The final countdown...

30 Surgery update...

31 Recovery update...

32 Back with the living...

33 Pathology report is in...

34 Home to Kentucky

35 Laying low...

36 So done with these drains...

37 Out with the drains!!!

38 Room to relax...

- 39 Pump, pump, pump it up!!!
- 40 ICU Kentucky/ Indianapolis
- 41 Back among the living
- 42 Back in the saddle...
- 43 Home again...
- 44 Figured out the error message...
- 45 "Rock" n chest
- 46 Na Nan A Nahhhh... Hey Hey Hey...GOODBYE!
- 47 Feeling good!!!!
- 48 Recovery Rebellion...
- 49 Susan G. Komen Race - Nashville
- 50 Crazy busy in Kansas....
- 51 Fall is here!
- 52 Happy Halloween!
- 53 My 3-month check up...
- 54 Surgery time again...
- 55 One last time
- 56 Heading home to heal...
- 57 Things are good!
- 58 One last surgery...

59 Surgery update...

60 Check me out!

61 Fall is here...

62 Third time's the charm...

63 The waiting game....

64

65 Giving thanks...

66 The results...

67 My plan...

68 Ringing in the New Year...

69 Finding the will to fight...

70 Another twist of fate...

71 My ups and downs

72 A time to believe...

73 The Legacy Book

74 Living it Lawrence style...

75 The power of perception...

76 Yet another surgery update...

77 Another bump in the road...

78 Side effects...ugh...

79 Race for the Cure - Kansas City

80 Time to get moving...

81 Loving our "normal" life!!

82 Costumes for the Cure!

83 Hanging on for the ride...

84 Happy Anniversary to me...

85 Go figure...

86 Results...

87 Woo Woo Woo...

88 Another day, another decision...

89 Happy New Year!

90 The book that captured my heart...

91 Time for the hair to go...

92 Activate Team Jamie Prayer Chain

93 The fun stuff....

94 This is a hard one...

ABOUT THE AUTHOR
(as written on her blog)

In 2006, while breast feeding my 9 month old daughter, I found a lump in my right breast. This lump changed my life. I was diagnosed with Stage III Breast Cancer and I was only 30 years old. I went through extensive treatment over the next year and became a survivor. 2 years later I had a recurrence in the same breast as the original tumor. Once again I went to extremes and fought to take my body back and became a survivor for the second time. Now at the age of 33, I have been told that the cancer has spread to my bones. This is the conversation that you never want to have with your oncologist. Not after the immense fight we have put up over the last 3 years. I am now considered to be Stage IV (metastatic breast cancer). It is a tough pill to swallow and we are struggling to understand why this has happened to us.

I have used this site to capture my journey since my original diagnosis. It is a link to my awesome support system and my outlet for the many feelings that this disease has forced upon our lives. To say that this has been a tough road is an understatement, but I will not lie down and let this disease run my life. I will fight with every ounce of my being to take my life back and put this cancer in check and I am more than happy to share my journey with you. You will find the site full of good news and bad. I tend to wear my heart on my sleeve so I don't leave much out when I write about what is going on. I also try to do it with a smile if I can so this burden doesn't get the best of our lives. I want to someday know that my daughter will be able to read this and understand my battle a little better. I hope it also enlightens those who read it and helps those going through similar situations to know that they are not alone.

Thanks for taking part in this journey with us... and we continue to be grateful for your positive thoughts and prayers. Your support has truly helped us as we continue to kick cancer butt in the Barkes/Pursley household. Please feel free to post your thoughts, pictures, questions or whatever suits your fancy- it gives me that extra boost of strength and courage knowing what an awesome team I have on my side!

Much love-

Jamie (Barkes) Pursley

Hope

1

MY DIAGNOSIS

Monday, October 25, 2006

My diagnosis...

Hi everyone-

Most of you are already aware of my recent diagnosis- for those of you that aren't I was told last Friday that I have moderately to poorly differentiated infiltrating ductal carcinoma. It is an invasive form of breast cancer. I had a lump in my right breast examined by my OB doctor last Monday on the 16th. He requested a sonogram be done on it that same day. That was inconclusive and they asked for a mammogram to be done the next day. That test was also inconclusive. All they could say was that there was a mass in my right breast- I could have told them that :) I do have a family history of breast cancer (my maternal grandma) so they had me visit with a general surgeon to get his opinion the same day as the mammogram. At my request he did a core biopsy and said he would have the results on Friday afternoon. He was certain due to my age that it was not cancer. Unfortunately he was wrong. We stayed in Kansas over the weekend to be with family and friends. Aaron and Kayden and I flew back to IN on Monday morning to meet with the doctor and find out more on Tuesday.

I can warn you that this is going to be a long email just so I can bring everyone up to date. I would have sent this yesterday- but honestly- I think my brain was on the verge of being overloaded with information. We were able to meet with the general surgeon to get more info on the diagnosis. He was as surprised as we were at the results. He has recommended pre-op chemotherapy to shrink the tumor- then a lumpectomy (surgically removing what is left of the tumor after the chemo) and then another round of chemo with some possible radiation. He referred me to a local oncologist that would be able to put together a treatment plan based on my specific cancer as well as identify the stage of the cancer.

Unfortunately- cancer at my age means that it is an aggressive form of cancer. It is rare- but not unheard of to be diagnosed at 30 and pre-menopause. The oncologist was able to fit us in yesterday afternoon and we spent about 2.5 hrs in his office. As of right now, we are waiting on the results of further testing on the biopsy done last week. These results will tell me if it is estrogen positive or negative. This helps determine what type of chemo drugs they will use in my treatment. It appears that there are no bumps under my arm at this time which is a positive sign that it may not have spread to my lymph nodes. Although that can't be determined for sure unless they do a lymph dissect - which they haven't done at this time. He did say that the tumor is mobile which means he can move it back and forth and up and down. This is a good sign that the tumor hasn't fixated itself to the interior wall of my breast! He told me that he was going to put me at a Stage IIA (T2 N0 M0 for those of you that are familiar with cancer lingo) based on the size (4cm x 4cm approximately), its mobility, and the fact that he can find no external evidence that it is in my lymph nodes yet. This is fairly good news as far as staging goes. Of course I would rather be something less then a Stage II- but it is much better then being a Stage IV.

He has recommend that we move forward with several tests that will help tell us what my heart function is at right now. Apparently a lot of the drugs can have a negative effect on your heart and they want to make sure you have a strong one before they start the drugs. Also- he is recommending that I talk with an oncologist at the IU Medical Hospital where they specialize in Breast Cancer. I have an appt. set up with another general surgeon- Dr.Robert Goulet 11/1/06 and also an oncologist Dr. Bryan Schneider on 11/6/06. It seems like a long time to wait- but unfortunately everybody in the region with breast cancer is trying to get in with these good doctors. In the meantime Dr. Jag the oncologist in Richmond is going to make sure I have all of the pre testing I need done so they don't have to waste any time in Indy. All we can do now is wait to hear what they have to say and then make a decision on when and what type of treatment they recommend.

Overall- it sounds like they should have me on chemo as soon as we can after meeting the second oncologist. Dr. Jag has mentioned that he would like to potentially do the chemo at a more rapid pace (once every 2 wks for 8 wks instead of once every 3 wks for 12 wks.) since I am young and should be able to take the strain it will put on my body. This is a very aggressive approach and has proven recently to have great success in the treatment of aggressive tumors. It will definitely be harder on me but most likely worth the pain if it helps accelerate the removal of the cancer. That would put me in for surgery at the beginning of the year- with another round of chemo after that. Hard to tell though until we hear more about the test results and hear what Dr. Schneider says.

I will lose my hair- and I will be extremely fatigued from the chemo according to Dr. Jag. He already wrote me a prescription for a wig. Ugh. Can't say I was thinking of adding wig shopping to my list of things I need to shop for- but if that's what it takes then bring it on! Aaron has already stated the obvious that I am not allowed to make fun of him losing his hair anymore since I am going to beat him to it- ha ha! He has been extremely supportive throughout all of this news. If he can make me laugh he has-and he has helped me digest this information and make sense of it. Kayden of course has no idea what is in store for us as a family- but hopefully she is young enough that she won't remember mommy being sick. I truly hope that is the case.

I can't tell you all enough how much I appreciate your support and thoughts and prayers during this time of uncertainty. It is going to be a long haul- but with the amazing support system that we have it is going to make it that much easier for us to overcome this. I know everyone is wondering what they can do to help- and until I know more about when and how they will treat me...we are stuck in a holding pattern. I promise to let you all know if we need anything. Several people have asked for our address so I am going to include it so you have it. I will keep you updated as we get more information. It should be in the next couple of days. Please feel free to call either of us- if I can't talk just leave a message and I will call you back. If I missed anyone please send this email on to them. You all know me well enough to know that I am not going to let this thing beat me. Wish us luck as we get ready to kick this thing! Talk to you all soon!

Lots of love-

Jamie, Aaron and Kayden

Admirable

2

DECIDING ON TREATMENT

Thursday, November 2, 2006

Deciding on treatment...

Hi everyone-

I am sitting here thinking about how to put my thoughts into this email- it is kind of hard to do when I have so much I want to say. As most of you know I can be a bit wordy at times :) But it is important to me to convey how much it means to me to have each of you worried for me and offering the moon to help make it better. It is amazing to me how far my news has traveled already and I am overwhelmed (in a good way) with the support of the friends and family that I have around me (near and far). It actually makes me smile to think that I have touched enough people over my 30 years to have created such a huge foundation of support during a time like this. That's a good feeling. Something like this puts things in perspective for you pretty quickly. I won't get all sappy on you- I just wanted to say thank you and keep it up! It is helping- a lot!

As far as our appt. at IU Cancer Center this week....we got a lot more information that I will try to compress so I can pass it on to you. I was able to meet w/ both the surgeon and the oncologist on Monday. My mom and Aaron both accompanied me to the meetings. The general consensus is that the tumor is between 5-6cm (not 4) and that there are some suspicious lymph nodes under my arm. This changes the cancer lingo a bit taking me from a T2 N0 M0 to a T3 N1 M0. It basically means that they think it has spread to my lymph nodes. Not good news unfortunately. They made a decision to do an ultrasound biopsy of my auxiliary nodes this afternoon. I had a CAT scan last night to check for cancer in my chest and abdomen-no results on that until later this week.

The treatment plan they intend to follow will be 16 weeks of chemo then a lumpectomy, then radiation therapy on the tumor sight (possibly on my armpit as well for the lymph nodes if they prove to be positive for the cancer). There are a lot of things that can change this plan- mainly tests they are in the process of running now, as well as some genetic testing that I have decided to do. But for now- assuming the cancer hasn't spread from the breast and lymph nodes into other portions of my body- I will be in chemo for 4 months total. It will be once every 2 weeks with a shot 24 hrs. after the chemo to help boost my immune system. I will be driving to and from Indy for the chemo and then the next day for the shot. No need to stay here since it is only 1.5 hrs from our house. The chemo will be starting early next week based on what we find out from the CAT scan and today's biopsy. It is hard for them to predict how I will react to the chemo as far as fatigue and sickness. They have assured me that they can help manage the vomiting and nausea. The fatigue is unfortunately something I will just have to deal with. My oncologist told me his goal is for me to NOT throw up at all during the chemo! That sounds good to me!!!!!!

They have tried to not overwhelm us with too much information about down the road stuff- we are focusing now on the present and finding out everything we possibly can about the tumor and the lymph nodes. Hopefully this helps bring you up to date on what is going on here for now. Sorry I haven't been able to send this out until today. I know a lot of you were wondering. My parents are both here today to help with Kayden as we get through all of the Dr. appts. this week. I truly feel that we have assembled a great team of doctors that have only the breast- I mean best care in mind for me during this :) HA HA! I feel like maybe we were transferred to Richmond for a reason-so I could be treated by a group of very strong doctor's that are on the cutting edge of all of the cancer treatments available currently. I have faith that we are making the right decision in choosing to be treated there. If somewhere along the line that feeling changes for any reason I will be the first to go elsewhere for another opinion. Again- pass this on to anyone I missed and let me know so I can add them to my list. Better go for now- I have to leave for the biopsy. Wish me luck! Thanks again and we will touch base soon!

Much love from Indiana-

Jamie, Aaron and Kayden

Real

3

MY FIRST CHEMO

Friday, November 10, 2006

My first chemo...

Hi everyone-

I thought I would take a few minutes to fill you in on the week. I did in fact have my first round of chemo on Monday morning. We met w/my oncologist Dr. Schneider first thing. He unfortunately did confirm that my lymph node biopsy came back as positive for cancer. This bit of information is unfortunate- but it will not change our mode of treatment. I had honestly expected it and can move forward now knowing that we have identified the issue and will resolve it at the time of the surgery with the removal of my lymph nodes. There are long term issues with this process....but in my mind- long term is a term that sounds pretty good to me right about now. We will learn more about the process closer to the surgery. Meanwhile- we also were informed that my chest scan was clear but there was a 7mm spot on my liver that has shown up. There are many different things this spot can be, of course one of them is cancer. Due to the size and location of the spot- my doctor has made the decision to keep an eye on the spot to see if it gets smaller or larger or stays the same through my first couple of rounds of chemo. Then they will do another CAT scan to check it out. I have had trauma to my liver back in 98 from my car accident so there is a good chance that it might just be scar tissue. Dr. Schneider isn't too concerned yet- he says it wouldn't change the mode of treatment at this time- so we are going to move forward as if the cancer has not metastasized. I am confident that he has made the right decision regarding this issue as of now. So no worries yet....

As far as the chemo goes. It was a pretty overwhelming process. I got to sit in a room of many other patients getting the same thing done to them. It was very hard to see. I felt very out of place because I swear I was the youngest person in there. I won't lie- I shed some tears here and there. I was lucky enough to get a great chemo nurse who was very understanding of my situation. She kept apologizing that I wasn't able to have a more private setting for my first round. It was all done through an IV in my right forearm. I will hopefully have a port (small drum like object inserted under the skin that can be used to infuse the drugs without going through a vein every time) by my next round on Nov. 20th. The chemo is very hard on your veins so the goal is to get my port in as soon as possible. They can even do it the same day as my next chemo (which is the plan for now). From start to finish it was only about 2 hrs. It shouldn't be that long next time with the port though- and a few less tears :) I left feeling pretty normal. On the way home though I came down with what I can only describe as the worst case of motion sickness ever. It pretty much sucked. They had given me some steroids in my IV to help w/ the nausea....but unfortunately it wasn't much help. Mom suggested we stop off at an outlet candle store to find some candles to help hide Roxy's skunk smell in the house- and I mustered up the courage to do a little shopping. For those of you that I haven't mentioned it to....Roxy was sprayed over a week ago and we are STILL dealing with the stink in the house. It is enough to make you throw up alone without the chemo. We found a couple of candles and I was able to take my mind off of the anticipation of getting sicker. I went to bed early and slept through the night. Woke up feeling pretty good Tuesday overall. Wednesday and Thursday have been jammie days w/ a forced shower. I feel pretty out of it and overall tired and achey. Not too nauseous though. I can't really complain. I have eaten dinner w/ the family two nights in a row and been able to watch Kayden play. She even took her first tentative steps on Tues. She is already on her own as of tonight with up to 4-5 steps unassisted at her own will. VERY COOL to watch! In addition to that she has her two top teeth popping in as of Sunday. It is like she didn't want me to miss any of her milestones this week so she got them all out of the way early :)

I know many of you have called and emailed and sent packages. I am sorry that I haven't been able to get back w/ everyone. But please know that each message helps lift my spirits. I promise if you call and I feel up to it I will answer- same goes for emails. Keep them all coming. My dad is working on a web site that we can use to post updates and you can post your own messages and pictures. Hopefully it will be up and running next week sometime. My next treatment is 11/20 then 12/4 and finally 12/18 for this particular round of drugs. It is supposed to start to accumulate in my system over time so we still are not sure what to expect. Just know that I am not in any pain- just pretty uncomfortable overall. Nothing I can't deal with! I promise! Talk w/ you all soon.

Much love from Indiana-

Jamie, Aaron and Kayden

Strong

4

THE DREADED HAIRCUT

Monday, November 27, 2006

The dreaded haircut...

Hi everyone-

Happy Thanksgiving! I just wanted to let everyone know how things were going here for us in Indiana. Aaron's mom (Kitty) came out and stayed with us for a week after my chemo week was over last time. I was feeling really good and we were able to spend most of the week shopping and decorating the house (something I have been wanting to do since we moved here and haven't taken the time to do!). I must say we did quite a good job! Now that I am stuck indoors for awhile might as well enjoy the view :) Aaron's dad was able to join us at the end of the week and we all enjoyed some fun time with Kayden and RV shopping for his parents.

After a week of feeling great I had to buck it up and go back in for round two this past Tuesday. It was moved to Tues. this time because they wanted to do my port surgery the same day as the chemo. We had to be at the hospital at 5:30am to check in for surgery. Then after the surgery was done (I was under so I don't remember much) Aaron took me up to visit with Dr. Schneider. He is very insistent that he sees me each time we come in. He did some external measurements of the tumor (which he will do each time) and checked on how the chemo had affected me first round. Unfortunately the measurements are still the same on the tumor- but he agreed with me that it does feel less firm which is a good thing. He was adamant that we should not expect to see a huge palpable change in it with just one round of chemo- or even two for that matter. The best news of all is that he was able to give us a tentative yes on possibly coming home for Christmas!!!!! YEAH! But of course I don't want to get too excited until it is closer. A lot of things could stop that from happening...but for now we have our fingers crossed.

As far as chemo goes- we were lucky enough to get a room to ourselves this time and Aaron and I both napped through most of the actual process. By the time we were done getting the chemo and getting some prescriptions filled we were headed home around 5:00pm. LONG DAY to say the least! It has been a bit rough this week due to the combo of chemo and surgery. The port is pretty uncomfortable- but I will get used to it as it heals and the swelling goes down. Dr. Goulet put it under my left arm just below where your armpit is so that it will not interfere with the radiation later. It has taken some pain meds to help me through the discomfort- but it hasn't been unbearable. Between those pain meds and the anti-nausea drugs I am feeling a bit off overall this week. Dizzy, queasy and tired pretty much cover most of the bases. It has lasted longer this time in comparison to the last round. But some of this may be due to the addition of the surgery this time.

My brother and dad flew in this Wed. night to spend the Thanksgiving weekend here (my mom has been here since Sunday). We postponed Turkey dinner until Sat. night when I was able to eat more of it. It was a pretty laid back weekend- we did a good job of putting some dents in the couch and catching up on movies. I was able to get out and do some low key shopping (more like leaning on the stroller or shopping cart and looking at people shop but who cares! It's still better than being on the couch!) this afternoon. That was a big step up in the activity level so everyone is happy here I was feeling well enough to leave the house.

As you can see in the Thanksgiving video we downloaded- my hair has been cut, once short early last week, and then again this weekend REALLY short since it has really started to fall out. I've been told nicely that it is a very "granola" look for me :) Ha Ha Robin :) I think it is more GI Jane- but who cares- it will be gone next week anyways...why stress over what can't do anything about?! I am finally at peace with losing it and will be able to totally shave it here in a couple of days. Needless to say- we are taking it day by day and each day seems to be better than the last. Have a great week- check back on this awesome website my dad has set up for updates whenever you can- just bookmark it and we will be using it to help get out info as we move forward with treatment. Feel free to sign the guest book or email me directly- whichever you prefer! Talk to you soon!

Much love and turkey leftovers from Indiana-

Jamie, Aaron and Kayden

Gutsy

5

SHAVING MY HEAD

Sunday, December 3, 2006

Shaving my head...

Hi everyone!

I couldn't sleep tonight so I thought I would put together some thoughts before I head back in for chemo on Monday. It has been a great week for me. I started feeling better late Monday night/ early Tuesday. I still have to take naps sometimes during the day...Kayden and I go down about the same time in the afternoon :) But overall I am feeling back to normal this weekend. We had the Hill's kids holiday party today at a bowling alley here in Richmond. Kayden got all dressed up to go see Santa and get her picture taken with him. When I took her up to put her on his lap she looked at me like I was handing her off to an alien. She wanted off his lap and slap some quick on it! The photographer got a couple of quick shots before she totally freaked! I haven't seen her be afraid of anyone before- must have been the beard!

I hear there was some ugly weather back in Kansas. We were lucky enough to miss it here. It was nice up until Friday and then we got some extreme winds and the temperature finally dropped, but nothing compared to what you guys got hit with. It was pretty chilly today but we still went out during the day without coats. Not bad compared to last year this time. We had 9 inches of snow on the day we left the hospital with Kayden. Speaking of which- she turns 1 this Thursday! Hard to believe how fast it has gone. Guess you can say it was an eventful year for us.

I finally shaved my head completely this past Wed. It is quite a sight to see yourself with no hair. Thank god my head is not oddly shaped. It actually doesn't look too bad without the hair. I let out a breath of relief when she turned me around to look at it. That same day I walked into a store without any hat or bandana on (feeling pretty proud that I was ok without anything) and I shocked a poor little girl and her sister. The older one kept telling her little sister to stop staring. It was an odd moment for me...to draw that type of attention, especially from a child. I'll be honest- it brought a sigh from me that I can't explain as anything other then sadness. It is weird to know that strangers are looking at me and know that I must have cancer- it is such a personal thing to have out there for everyone to see. I can tell that it makes people uncomfortable at first and then you see the...ohhh it must be cancer cross their face. It is hard not to be bothered by that- I don't want people to feel sorry for me or feel bad for me. I want to tell them "It's ok- I am OK!" But that isn't feasible either. It's been a bit of a mental adjustment for me to not worry about it too much. So that has been my battle this week-not worrying about what other people think of my baldness. I do have two wigs that I can use, but I don't feel right in them either yet. So for now it is bald at home and bandana or hat in public... in time I think I will find my comfort zone and hopefully everyone else will get used to seeing me this way! Kayden on the other hand- hasn't even batted an eye at the new do. Guess I am still mommy with or without hair- good to know it wasn't based on my good looks in general! Ha! Ha! Such a comedian at 1:30 am in the morning. To be honest- as far as feeling wise- I feel great bald. It is total low maintenance! Shorter showers, less get ready time. I could get used to this- although I wasn't quite sure where to stop my make-up at first :)

Anyways. I wanted to say hi to all of you that are checking back to the website. I absolutely love the postings. I check it every day to see what is new. I hope you all continue to leave messages, it truly brightens my day to read them. I wish I could take time to respond to each message to say thank you and catch up- but for now I have to realize that that is not possible. Just know that I appreciate the thoughts, cards, and care packages with all of my heart. Better try to go get some sleep. We are off to Indy tomorrow to pick my mom up at the airport and then I plan to get some more Christmas shopping out of the way while I can! Think of me on Monday as I get #3 out of the way- only 5 more to go after this one!!!!! I will post again later in the week after I start to feel better. Please pass the word to anyone that doesn't already have this web site yet. It has worked out good so far! Hope everyone has a great week!

Much love from the middle of the night-

Jamie

Laughter

6

BIRTHDAY GIRLS

Wednesday, December 6, 2006

Birthday girls...

Hi Everyone!

It is about that time that I checked back in to let you all know how things are going. I am officially 30 something now. Ugh! I had a great birthday yesterday! It was also a really good chemo week for me last week. It was WAY better then the last round w/ the combo surgery. Overall I felt better sooner and the queasiness was not near as bad. I would say the only downfall has been that I am more tired this time. I spent some time in bed Tues.- Friday but it was not because I felt sick, more so because I was wiped out. I am also coming down with a pretty annoying head cold that has messed with me the past couple of days. Hopefully I can kick that soon so I can enjoy my off week. Aaron's mom and dad and sister will be here on Thursday night to spend the weekend here.

My appt. went well this week with Dr. Schneider (the oncologist). My port is healing well and he was very impressed with my bald head. He measured the tumor at 5 cm x 5.5 cm (used to be 5 cm x 6 cm). So that was great news! It is definitely feeling different as far as to the touch which means that what we are doing is making some positive progress. I made an appt. for some genetic counseling/testing to be done in January at the same hospital I am doing my chemo at. If I qualify for the testing (they counsel you first and do a family history to see if it is necessary) then they will be able to test to tell if I carry a particular gene that is connected to cancer. This information may change our decision on how to proceed with my surgery. It could mean the difference between doing a lumpectomy (taking only the tumor out of my breast) or a mastectomy (taking the full breast)- or possibly a bilateral mastectomy (taking both breast) and possibly the ovaries too. There are many factors that will play into the decision. I wish I could give you a better explanation but I am still a bit in the dark on the subject so hopefully we will learn more in January and I will share that with you when we know more. So for now we are celebrating the smaller measurement! Also- it looks like our plans to be home during Christmas week are still on. In fact- I will actually be able to spend one extra week in KS w/ Kayden due to the rescheduling of my Jan chemo date to the 8th instead of the 1st. YEAH! I call it my Chemo Vacation :)

We were able to celebrate Kayden's birthday on Thursday- I was feeling pretty good by the evening. She was quite the birthday princess. She drug around a helium balloon most of the afternoon and tried out some of her birthday toys before I could get them wrapped. Sneaky little thing! She gets her mind set on doing something and if you try to stop her she is like a mad bull. She's proven to have a pretty big attitude for such a little girl. Hopefully it is a phase! We invited over our neighbors (they have a big family w/ 7 kids) to partake in the party. Needless to say there was not lack of noise or activity as she opened her gifts and enjoyed her birthday cupcake. It was a fun day for everyone. She went to bed with a glazed look of contentment on her face. By the way...she loves the cards and opening boxes that are sent here for her and mommy. It is a favorite activity around here! So thanks again to everyone that has sent gifts and cards for us both!

As far as mental health goes this week.....still doing pretty good overall. It has been weird to feel so wiped and not just want to pull the covers up and wish it all away. Trust me- I have those moments where that is exactly what I do. Usually Roxy or Uno are there to help me keep me company under the covers :) I have been so fortunate to have such support and help w/ the house and Kayden during this past month and a half. My mom and Aaron's mom have stepped up and between the two of them there have been only a few days with me on my own. Kayden has been in Grandma heaven! Every day is a party for her lately.

Unfortunately, all of the help this round has left me able to fall into the easy couch/nap/bed routine where I forget to motivate myself to get up when I do feel better and do something active. This was a problem that I faced this week for the first time since I was feeling better overall, but still had the help around the house. It was too easy to let my mom do all the work while I was "taking it easy" on the couch. Aaron brought his concern to my attention this weekend as a concerned bystander/husband. He helped me see the potential hazards of how letting the "take it easy" road could easily become a habit down the road that wouldn't be an easy habit to break. He is right- I don't want the cancer to become an excuse for me to become complacent. Yes I need to maintain my health and listen to my body- but it doesn't give me a license to be lazy. That is not fair to anyone around me, especially down the road when life goes back to normal (which will happen). So we had a heart to heart with my mom, Aaron and I and we talked about how important it is to stay physically active as much as my body will allow me to both during my chemo weeks and my off weeks. It is not easy to admit that you maybe aren't trying hard enough so it was a humbling experience- not one I ever expected to have. But this cancer has a sneaky way of creeping up on you and trying to take advantage anywhere you let it. I let it get the best of me this week as I sat around. This cancer doesn't get to take my motivation to be a good mommy and wife away from me- I put my foot down. No more... it is my personal goal from here on out to not let myself turn into a hermit afraid to be physically active. I know I will feel better for it physically and mentally, and as a member of this wonderful family! Hope this message finds everyone well. That is it for now- I will post again next week!

Much love NOT from the couch-

Jamie

Determined.

7

LOW COUNTS = NO CHEMO

Thursday, December 21, 2006

Low counts=no chemo...

Hi Everyone!

I hope this update finds you almost finished with your holiday shopping and wrapping! I think I am the most organized I have ever been this year. I was done wrapping last week!

It has been a tough week here for us. We got news on Monday while we were at the hospital for chemo that my white blood cell counts were too low (nuetrophyls were at 700 instead of 1200 for those of you that are familiar with the counts) for me to get the chemo. We made an appointment to come back on Wed. (yesterday) to try again. They told me to go home and rest and my body, in time, would naturally bring my counts back to where they needed to be. So I did- and we went back yesterday for round two. Unfortunately, my counts had gone down even further to 400 instead of 700. It was hard news for the nurses to deliver- they all knew that I was really wanting to be home (in KS) for Christmas this year. Dr. Schneider's nurse, Danielle (whom I love), came up to the chemo infusion center personally to deliver the news that again I would not be able to get chemo due to my counts. She explained that the shot (Nuelasta) I get after chemo each time is supposed to help keep my counts higher than 1200. The cold that I was fighting last week had apparently taken up all of the good cells in my fight to get over it. That left my body weaker than it normally would have been when it came time to get the chemo. This is my version of what she said- it isn't the technical version she gave me :) Layman's terms. So again we came home to ride it out and try again this Friday. I have made arrangements to get my blood work done in Richmond in case my counts again are too low- that way we don't waste the gas to drive to Indy for nothing. I am tentatively hopeful that it will happen- but am also realistic that it might not. Danielle explained that most likely I was at my lowest point on Wed. and it usually takes 3-4 days for the counts to come back up. She is as determined to get me home for Christmas as I am. If I cannot get treatment on Friday then the earliest I can get in next week is Wed. We already have me on the schedule in case that is what needs to happen. By then I will for sure be able to do it- it just means that I will feel pretty rough through the weekend.

On a positive note, we were able to meet several people while we were waiting in the infusion lobby on Monday and also on Wed. I exchanged information with 3 different women that are all going through different stages of their chemo. It is amazing how quickly you can strike up a conversation with a complete stranger when you have such a common bond. One of the women even lives here in Richmond. I was happy to have someone to chat with and share things with and I look forward to getting to know each of them better! So it appears even though we weren't able to get chemo- I was there in Indy for a reason- to meet those women!

We haven't made any decisions on when we will be heading back to KS yet- it really depends on when the chemo happens. I can tell you that even if I get treatment next Wed. we will still come back. I hate the most that it will shorten Aaron's time in KS since he has to fly back on the 1st to be at work on the 2nd. I on the other hand, am able to stay that week of the 1st and will most likely head back on the 6th. I knew when we first made the plans to come home that there was a possibility of set backs like this. It is just hard to actually have to face them. I am now quarantined to the "bubble" (our bedroom) with an occasional dog or cat for company, my brother's extensive movie collection, and of course the latest "People". I am determined to not get sick again and with my counts so low I am extremely prone to infection right now. So for now Aaron's mom is taking care of Kayden (she was coughing a lot yesterday). Aaron slept on the couch last night since he was feeling like he might be coming down with something. We are doing everything in our power to keep me feeling well. Just a note of caution to the people that I may be seeing when we are home--Please be sure to do your best to wash your hands between now and then (tip: scrub for at least 30 seconds and use the paper towel to shut off the water so you don't pick back up your germs). This time of the year is horrible for germ passing and washing your hands will help cut down the spreading of germs tremendously. My counts should be back up by then but it will still be important to limit my exposure to colds and flu as much as possible.

I am doing ok with the news. It was bound to happen sometime, it just figures that it would be now when we have plans for the holidays. Oh well--this too shall pass. I was pretty discouraged Monday but have since put things in perspective and realize that

I need to listen to my body and in time it will be ready. It has given Aaron and I a reality check that I am susceptible and we need to be sure that we are taking every precaution necessary to keep me well. I wish I had better news for you to be reading, but I wanted everyone to know what our situation is for the trip back to KS. I will let you know if chemo happens Friday or not...keep your fingers crossed, think positive thoughts, and say a prayer for us. I know we will have a wonderful Christmas no matter what state we wake up in that day, but just in case, I made sure to send Santa a text message to let him know he may need to bring Kayden's toys to Indiana this year :) He appreciated the heads up and is on standby and ready to go wherever she may be........

Much love from the "bubble"-

Jamie

Human

8

CHRISTMAS IN INDIANA

Friday, December 22, 2006

Christmas in Indiana...

Hi Everyone!

Well.....it looks like we will be spending Christmas in Indiana this year. I got my lab work done in Richmond this morning and my counts were still too low to do the chemo. I have moved from 400 to 520 on my absolute nuetrophyl count (ANC), and my white blood cell count is up from 2 to 2.1- but it needs to be at 4.5 to be ok. We are disappointed- but have to look at the big picture...the chemo is what is most important and we realize that. My parents and brother have decided to come to us to celebrate Christmas. They will arrive Sunday morning and Kitty will head home to be with Bill and Jen and Nate for the holiday. Scott has to work Tues. so he will fly home on Christmas afternoon and my parents stay and catch a ride home in the RV with us next week. I am excited to have them here to celebrate with us- hopefully it will provide some well needed Christmas cheer around here after the week we have had. On the bright side...at least I will feel good for Christmas!

I am scheduled for chemo now on Wed. of next week at 8:30am (my Dr. is confident that I will be good to go by then). Just in case I will get my blood work done on Tues. afternoon to check my counts one last time. Then we are going to hop into the RV and head on home to KS when I am done with chemo on Wed. It will shorten our original plans and I won't feel 100% through most of the weekend- but we still really want to come home. I think I need to come home to rejuvenate my positive attitude :) I am a little low on positive thoughts today- I have to wonder if I didn't end up on Santa's naughty list this year! Just kidding. So the plans are to be home next Wed. night. Aaron will stay through the 1st and I will stay through the 6th. For those of you that know what a horrible packer I am (I procrastinate and take forever to pack)- you can appreciate the fact that I am already packed for the trip (just in case we got to leave today). That tells you how ready I am to be home :) I hope everyone has a wonderful Christmas and we can't wait to see you soon!

Much love from Indiana-

Jamie, Aaron and Kayden

Loyal

9

STARTING THE NEW YEAR

Thursday, January 4, 2007

Starting the new year...

Happy New Year to everyone!

Sorry it has been a bit since my last update. It has been busy for us since Christmas. After finding out that my counts were once again too low for chemo last Thursday, my parents and Aaron, Kayden and I hopped into the RV and headed back to KS for a much needed trip. With my doctor's approval of course :) It was a short trip- but I came home feeling rejuvenated mentally. I told Aaron that needed to refill my positive attitude because I was running a little low after the constant bad news on my counts. I was able to see a mixture of friends and family in both Manhattan and Topeka over the long weekend. Of course I wish I had been able to see more of everyone, but our time was limited. I was just thankful that I was able to be there at all. It is hard to explain the feeling of comfort that washed over me as we pulled into town. It was like the feeling of a huge warm hug. All of the love and support you have all sent us to Indiana has done wonders for our spirits...but nothing compares to being there to feel it personally. Kayden has a ball opening more presents and entertaining everyone with her constant activity and chatter- which was very funny to those of you that don't have to chase her all day! Her uncle Nate was finally home from Iraq and excited to see how much she has changed over the last 5 months. We are very glad to have him home safe and sound- and hopefully for good! We are keeping our fingers crossed.

She was also able to meet some of our friends she hasn't seen since she was just a baby. I do believe she may be setting the record for unofficial uncles and aunties. She will be one lucky little girl with the plethora of unnecessary information she will obtain from these uncles in particular. I can already tell it is a race to see who can teach her what she doesn't need to know first! Got to keep an eye on those boys! And it is certain that she will continue to evolve into the fashion diva she is already starting to be with the help of her aunt Jen, Uncle Scott, and of course Auntie Robin! What other 1 year olds can accessorize with such flare? Thanks again to everyone for making our trip home so wonderful!

I am sitting here typing away on my new Apple laptop my dad got me for work. It will make it easier for me to update my web site, even from bed if needed! As far as chemo goes this week I was scheduled to go in yesterday morning to Indy to get my blood count and hopefully chemo. My mom rode back with us from KS and she came to the appointment with me. Unfortunately it was a NO GO again. My white blood cell counts were even screwier then last time. The Dr. is still scratching his head at was is causing the delay in the counts stabilizing back to normal. He decided to run some additional lab work and also called for a bone marrow biopsy to be done while we were there in the hospital. It was a fairly painless procedure. They sedated me so I was awake but didn't care and took some tissue from my back left hip. Apparently I chatted throughout the whole procedure (surprise) and even admitted that I knew I was talking too much like when I am have had a few too many glasses of wine. My friends will laugh at this I am sure :) I was able to talk with Danielle, Dr. Schneider's nurse, yesterday after we got home- she explained that they wanted to get a better understanding of what was happening in my marrow since that is where the blood is produced. The main concern is that the cancer could have spread there- the biopsy will be able to tell us if it is there or not. We hope this is not the case as that would be considered incurable metastasized cancer. There are many other things that could be causing the counts to be up and down- so I have promised myself not to get too upset (easier said then done) until we have more information. They expect to have results back by the end of the day Friday or Monday at the latest. I started to look up bone cancer online and decided that wasn't going to help me stay positive- I encourage you to wait as well. I know that what ever God hands me in the coming days will be something that I can handle. Isn't that the rule? God only gives us what he knows we can handle? Well- I have to trust that is the case. I know that in order for me to live the life I want to live as a wonderful wife and mother, friend and daughter- that I will do whatever it takes to make sure I am around to make the most of what I have built in my life. I appreciate all of your support and prayers. I can honestly say that my prayers have included all of you in them as well as wishes for positive thoughts. No matter what we find out this next week I am prepared to deal with it. Aaron and I have vowed to keep our heads up and to support each other when the other is down. He is my rock when I need it and I am trying to be his. Our families have continued to support us as we struggle to make sense of the situation...without them I know we would not be in the good place that we are now. I love them very much for that. I had better go for now. I promise to let you know what we find out.

Much love and prayers-

Jamie

Courageous

10

GOOD NEWS

Friday, January 5, 2007

Good news...

Well...I got the call late yesterday afternoon from Dr. Schneider. The cancer HAS NOT spread into my bones or marrow. Whew!!!!!! Talk about a sigh of relief. I couldn't stop shaking after I got off the phone. I guess I didn't realize how worried I was until it was all over. I had a cable repairman at the house looking at our internet connection when Dr. Schneider called. He stood there waiting for me while I talked w/ the Dr. It was all I could do not to hug him when I got off the phone! "Hey Leo the cable guy... good news....I don't have terminal cancer!!"" Bet he doesn't get to hear that at every house call.

According to the biopsy slide, my marrow looks like it is on it's way to recovery. He said it didn't look as if it was infected with a virus either. He said he had consulted with at least 12 different doctors on the case and they are all as stumped as he is as to why my counts have taken so long to stabilize. He had a hematology/leukemia doctor look at the slide with him at IU and they are both in agreement that the marrow looks healthy enough, it just isn't producing the white blood cells like they want it too. He said that there is a slim possibility that my immune system could be attacking my white blood cells (like with Lupus) but that would not show in the tests they did. We are scheduled to see the doctor on Monday morning to discuss where we go from here. They are going to do another blood draw to check the counts again. If by some miracle my counts are up they will administer the chemo on Monday. I may have to meet with the hematologist also. I am definitely feeling better now with the good news, even though they don't know what it is yet that is causing the low counts. Just about anything is better then the cancer having spread. It is about time we got a break in this journey. Thank you for your prayers and thoughts- I know they helped! I will update again after I meet with the Dr. on Monday. Have a great weekend! I know we will!

Much love and excitement from the Pursley house-

Jamie, Aaron and Kayden

Fighter

11

BACK TO CHEMO FINALLY

Tuesday, January 9, 2007

Back to chemo finally...

Hi Everyone!

We met with my doctor yesterday morning to further discuss the situation of my counts. He talked about several different options he has come up with that we could revert to as plan B if my counts did not stabilize this week. One of the options was attempting to do another Nuelasta shot to give my immune system a boost (this was not an option until now because the last shot I got from Chemo in Dec. needed to be completely out of my system). We also discussed the possibility of needing to move forward with surgery (removal of the entire breast) as early as the end of this week if we were not able to get the chemo in. He has met with my surgeon already and Dr. Goulet had agreed to get me on the schedule if needed. Then we would do the chemo after surgery when my immune system was better ready to deal with it. After much discussion about our options he repeated to me that his ideal situation would be to get me in for chemo that day and get me back to my normal schedule. He sent me off to wait for my blood test results and we all crossed our fingers. Aaron and I sat in anticipation in the infusion center lobby. Either Danielle would show up or I would get a phone call at the desk saying come back downstairs to talk w/ Dr. Schneider again (meaning my counts were not back up), or a nurse would call me back to the infusion center to get my chemo (meaning my counts were up where they needed to be). It was a long 45 minutes of hearing everyone else's name called, and Aaron messing with me pretending my name had been called and I hadn't heard it...meanie. Just when I found myself starting to have visions of some new double D's in my near future- they called my name. I looked up expecting to see the receptionist waving a phone in her hand for me to answer....but it was not a phone call for me. It was the chemo nurse with a big smile waving me back to get my chemo! The nurses were all congratulating me on my great counts. It turns out my white count had gone from 1.2 to 8.4 since last Wed. (well above the limit) Yeah! Back on schedule! It took about 4 hours since they did the new drug this time (Taxol). I am feeling great today- and hope to continue to feel good. This drug isn't supposed to be as hard on my body as the last drug. We will see. It is still going to be a test of my immune system to make sure I don't get so low again. If that happens we may have to go back to the drawing board. So for now- no surgery until after chemo is finished assuming I can keep on schedule from here on out. Keep your fingers crossed and I will keep you updated! Thanks for your prayers and cards. We continue to be amazed at the support system we have in place. You are all amazing! Talk with you soon-

Much love from Indiana-

Jamie, Aaron and Kayden

Genuine

12

REALLY FEELING THE CHEMO

January 26, 2007

Really feeling the Chemo...

Hi Everyone!

Well- it has been several weeks since I have made an entry so this is going to be a long one. I promise I didn't fall off the face of the Earth as some of you have wondered. I have gotten several calls to make sure I was doing ok :) Glad to say I have been keeping so busy I haven't had time to ramble. I was feeling well after my 1st Taxol treatment, which was my last entry. I kept busy trying to catch up on work for my dad. I didn't realize how behind I was! Overall- the first round of Taxol was easier on me then the AC treatments (1st drug I had). I was sore and had some massive headaches, but my appetite was still good and I was able to function on a daily basis....just a little uncomfortable for the first week. The second week was smooth sailing. We even had a house guest over the weekend. Christy- a co-worker of Aaron's at the plant that had moved to Tennessee was with us Friday and Saturday night. She attended a surprise birthday party for another co-worker of Aaron's with us while in town. We had a great time! It was good to get out and socialize with everyone even though I am not able to participate in any alcoholic beverages :) We were home by midnight and ended up with a sick baby all night...our first ear infection. Ugh! Christy was a huge help throughout the night- we tag teamed it and were able to get a little sleep. Kayden is now on antibiotics and doing much better! It was not fun to see her in such pain. Hopefully we don't have to do that again anytime soon.

I had an appt. with the genetic counselor at IU on Jan. 17th. It was a long meeting with an overload of information. I thought Aaron was going to fall out of his chair in agony after the first 1 1/2 hours, but he hung in there. Sitting still is not one of his strong suits. There was a lot of complicated information given to us that I am not going to try to explain at this time. The bottom line is that there seems to be only a 10% chance that my cancer was caused by a hereditary gene. As I have said before...we hope that this genetic information will assist us in making some of our surgery decisions. If the cancer is due to an inherited gene- then my chances of reoccurrence go way up. Hence the possibility that we may opt to be proactive and have both of my breasts removed as well as my ovaries. We were warned that the results can come back as unverifiable- which means they can't say for sure if I am positive or negative for the cancer gene. This was good to know- so we don't put all of our eggs in the genetic results basket when discussing surgery. Once we get our results back (21 days) I will hopefully be able to fill you in more.

Aaron had to head back to Topeka on the 21st for work meetings and I was scheduled for chemo on the 22nd, so my friend from college, Julie (Jump) Mitchell flew up to stay a few days with me to help out. I picked her up on Sunday night late- about the same time the Colts won their play off game. I was sure we were going to get stuck in the game traffic- but we got lucky and missed most of it. She took me to chemo on Monday and Leslie watched Kayden for me. It was a good meeting with Dr. Schneider. The tumor is still measuring similar to last appt. but continues to feel different to the touch. It sounds like we will be discussing surgery more at my next appt. He did confirm that we will only be doing 4 total treatments of the Taxol. He didn't feel it was necessary to make up the AC treatment I missed due to my counts. My blood counts were good again this time and I was able to proceed with my 2nd round of Taxol as planned. They altered my steroids a bit this round because they thought last time my headaches had been caused by withdrawal from the steroid, dexamethosone. The first time they gave the steroid in my IV all at once the same time as the chemo. For this round they had me take it orally the night before chemo, the morning of and also the next day. This seems to have helped with the intensity of the headaches. I felt great again on Tuesday, the day after chemo. Julie and I were able to hit the Gap Clearance Outlet in Cincinnati that I am always telling everyone about. We had a ball and Kayden was a rock-star shopper. By Wednesday late morning the ache from my Nuelasta shot started to creep in. It starts in my shoulders and spreads to my jaw and upper back. Eventually it affects my whole upper body. There isn't much I can do to deal with this. It is a good pain as I have said before because it means that my Nuelasta shot is working. It is spitting out new baby stem cells to help replace the ones we are killing with the chemo. It helps me keep my counts up and ward off all of those germs just waiting to attack me. Aaron made it home late Wednesday and was back to work on Thursday. I had the headaches again this time- but not near as bad as last time. I tried a Vicodin to help with the pain and ended up throwing up from it. UGH! So I switched back to regular Ibuprofen. Julie headed home Thursday afternoon. We had a great time catching up and playing with Kayden! She was a big help throughout the week.

I woke up Friday feeling like I had a horrible cold. Danielle (my nurse) says that the Taxol can create cold like symptoms. It is hard to tell if I am truly coming down with a cold or it is just symptoms from the Taxol. I am supposed to take it easy and make sure to drink lots of fluids. I also started having the bone/joint pain he had warned me about. It feels similar to the growing pains I had growing up. It starts in my hips and shoots down into my knees. Not horrible. Just a bit uncomfortable. The numbness in my fingertips has continued- it feels like they are asleep. Sometimes it is in my feet too. Again- not horrible pain- just a bit uncomfortable. Looking back at my entry- it sounds like I have just complained the whole time. Sorry! So many people want to know how I feel and how the chemo reacts with my body. Well- this is it, no sugar coating it. I continue to hold on to the fact that this is better then being sick to my stomach and not eating like I was for the AC treatments. I can deal with being uncomfortable. I just feel bad that Aaron and Kayden have to deal with my moods while I am uncomfortable. I try not to complain too much....but I have my days.

Overall- I have been able to stay busy with work and Kayden the past month. It feels good to be able to function on my own again- even if I have to ask for help once in a while. My next appt. is on the 5th of Feb. I expect to come back from that with quite a bit more info on our plans for surgery. I promise not to take so long to update again! Hope all is well for each of you. Bye for now- my fingers are worn out!

Much love and hugs from Indiana-

Jamie, Aaron and Kayden

ps. I am working on being able to say Go Colts for the Superbowl- These fans are almost as crazy as our Chief's fans!

ial Caking

13

GENETIC TESTING

February 4, 2007

Genetic testing

Hi!

I decided to do something different today. I am writing from my chemo chair here at the hospital. I have 4 hours to kill- might as well be productive! I was able to see a lot of my friends I have made during my infusion today. It sounds like everyone is doing well with their treatment which is great to hear. I was even able to make a new friend today. Earlier in the year while we were waiting in the lobby at Dr. Schneider's office there was a girl filling out office paperwork with several members of her family there. It is usually a sign of a first timer and you have to assume they have been diagnosed recently. It was all I could do not to go over and hug her that day as she was crying with her family. I ended up giving her dad a pack of Kleenex for her to use and telling him to hang in there. Well- she was sitting in the chair across from mine today when I sat down for my chemo! We were able to chat for a bit and swap stories. She is 25 and battling ovarian cancer. Scary! It was great to get to know her. We exchanged numbers and will hopefully keep in contact. It always feels so gratifying to talk with other people in a similar situation. I truly see myself doing that a lot in the future as I start feeling more like myself. Any help I can offer others to make it through their treatment makes me feel good!

As far as my appointment today- my counts were great! I was worried since I had started coming down with another cold late last week. I was terrified I would be set back again. Hopefully it was a fluke thing and we won't have to deal with it again. Only one more to go after I finish today! Now for the good news.....the tumor measured smaller in his examination today! It was 5x5 cm last time and today he measured it at 4x5 cm, not bad for two weeks! Guess the Taxol is doing its job! We talked a bit about surgery also. Dr. Schneider couldn't go into details since it is not his speciality, but he was able to answer our numerous questions about some what ifs and what to expect for the next few weeks. He also agreed to do another CAT scan before surgery to ease my mind about my liver. Dr. Goulet my surgeon is our go-to for further details about my surgery date and what type of surgery we will be doing. We will be meeting with him the week of my last chemo treatment, Feb. 19th, as well as a plastic surgeon if necessary. I know a lot of you are wondering, but there is still no decisions on exactly what surgery we will be doing. Dr. Goulet will go over that with us when we meet and he will be the one to discuss what he feels will be our best option for my situation long term. It will be a load off my mind when I can actually know what I need to prepare myself for as far as surgery.

We also had an appointment with the genetics department today as well. The results are in......NEGATIVE- no gene mutation was found in my DNA. This means that my cancer was not due to an inherited gene, it was just a chance occurrence. This also means that my extended family does not have to be concerned that they are at an elevated risk for developing cancer either. But most importantly this means that Kayden's risk for cancer is not increased because of a potential gene mutation passed to her by me. Whew! She will always need to be proactive about being tested and doing self exams....but she isn't more prone to cancer because of me. We were so relieved to hear this very good news!

On another note....many of you may already know this, but Aaron has decided to run the 5K Race for the Cure (Susan G. Komen Breast Cancer Foundation) in Indianapolis on April 21st. This was all started because a friend of mine, Lisa Schrader, here in Richmond decided to run this race in my honor with her husband Adam. I thought it was a really cool idea and Aaron got to thinking that if Adam could do it then he should too! For the record neither of the guys qualify as actual runners :) In fact, Aaron says he has never run more then a mile and a half at once...ever! They are going to train for it even!Aaron and Lisa both have web pages where you can make donations to the foundation in their honor. All proceeds will stay in the Indiana area where I am being treated so we felt it was a great chance to show our support for the cure, where it will help me most! He has already exceeded his first goal of $1000 in less them 48 hours so we upped his goal to $2500. He has been running in place and humming the Rocky theme song ever since he signed up this weekend. Haven't actually seen any "training" per say yet :) But he has a few months. No offense honey...but a tip....cutting out cookies during the week won't cut it for training on this one :) Better get to work! Don't think I won't be there at the race with a video camera in hand to document the finial moments for all to see on the web site! Better eat a light breakfast that day so you don't lose it on the finish line. I included the web site below.

The web site is http://race.komenindy.org

Click on Find a Team or Participant and search his first and last name if you want to see his page or make a donation. We appreciate all of the donation we have received so far! It is very generous to show your support for this great cause!

My mom is flying in this evening to stay through the weekend. She is needing a Kayden fix- it has been almost a month of not seeing her. Great timing since it has been snowing since about 11am this morning- it will be nice and cold with lots of snow when she gets here! Paybacks for spending last week in Hawaii :) It is really coming down like a good KS snow, hopefully we can go sledding in it before it is gone! That is it for now...more later!

Much love from our winter wonderland-

Jamie, Aaron and Kayden

Grounded

14

CHEMO SIDE EFFECTS...

Monday, February 12, 2007

Chemo side effects...

Hi Everyone!

Hope your weekend was great! We had quite an exciting one here so I thought I would do an update to fill you all in. First of all- I felt pretty good this week. My headaches were much better and my aches and pains didn't seem to be as long lasting as the past couple of treatments. My "growing" pains in my legs and knees has spread to my elbows this week, but not bad at all. Just a little twinge now and then. Probably the one thing that has increased as far as discomfort over the past several weeks is my nerve/sensory issues in my fingers and toes. The Taxol can cause nerve problems in your hands and feet. I am taking a B-12 vitamin everyday to help with it but it doesn't eliminate it. At first it just felt like my hand or foot was asleep, a sort of numb feeling every once in a while (more-so in my hands then my feet). Then it progressed over the Taxol treatments to a tingling sensation, or pins and needles feeling. Now it feels like my fingertips are EXTREMELY sensitive. It is actually uncomfortable to touch the keyboard as I am typing. I tried to help my mom put clean sheets on the bed and it was almost unbearable for me to touch even the soft sheets and blanket. It feels worse in my right hand- but that may be because I am right handed and do more with that hand. I keep using lotion since the sensitivity seems to dull when they are not dry, but it is a pretty constant annoyance for now. It is hard to explain other then to say the fingertips feel numb, yet also feel extremely sensitive. Weird I know, but that is what has bugged me the most this week. Definitely could be worse- so I refer to this as bearable or just uncomfortable. Speaking of worse....got to fill you in on our weekend here at the Pursley household.

I will spare you the details (trust me you do NOT want to hear them) but here is the clean version. My mom was still here on Friday so we decided to go out to a local Mexican restaurant to eat. They had a live Mariachhi band that Kayden was fascinated with. They kept flirting with her and singing to her. It was cute! After dinner we came home for a night of vegging out. I was in bed by 10pm because my legs were bugging me and I thought sleeping would take my mind off of it. Unfortunately I ended up having something different then that to take my mind off of it. By 10:30pm I realized I wasn't feeling quite right and ended up in the bathroom throwing up. I went back to bed hoping it was a fluke thing- not so much. I was back in there throughout the night. Aaron had fallen asleep on the couch and came in around midnight to go to bed and found me sick. He went back to sleep on the couch and realized he was going to get sick too. Throughout this ordeal I was taking my temp because I am supposed to go to the emergency room if I have a temp over 101 degrees. Sure enough- by 2am I was up to 101 temp and my mom had to take me into the ER since Aaron was still getting sick. While at the ER they gave me some anti-nausea meds through my port. They also ran some tests to check my white count to see if it was a bacteria causing the problem. My white count was up so my Nuelasta shot had done its job this week. I was pretty out of it from the meds they gave me so I can't tell you much else of what happened other then it really sucks to not be able to get sick in your own bathroom (too much info I know! Sorry!). Anyways.....it gets better.....my mom ends up getting sick while waiting on me at the hospital. So I sent her home to be more comfortable and told them I would call when I was being released. Skipping past the gory details....I was sure it was food poisoning, but the ER doc said it was a nasty stomach virus going around that we had all been exposed to. It was hard to believe him in my medicated/sleepy state- he looked more like a super hero action figure as I looked up at him from my hospital bed. He was really tall and had a super broad upper body. Looking up at him it was almost fake looking like out of a cartoon. I remember telling myself to listen to him and stop thinking about which super hero he be and what his name should be. It was actually a very funny/ridiculous conversation I had with myself looking back now :) I should have been paying attention to what he was saying...I still don't think I caught everything he told me cause I was so distracted by his appearance. Sorry ER doctor whoever you are- hope I didn"t miss anything important :) Gotta love the good stuff they give you at the hospital! Needless to say it was not a good day for the Pursley (plus mom) household on Saturday. I was released around 7am and our friend Jackie, bless her, came to pick me up after an early morning call from Aaron. I ran into the automatic doors as I left the ER- felt like I had had a few to many margaritas :) I don"t know how Jackie kept a straight face, it had to be funny watching me pretend to be OK. Good thing I didn't tell her about my super hero encounter :) We had to ship Kayden off to the Kulp's (our neighbors) and literally we all laid in bed most of the day recovering. Kayden did throw up one time on Saturday night- but has been fine since. Thank goodness! I wouldn't wish this virus on ANYONE!

Happy to report we were all feeling somewhat better by Sat. evening. Mom was able to fly home on Sunday. I think I will even brave breakfast today! So I did not make it through chemo without going to the ER like I had hoped. Oh well......at least it wasn't the chemo's fault that I was sick this time. Hope I didn't gross you out with our gory weekend! Better go for now. Kayden will be up soon and we have to prepare for Grandma Kitty who is coming this week to play! Don't forget to keep checking out Aaron's site for his 5K race. He is doing great in his fundraising efforts thanks to all of your generous donations! We continue to be amazed at what wonderful people we have surrounded ourselves with over the years.

The web site is http://race.komenindy.org

Click on Find a Team or Participant and search his first and last name if you want to see his page or make a donation. We appreciate all of the donation we have received so far! It is very generous to show your support for this great cause!

Much love from our soon to be sterilized home-

Jamie, Aaron, and Kayden

Giving

15

SURGERY NEW

February 20, 2007

Surgery New

Hi Everyone!

I met with the surgeon, Dr. Goulet, yesterday and the verdict is in...they will be doing a lumpectomy on my right breast! YEAH! I went into the appt. prepared to have them tell me I had to have a mastectomy. In that case I was going to tell them to do both breasts while they were there. What a relief to hear that he is confident we can have just as successful results with a lumpectomy. For those of you that are not familiar with this procedure, it involves making an incision in the breast above the tumor location. He will then remove what is left of the tumor and then also some of the surrounding tissue. They will test the tissue to see if they get what is referred to as clear margins (tissue that does not have cancer cells in it). As long as they can get 3mm worth of clear margins around the tumor sight it will be considered a successful surgery. If they are unable to get clear margins then we will have to discuss other options on how to proceed. But we won't get into that unless it is necessary. The survival rate will not be any different whether I have a successful lumpectomy or a mastectomy. That was good to hear. There will of course be a chance for reoccurrence because I will still have breast tissue. But they don't feel that there is any reason to think that this will be a problem since I will be monitored closely for the rest of my life. I feel confident that this is the best decision surgery wise and Aaron and I were both very happy to hear I am able to keep my breasts. As much as it would have been fun to get a new bigger pair :) I am relieved to not have to go down that road- at least not yet. By the way.....the tumor measured 3x3 in my appointment yesterday- down again from last appointment! Dr. Schneider was even impressed at the shrinkage. I also finished my last round of chemo yesterday. It felt weird- I was so worried about the appt. w/ the surgeon that I kind of forgot that it was my last chemo. Nice to have behind me for now! Hopefully I don't have to see the chemo chair again-EVER!

Another piece of good news is that Dr. Schneider and Danielle asked me to take part in an event in June this year. Dr. Schneider is going to be accepting a donation check from the Elks Club of Indiana at their State Convention in French Lick, IN. Each year they donate hundreds of thousands of dollars to doctors at IU (Indiana University) and PU (Purdue University) to be used for research in Cancer. A doctor is chosen at one of the hospitals to accept the check and that was Dr. Schneider this year. In addition to the check acceptance- they have a patient come and talk about their experience with cancer and their treatment by the hospital. I have been chosen as the patient to speak this year! I am really excited. They do a professional brochure with Dr. Schneider and I in it, and they take professional pictures for it (which we get copies of). This brochure is also used at the National Elks club convention to represent the Indiana Elks philanthropic efforts. It is an honor to be chosen this year and I can't wait to do it! Aaron and I get a free room for the night at the resort the conference is at and we are thinking about making a weekend of it to celebrate his birthday.

I have also recently started meeting with the local branch of a group called the I.W.I.N (Indiana Women in Need) Foundation. They raise money to provide financial support for personal services (childcare, massages, transportation, meals, etc) for women in Indiana going through breast cancer treatment. Aaron and I were able to take advantage of this service for our own situation. I am helping to plan a wine tasting event here in Richmond that will be in April. I met for the first time with these women last week and was able to offer my services in developing their marketing material for the event. Fliers and donation cards for the event. I look forward to having something to feel like I am starting to give back and help other women in my situation. I hope to continue to do this and hopefully talk to people about my experience as much as possible. That is my personal goal for the future. We actually have an event this weekend in Indianapolis that is an IWIN fundraising event- its a Pink PJ party and several of my Pi Phi sisters (Mitchell, Roberts and Jackson) will be joining me to go to the event as well as my mom, my Aunt Cindy and Leslie Goertzen (our friend in Richmond that has helped us with Kayden throughout my treatment). It will be lots of fun. We are all wearing pink PJ's and enjoying a night of fun spa services and music! I am really looking forward to the event!

The web site for IWIN is if you are interested in checking it out: http://www.iwinfoundation.org/

I have been feeling very good this past week. Still having neuropathy issues in my fingers and toes, and that will probably be worse this week since the Taxol has accumulated in my system. It is worth it though since the drug has been so successful in shrinking the tumor. Kayden is doing well. She is developing quite a little personality. Now if I could just get her to stop trying to get strangers in the store to pick her up we will be good. She has definitely never met a stranger. We have been slowly learning some sign language in the past couple of weeks. She is currently abusing "more" and "done" so we are trying to teach her food, drink and wait so we can tell what she wants more of and also that no she can't have it RIGHT NOW like she wants. She is talking in Kayden speak for now. She even reads to herself from books. It is cute! She says a few words like dog, dad, hi, bye, night-night, etc. Temper-tantrums are also starting as she knows more what she wants. She is also currently obsessed with our cat....much to Uno's dismay. But he and Roxy have been great with her considering she likes to give open mouth kisses one minute and then tell them no and swat at them away in the next. She is growing up right before our eyes and she is only 14 months old.

The web site for Aaron's personal race page is:

(Click on Find a Team or Participant and search his first and last name if you want to see his page or make a donation.) Again- we truly appreciate all of the donations we have received so far, he has already hit $3000! So far he has raised more then any other individual or team! You guys are the best. I will keep you updated as we get a surgery date set- all we know now is that it will be the week of March 12th. Better go for now much to do today.

Much love from our house to yours-

Jamie, Aaron, and Kayden

Adventurous

16

MOVING TO KENTUCKY

March 13, 2007

Moving to Kentucky

Hi Everyone!

I have to start off by apologizing for the delay in my getting this update posted. It has been a very interesting week here in Indiana. First of all for those of you that have not heard it through the grapevine- my surgery date is now on the 20th of March. It wasn't technically moved- I just misunderstood the nurse when she told me over the phone what week my Tuesday surgery was scheduled for. So it was my mistake. We now have a week more to re-prepare for it. I didn't find out until this past Friday afternoon about my mistake. Good thing I checked! Talk about chemo brain....

And I was not able to update this weekend because Aaron and I made a quick road trip to Bowling Green, KY. Again for those of you who haven't already figured it out or heard it through the same ole grapevine- Aaron has accepted a new position within Hill's Pet Nutrition as the Operations Manager for the Bowling Green, KY plant. He is very excited at the opportunity to take on this role. As far as timeline goes- his first day with the new plant is scheduled for April 16th. He will be living in temporary housing in Bowling Green during the week and then commuting home to be with us on the weekends. I will not join him until my radiation is done in Richmond. We are expecting that to be early June.

Both of us are extremely sad to leave this tight knit support group we have here in Richmond. It will be hard for me especially to leave my safety net of individuals that have stood behind me during our time here and throughout my treatment. You know who you are- so I won't say good bye yet. It brings tears to my eyes to think about how quickly this town had opened its arms to us in our time of need. That is not an easy thing to leave. My heart will have a special place in it for Richmond, Indiana- not only as the place Kayden was born- but as a place full of very generous individuals that I consider family. We have made a decision to stay at IU with Dr. Schneider even after we are no longer in IN. It is a 3 hr. drive from Bowling Green to Indy so very do-able. In fact, I have a feeling that we will continue to be with Dr. Schneider no matter what state we are living in for a long time to come.

As we begin to get the house ready to list with a local relator I find myself thinking back to our last move from Topeka to Richmond. And I thought that one was hard......but look what we had in store for us in Indiana. I can only imagine what we have waiting for us in Kentucky :) All good stuff I hope- I feel like we put in our time this year and it is about time for us to move forward and start enjoying life again. Just in time for spring! I have to go for now....I will post again before surgery hopefully. I promise more next time. Much to do and things to clean here tonight!

Much love from us to you-

Jamie, Aaron and Kayden

p.s. The race is coming up on April 21st! Aaron has been training hard! He is still the top fundraiser in the individual category.

Open.

17

SURGERY UPDATE

March 20, 2007

Surgery update

Hi Everyone!

This is Aaron here to provide everyone with a quick update on Jamie's big day. I apologize in advance if I am not as entertaining of a writer as Jamie.

To cut to the chase, the day's events went very well! Jamie is sitting with me now in her hospital room, hopefully cancer free! She is simply too tired and groggy to make this entry herself.

Our day started at 3:30 this morning with an alarm to get ready for surgery. This was after Jamie kept us up until 11:00 pm with a mixture of nerves and some last minute phone calls. We hit the road just after 4:00 am to meet Jamie's 5:30 check in time. Things here at IU run fairly efficiently and we were in a staging room with Jamie in her hospital gown before 7:00. Jamie's parents and Aunt Cindy arrived in true Barkes style with only about 15 minutes to spare before they kicked things off. We had a brief meeting with her surgeon Dr. Robert Goulet. His confidence prior to Jamie's surgery was very comforting. The surgery went well taking around 2 hours. After completion of the surgery Dr. Goulet joined us in the waiting room to update us on Jamie's status. The surgery went as planned. They started with the lymph node dissection, removing approximately 15 lymph nodes (that seems like an avg. number from our discussion with others who have been through this process). During this portion of the surgery there were no significant issues identified which would require further removal of her lymph nodes. They then transitioned to the lumpectomy which also went well. They brought her up from recovery around 1:00 pm. She was glad to see us but needed some rest. My parents, who are staying at our house to watch Kayden, were able to join us for a short time in the afternoon. Jamie was very happy to see Kayden. She was VERY entertained with the controls on her Mommy's hospital bed and was able to get into about everything she shouldn't get into.

It is nice allowing her to enjoy the time with her grandparents, without having to explain to her why her Mommy is sick.

We expect to hear the results of the pathology report by the end of the week. This will provide the "clear margins" status you always hear associated with cancer related surgeries. Her spirits are up as usual and she is taking it slow. Keep us in your thoughts and prayers as we wait to hear the results from pathology. She will probably be updating on her own in the next day or two.

Much love from us to you-

Jamie, Aaron and Kayden

Positive

18

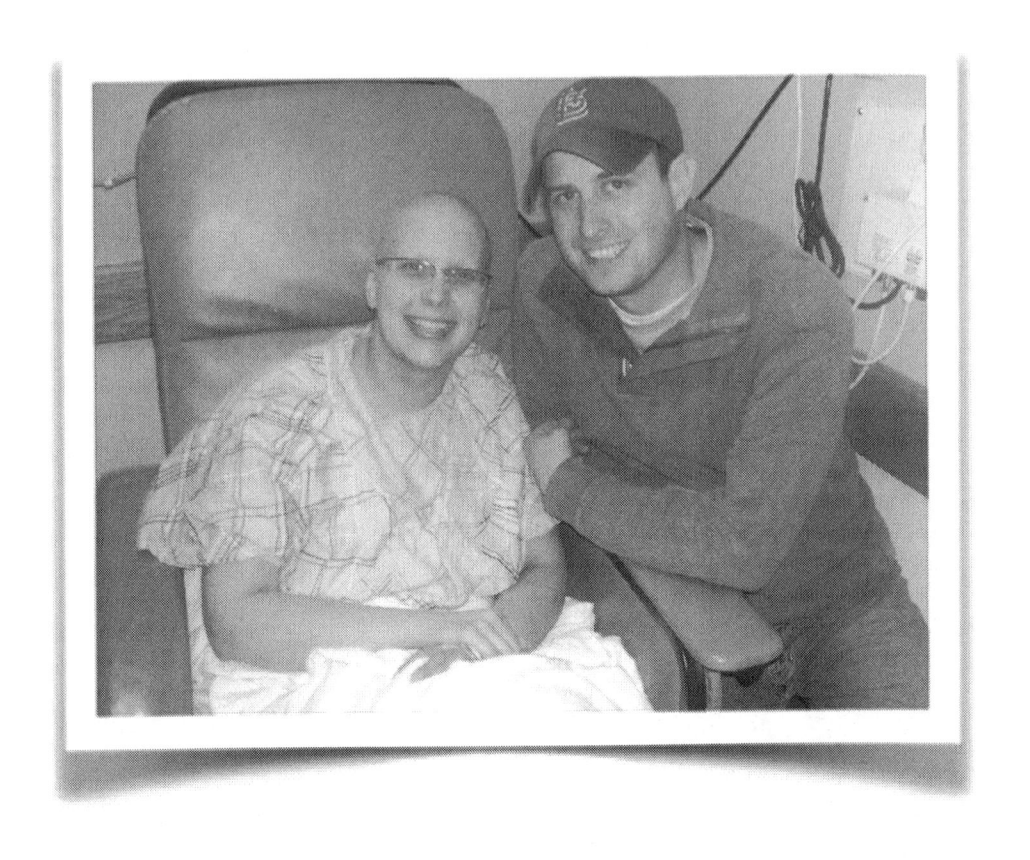

POST SURGERY

March 23, 2007

Post surgery

Hi Everyone!

I know a lot of you have been waiting for this update to see how I am after surgery and also to hear the pathology results. Well- here goes....

I was released from the hospital on Wed. morning around 10:30 am. They had me on some good stuff that made me sleepy so I told the nurse I needed to take a nap before we headed home. It was 12:30p before we actually packed up the room and headed out. Stayed a little past my welcome :) But boy was I tired! I slept the whole way home and was pretty groggy the rest of the day from the pain pills. My breast didn't (and still doesn't) hurt near as much as under my arm does from my nodes being removed. I can't really move my right arm much. I keep it folded across my stomach because that is the most comfortable. I have to sit and sleep with several pillows underneath it to keep it from pulling at the stitches and drain. Slowly each day I am able to move it around more and more. I met with a physical therapist to learn some exercises I can do to get it back to normal. Today I was able to actually type for the first time. I had to eat and do everything left handed for the first two days. Kayden isn't happy since I can't pick her up, but my mom is still here to help out and is more then happy to give in to her wishes :) I was able to cut back on the pills today as the pain has subsided a bit. Yesterday we had a scare where I actually fainted while my mom was emptying my drain (it comes out from under my arm). I knocked my head pretty good on the baseboard of the bathroom- but I wasn't out much more then a second or two. Not sure why it happened. We have been very careful since then to make sure i am sitting down more and being careful to not stand too quickly. Overall I feel pretty good today....just really sore on my right side. There is one particular nerve that runs from my arm pit to my elbow and it must be touching my drain somehow because it sends out a shooting pain every once in awhile if I move a certain way.

Overall- a very bearable recovery. I just can't wait to be able to lift my arm and take care of Kayden on my own so my poor mom can stop putting her life on hold for mine. I truly appreciate all of the help we have had from our families. They have truly dropped every thing to help us when we need it. We couldn't have done this without them.

As far as the pathology results. Dr. Schneider (my oncologist) called this afternoon on behalf of my surgeon, Dr. Goulet, to give me the results. The goal was to find no cancer anywhere in the tissue they sent off- that would have been our ideal situation. Of course, that is never how it works out for us. There was still some tumor remaining- it measured 2.8 cm. This was very close to the Dr.'s last measurements. They also confirmed that there was dead tissue surrounding the tumor that showed signs of chemotherapy. That tells us that the chemo did have an effect on the cancer- it just didn't eliminate it completely. They also told me that they took 34 (not 15 as we thought) of my lymph nodes. Out of those 34- 8 of them were positive for cancer. This was a bit disappointing for me to hear. I was really hoping we would hear that there was no cancer left in the nodes. Obviously the lymph nodes are the gateway to my other organs- it makes me even more nervous to hear how much more risk I have to it spreading. But those nodes are now out of my body- that is the good thing. I am cancer free as of right now. As far as margins go- they were hoping for 3mm of clear margins and they were only able to get 2mm from my tissue. The surgeon seems to still be happy with that and doesn't feel there is a need to go back in to take more tissue at this time. I have a follow up on Wed. 28th to get more info and also to discuss my radiation schedule. I will be able to fill you all in more after that appointment. So overall- we got very good reports back. They do not need to go back in to take more tissue or nodes out- and I am able to start the last phase of my treatment to make sure we get any microscopic cancer cells that may be floating around still. I am cautiously happy with the news....I wish of course that we had heard there was nothing left- but realistically there isn't much to do now but move on and do everything we can to keep me cancer free- for GOOD! I truly appreciate all of your support and prayers this week. I will keep you updated as we get more information. I have included some of the pictures that we had taken for the Elks brochure that they are using for the conference that I am speaking at. They sent out a photographer to take pics of us at home to use alongside my story of cancer, unfortunately Kayden was more interested in the camera then having her picture taken that day. She preferred to sit on the photographer's lap then sit with me. Roxy stepped up and had her time in the spotlight with no complaints at all :)

Much love from us cancer free people to you-

Jamie, Aaron and Kayden

Sympathetic

19

MOVING ON TO RADIATION

April 4, 2007

Moving on to Radiation

Hi Everyone!

Happy Wednesday! I have been telling myself it was time to do an update earlier this week- but I decided to wait so I could include my radiologist appt. in Richmond info. I had that appointment today- but I will get to that in a bit. First I want to tell you all how I am recovering from the surgery. The week I came home was tough. I couldn't move my right arm much so lifting Kayden and changing diapers was pretty much out. My mom stayed on a week longer then everyone else that was here for the surgery to help me out. I couldn't have recovered this quickly without her help. I was able to rest and focus on getting better. It has been good so far in the 2nd week of recovery. I am still sore and still taking the pain meds- but I am at least able to get myself dressed and type with minor discomfort. I have been told by many that my physical therapy stretch's they asked me to do are very important in order to get my full range of motion back in that shoulder. I am going to have to really focus on doing them each day- it is easy to get busy and forget. I guess the good part of that statement is that I am staying busy. That is actually an understatement...we have been crazy busy. We have listed our house with a relator here and we have been to KY twice to house hunt. We made an offer on an house in Bowling Green on this last trip and it was accepted. So we officially have a place to live in as of May 18th. It is currently under construction so I am looking forward to having a hand in the finishing details! We haven't had any interest in our house yet- but we hope that the showings pick up in the next few weeks.

As for my radiation appointment today in Richmond...we met with Dr. Kumar (add another name to my ever growing list of doctors). He will be my radiation oncologist. He seems very nice and did a good job of explaining things to Aaron and I about what to expect for the next couple of months. It looks like I will go in on April 11th for what they call a planning meeting. He has requested a CAT scan, mammogram, and bone scan to get baselines prior to my radiation. Those will all be done before I start. At my planning meeting they will map out the different areas where we will target the radiation. . Due to the high number of nodes that were positive for cancer they will increase my areas being treated to include the breast, arm pit and shoulder (where the lymph nodes he left in on my right side reside- referred to as region three). I will have 33 total radiation sessions. They are 5 days a week getting weekends off. It will take approximately 20-30 minutes each day. I will meet with Dr. Kumar every Wed. that I am receiving radiation. The side effects are fatigue, and skin irritations. They have also informed me that they would prefer I didn't wear a bra during the whole time I am being treated. She had to pick my jaw up off the table when she mentioned that part. ugh! Sports bras can be worn sometimes if I am in public- but if I incur any skin breakdown (cracking and splitting of the the skin from the radiation and friction caused by the bra) then I am doomed to let 'em hang for a while. Oh well. it could be worse I keep telling myself. It sounds like a simple process it will just take a while to get used to it. I am sure I will get into a routine over time. From what I understand- I will have one funky tan on the right side of my upper body once it is all done. Maybe I can start a new trend? ha ha! Let's see if Brittany can jump on that bandwagon :)

It has been hard this last week not to dwell on the fear that the cancer is growing in me again. I have had a couple of minor breakdowns when I start thinking about Kayden and all of the things I want to share with her and experience with her. I thought I would feel this sense of relief when the tumor was gone, but I actually feel more dread then relief. It is like a dark cloud is hanging over me waiting to rain on my parade. So I have been trying to keep positive thoughts in my mind rather then let the worry creep in. I won't lie to you- it has not been easy. I guess this is the wall they told me I would be hitting once we got through the chemo. I guess it is natural to go through...I don't want to live the rest of my LONG life in fear that cancer is going to raise its ugly head again and wreck everything I have strived to regain. It is going to take some time for me to get past this. I don't know if I will ever be able to completely get past it. I guess I just need to take it one day at a time and move forward from there. That is the best I can do for now.

On to more positive things, they did an article on me in the local newspaper. It was a very cool spread with a picture of Kayden and I and Roxy (our dog). I will try to scan it in and post it. Or I can email the story to you if you are interested let me know. I got a few extra copies to keep :) It has been busy so I apologize for the late posting, but busy is good! It leaves me with less time to worry and more time to be productive and catch up with all I am behind on. Hope all is well with you. Have a wonderful Easter weekend. We will be headed back to KY to pick out some things for the house. Till next time......

Much love from us to you-

Jamie, Aaron and Kayden

Dignity

20
HOUSE HUNTING IN KY

April 15, 2007

House Hunting in KY

Hi Everyone!

It's one of those nights where I can't seem to get to sleep so I decided to be productive and share all the new news with you :) I had a busy couple of weeks as usual since I last checked in. My good friend from college Leigh came to Indiana to visit me all the way from Hawaii where she is a nurse/yoga instructor. I haven't seen her in over two years so it was great to catch up and hang out. In fact I am sitting here listening to my new music I downloaded (at her recommendation). It is a singer named Jack Johnson, he's from Hawaii. It is fun upbeat music that is perfect to journal to- thanks for the tip Leigh. I am solo tonight as Aaron's first day at his new job in Bowling Green starts tomorrow. He is staying in an apartment there during the week until Kayden and I join him in early June. He seems confident that he will really enjoy this new role and is excited to get there and dig in. I think it is a lot harder for him to be gone from us for so long now that Kayden asks for him and can really appreciate her daddy time. It sure is different then mommy time that's for sure. How is it that dad's are always able to make things more fun and exciting?? And leave the biggest mess in the wake of the fun :) Just kidding honey! I have a feeling it will be pretty lonely around here for the next two months while we have to hold down the fort in IN.

I am feeling great. No crazy chemo drugs left in my system. I am really feeling more like my old self each day. My side effect of the chemo have pretty much worn off. Still having my memory slips- but some of that is from trying to multitask like a super hero. It is pretty hard to keep the house clean when you have a 26 lb. tornado following you around and undoing everything you do with an evil giggle while doing it. I think she knows exactly what she is doing and is having a ball doing it. It is a never ending project to keep up with my little firecracker. I guess I shouldn't expect anything less from her. She is turning out to be mommy's little mini-me since we spend so much time together. She gives the best hugs and loves to press her cheek against mine to show me affection. I think she learned it from hugging the animals and loving on them. Might as well love on mommy the same way! It just melts you heart. Then she runs up and turns off the TV or empties a full kleenex box with a squeal. Oh well.....what can I say- she keeps it interesting around here. At least I can keep up with her now!

I met with my radiation oncologist, Dr. Kumar, at Reid Hospital, here in Richmond, this last week to map out the radiation path they will use on my body. I had to lay on this big table and they moved me all around into the position and marked on me with black marker. All of this is needed to target the proper areas that were affected by the cancer. I had to hang on to a bar above my head with both hands so good thing I have been working on getting my right arm back into shape or it would have really hurt to have to hold that bar like that for so long. I had to also get a baseline CAT scan and mammogram before starting the radiation that same day they mapped me out. I almost passed out during the mammogram when the machine started squeezing my boob. It is bad enough getting squeezed when you haven't had surgery on it.....but add the surgery and the fact it wasn't totally healed up and you can only imagine what I felt. I think they heard me yelling on the second floor. The poor lady doing it felt terrible she was trying so hard to do it quickly. I was just worried I might pass out and fall to the floor with my boob left in this stupid machine. I didn't come this far to lose my boob to the mammogram machine- I can tell you that much!!! When I walked out to go get dressed the whole waiting room of women in line for their mammogram stopped still and stared at me with this panicked look. I was so embarrassed! I sailed out of the room trying to explain it doesn't normally hurt THAT much and they shouldn't worry. I didn't stick around to see if I scared any first timers away. I now understand why Dr. Kumar wanted me to wait a bit longer to start my treatments- to let my scars heal. I pushed him to move it up so I could be back with Aaron sooner then later in KY. Oh well. I lived- but I hope to not EVER have to do that again after any type of surgery. YEOUCH!

My arm is still a bit sore but it is definitely getting better each day. I am no longer taking any pain meds as of last week. I feel much more clear headed and able to function as far as daily activities. Nice for once. it has been awhile. Wish I could be home with everyone in KS to enjoy this cloud free time in my treatment. We have just had too much going on though with Dr. appointments, working on the house and traveling to KY to get our new house lined up there. I know for sure we will be home for the week of July 4th. If possible it will be even sooner then that...but I am not holding my breath since I am tied to radiation every day (except Sat. and Sun.) for the next 6 weeks. Gives me something to look forward to!

My hair is starting to really grow back. It is very dark and soft. My eye brows and eye lashes are creeping back in too!!! Boy I didn't realize how much I missed them until they started to come back. I think Aaron is glad to see them too :) I had a little kid yell Brittany as I was leaving a Wendy's the other day with Leigh. I only wish!!! He must have been standing pretty far away to make that mistake :) She is ruining it for all of us that started this bald trend! Get off the band wagon Brittany! If you really want to make a statement you have to go all out with the eyebrows and lashes! Anyways...I am tired and if I don't sleep soon Kayden will run circles around me tomorrow. Bye for now!! Till next time....

Much love from Indiana-

Jamie, Aaron and Kayden

Outspoken

21

KOMEN RACE IN INDY...

May 15, 2007

Komen Race in Indy...

Hi Everyone!

I am here finally!!!!! Many of you have politely questioned me as to when I was going to do a new update.....hint hint! So much has happened in the last month, I may have to do two entries so my hands don't cramp up! Aaron completed his Race for the Cure! I have many fun details on that...and pictures! I have been doing my radiation each day. I have had some visitors, both family and friends. I will give you all a condensed version of everything as I don't want you to fall asleep on me while reading it.

The race for the cure happened on April 21st. it turned out to be a beeaauuttiful Saturday, even at the crack of dawn when the runners had to be there to check in. It was Aaron, our friends in Richmond Lisa and Adam Schrader, our brother-n-law Nate, and a surprise entry at the last minute (after some heavy peer pressure) Grandpa DAVE! Team Jamie had 5 people running in the competitive 5K race! It was a great time. We were able to see the gang take off with the big group. We had decided to do the family 1 mile walk with Kayden so we headed on that while they raced. My mom, Jen (Aaron's sister) and I had planned to be at the finish line to see them cross- but unfortunately there about 1,000 other people doing this short 1 mile walk with us, and little miss I can do it myself decided she wanted to "walk" most of it with us. She was quite a spectacle touching all of the dogs, shrieking, talking, waving and stopping in front of everyone with no notice. She had quite a back up at one point. The best was when she was asking people to share their snacks if they appealed to her :) She has truly never met a stranger! Channel 8 even taped her enjoying herself on the walk. We never got to see if she made the news or not. Needless to say we didn't make it in time to see the group cross the line. Nate and Aaron did the full race without stopping (riiiiigghhhhtttt!) and finished in 27 minutes. Adam finished first of all of the group and Lisa came in just behind the guys, and last but not least...Grandpa Dave came in at a very respectable 37 minutes. I had to promise I would do it next year with them- it was such a powerful day. Aaron was one of the top individual fundraisers thanks to all of your generous donations. I have many pictures and videos from the day that I have included to the left. If only I could have seen them all cross the line at the end! Sorry to let you all down! I hear it wasn't pretty though! They were all cooled off when we got there :(After the race and walk we walked around the crowd and danced a bit with Kayden to the outdoor DJ, and shopped for Cure attire and enjoyed the rest of the morning. It was a great day for all!

As you know I started my radiation 4/18/07. It hasn't been too bad so far. I am just now after 18 sessions of it starting to show some skin coloration change and it is starting to be itchy like a sunburn. I use Aquaphor (a jelly like lotion) on it to help soothe the skin and that helps so far. Still letting the old gals swing loose as directed. It is so embarrassing sometimes! I cheat and wear my bra sometimes if we are headed out of the house. I have been a bit tired from the radiation so far- but it's hard to tell if it is from the radiation or from Kadyen. She is full of energy and into everything she can get her hands on. She has been a blast to be around and never ceases to amaze us with her resourcefulness.

We had a bit of a scare last week. We spent an evening with some of Aaron's co-workers and I partook in several beers over the night. The next day I started feeling dizzy. I was sure it was a reaction to one of my medications so I went to bed early and hoped it would be gone by morning. Unfortunately it was not any better. After talking with several of my Dr.'s they thought it might be a sinus infection, but just in case they scheduled a head MRI to check for cancer in my brain. That is some thing I haven't gotten used to yet- the automatic jump to the worst case scenario when something is wrong with me. I felt pretty terrible from the dizzy spells all week, and it didn't help having to wait 4 days to get in for my MRI. It was a pretty miserable week. I couldn't drive, or take care of Kayden, or do much of anything. The Goertzen's pitched in and helped me out with Kayden and getting me to radiation. It was a lot of help to be able to lean on them with Aaron being in KY. I started an antibiotic to help treat any infection that might be causing the symptoms. By Thursday I started feeling worse and had a fever by late afternoon. My MRI was scheduled for 5:30 pm and by 4:30 pm Dr. Schneider had decided to send me to the ER for a work up to see what was going on. So I headed to the hospital with Leslie and Aaron was able to meet me there. They did my MRI and also a spinal tap to check for meningitis (my neck was sore). There was a lot of concern that since I was already on antibiotics my symptoms might not present as severe as they should depending on what was wrong with me. After a tense hour of waiting for the MRI results we were relieved to hear that there was no sign of cancer in my brian, but there was some sinus infection showing up. The spinal tap came back clear of any sign of infection also. So the diagnosis was sinus infection and a possible viral infection of some sort. They told me to go home and take it easy and wait out the infection. Fun Fun. But boy was it good to hear the cancer had not spread! Whew! I had several more days of feeling pretty bad. Robin came up to visit me over the weekend and was a champ at holding down the couch with me. It was disappointing not to get to partake in all of our shopping we had planned to do. But oh well...guess I can't control everything as much as I would like to. It never fails every time I want to plan something- I get sick. Ugh! My mom flew in the same night that Robin flew out so she could help with the house and Kayden. I was still feeling pretty bad even on Monday. I just didn't feel right and it was starting to worry me.

I called Dr. Schneider on Tuesday and told him I was still feeling bad. We recounted all of my symptoms and what I had done medically so far for them. It turns out my radiation Dr. had told me to stop taking my Effexor (anti-depressant that was helping my mood/hot flashes). According to Dr. Schneider- you cannot stop taking an anti-depressant cold turkey. It is like a steroid, you have to ween yourself off of it or you will have severe side effects (such as dizziness, nausea, etc). I started taking it right away and within 6 hours I was feeling better. So in the end- I had several things causing my symptoms and it was a matter of figuring out what they were in order to get me back to normal. I am happy to say I am finally feeling like myself today, I was beginning to wonder if that would ever happen again. I am feeling the fatigue from the radiation a bit- but that I can handle with an extra nap or two during the day. Glad to be back! That's it for now....my hands are tired of typing. I will do another update later this week to fill you in on our upcoming move and everything else!

Much love from KY and IN-

Jamie, Aaron and Kayden

Relentlessly Optimistic

22

OUR SUMMER IN A NUTSHELL

September 23, 2007

Our summer in a nutshell

I have decided to move towards a blog type update. Now that I am officially cancer free- I thought it would be a great time to spice up the web site and make some changes for a fresh start. Since things have calmed down and we are getting back to a normal lifestyle I want to feel like I am just journaling rather then sending out messages about my health. Don't get me wrong- I will still keep you updated, but just through this blog. So from now on you need to check 'My Blog' for new updates not the 'My Ramblings' page. Hopefully this will make it easier for me to do my updates and for you to follow them. You can still add a comments like before, you will just add comments to my latest blog instead of the guest book. All the comments that have been added up to this point are all in my first blog labeled 'Comments from friends and family' We'll see how this works...let me know what you think!

We have crammed so much into our summer! We have been to Cincinnati to see some tennis with my parents, to Columbus, GA to see Aunt Jen & Uncle Nate (and Bacon the pig!) and the Ft. Worth Pursley's, to Auburn, AL for a K-State game, to St. Augustine, FL for some beach time, and to Kansas to do the Race for the Cure in KC, and back to KS again followed by a quick trip to Waynoka, OK with all of Aaron's buddies for some 4-wheeling in the dunes. Whew! And this is all since August! Fun Fun! I am feeling good overall, still a bit tired sometimes, but I catch a nap when I can during the day. It has been a crazy schedule but we are loving every minute of our freedom.

As far as where I am in treatment at this point...still hanging in there with my trips every three weeks for chemo. I continue to be cancer free. My follow up apt. with my radiation Dr. in early August went well. Everything is healing properly and there is no lingering effects that we can see. I did a bone scan while I was in Richmond for my radiation appt. and that came back clear! That was very good news! I am in my 5th cycle of the study (out of 18), each cycle = 3 weeks. I have had very minimal side effects overall with this treatment. The hand-foot syndrome they warned me about is the only real thing I have had problems with.

My fingers and toes have gotten very dry and the skin is cracking in the creases. It can be treated with lots of lotion and B-6 supplement which I take every day. I also seem to be back in Menopause. This has caused my hot flashes to come back again, and also my ankles and wrists have been really sore. The Dr. tells me that this is from my low level of estrogen. Apparently estrogen helps lube your joints or something along those lines. I only have 5 weeks left of the Xeloda (pill portion of the study). That is what is causing the hand-foot syndrome. Can't wait for it to be done! After that I will just have my chemo every third Monday that I have to do, which brings on a headache (treatable with Tylenol) the day of treatment and sometimes the day after along with some general fatigue. Dr. Schneider has been very happy with my progress and continues to be a great support on my journey through this. Several of my friends I have met through treatment have had to go through mastectomies recently and I continue to thank my lucky stars that I was able to avoid that route (for now at least). Please keep Val and Gayle in your prayers as they heal from their surgeries. I admire them both for their strength and determination to do what they have to do to beat this nasty disease.

Kayden has been doing great. She is such a little person all of a sudden! She walks around with a purpose and is so particular about certain things. It is a hoot! She loves to draw right now. She has already signed our brand new hardwood floors with a green Sharpie (magic eraser removed it and the shine to the floor), our couch and the pillows on it with a ball pen, and my wall in the office walls with hi-lighter to name a few of her favorites. She is addicted to a 1985 Care Bear Movie I recorded on our DVR. Aaron and I have watched it no less then a million times. It teaches her about friendship so I guess that is better then Shrek or Cars in the end. She is still loving her daycare she goes to 2 days a week.

Aaron is still working hard as ever. He goes out of his way to make time to be home with Kayden and I. He went to my last appointment with me. That was nice to have someone to drive on the way home. I tend to get tired after the long day at the hospital. I think we have decided that he will try to come every once in awhile to help break up my trips. He is really loving his job here in Bowling Green. I think we are going to be very happy here- it is a nice change of pace for us. We have already traveled to Nashville to do some shopping and for dinner as a family. It is a short drive, only about 50 miles away from us. He has been a lot of help around the house (yes honey I do notice and I do appreciate your help!) when I am feeling tired. We are meeting people in our neighborhood and we take walks almost every night as a family. I went home in August to attend a bachelorette party for my friend Julie that is getting married (next weekend!). We had a blast. I forgot how nice it is to fly without a toddler- how relaxing! I was also able to surprise a group of girls (mostly my Pi Phi sorority sisters) that had put together a Team Jamie for the Kansas City Race for the Cure. They all met before the race early on Sunday morning and I showed up and walked through the door as the surprise addition to the team. You should have seen all of their faces :) There were girls there I hadn't seen since college graduation. It was so great to see everyone and catch up while taking part in the 5K race (which we walked and talked during). It was pretty cool to be honored by this group- I felt pretty special! I will post some pictures from the event when I get them (just giving you a hard time Kelli!) I also had a group of girls come visit me in KY a couple of weekend later. Liz even came all the way from California to see me! I used a pic of the group at the top of this entry. We stayed one night in Nashville and went to a girls dinner and toured some of the honky tonk bars as they call them near Printer's Alley...which by the way I was calling Painters Alley until I read the big sign down there and corrected myself :) We had a great time catching up and just hanging out and shopping. I think those girls weekend should be mandatory once a quarter- what do you say girls? We came back to Bowling Green and spent a night here with Aaron and Kayden. It was a very refreshing weekend. I can go on and on about our trip to Alabama to see KSU get beat by Auburn (ugh!) and all of our other fun excursions, but I am seriously getting a hand cramp from typing- so call me or email me if you want more. I have also started a new portion of the web site, my picture page! It is a much better way for you to see the pics I post. Hope you enjoy! By the way- for those of you that seem to check all the time for my updates- let me know and I can add you to an email I can send out to announce new updates. That's it for now....

Much love from Kentucky-

Jamie, Aaron and Kayden

Loving

23

HAPPY 4TH ANNIVERSARY TO US...

October 4, 2007

Happy 4th Anniversary to us...

So yesterday was our 4th Wedding Anniversary...Whew! Who knew so much could happen in a year. I sadly couldn't even remember what we did last year to celebrate #3 (I will blame this on continued chemo brain). Aaron actually remembered and I didn't. How sad!

Anyways....we had a babysitter all lined up and we went out on the town just the two of us for dinner and a drink. It was a perfect way to spend our evening. Good food, good drinks, and good company. I hate to say that all I did was get a card for my honey (yes, it was Hallmark Tressa!), but I made it all mushy inside and told him how much his support has meant to our family in the last year. Sitting here thinking about it today I don't think a card can do justice for what I would like to express to him. He has been a rock for the last year. Always working hard to support our family, while still being a good husband and daddy. I am sure he answer the question "how is she doing?" more times then he wants to think about.

I don't think that the spouses ever get enough credit for all the support they provide during something like going through cancer. It is a tough road to walk not being able to fix something in the person you love. I have been able to sit back and focus on myself mainly because of the people that surround me with their support (especially our families). So as I look back at the last year...honey, you have been so much more then just a husband to me. I am so happy that I have you here by my side, through the good times and bad, and in sickness and health (boy, you sure didn't know what you signed up for on that one did you!?).

My silly card may have brushed the surface on how much you mean to Kayden and I, but I thought that you should get some credit outside of our little dinner last night. So I am proclaiming you to be #1 in our eyes...I hope you truly understand how much I love you and am looking forward to spending many, many and maybe one more many for good measure :) more years together raising our beautiful daughter.

Committed.

24

OCTOBER IS BREAST CANCER AWARENESS MONTH

October 10, 2007

October is Breast Cancer Awareness Month

So I had chemo this Monday. I drove myself again this time. I got sick a couple of times ago and Aaron went with me to make sure I could drive the 3 1/2 hours home after my last appt. I feel really good so far this week, not even really tired like I normally am. I didn't even end up with my headache I usually get. I always make sure to stop and take a few breaks (there is two different outlet malls I tend to visit on the way home!) so I don't get tired. I left the house a 7 a.m. this past Monday and didn't get home until 10 p.m. It makes for a long day- funny, when Aaron drove me we were home by 7 p.m. Guess he must have that efficient stopping/driving thing down better then me. I only have two more weeks of my Xeloda portion of my trial. Xeloda is a pill that I take in the a.m. and p.m. for two weeks and then have a week off. It is what has caused my hand/foot syndrome which is a very common side effect of this particular drug. It causes increased sensitivity, cracks and peeling of my hands and feet, and some minor pigment change in my hands. It is nothing I can't put lotion on and relieve though. I am on my 6th and final cycle, so after next week I will only have to go in and do my Avastin chemo (through IV) once every three weeks until May 2008. A lot of you have asked where I am at in my treatments recently, I hope this answers most of your questions.

I think I may have mentioned that my 1st diagnosis anniversary is coming up on Oct. 20th. I am going to play in a tennis tournament with my mom here in Bowling Green. It is called the Hope Tournament- to raise money for Breast Cancer Research. I get to play free since I am a survivor! It seems a fitting way to spend the day. I even have a pink tennis skirt to wear :) We will take some pictures and post them so you can see us in action! Anyways... better get to work- Kayden is at daycare today and my moments alone are precious and must be used sparingly!

I almost forgot...October is Breast Cancer Awareness month. Ladies, be sure you do your monthly breast exam (or for the guys- tell a woman you love to do theirs) and commit to doing it every month from here on out. Just write a note on your calendar and DO IT. Also make sure you have not skipped your mammogram for those of you that are old enough to do them (typically 35+, earlier if you have a family history).
Remember...it can happen to anyone. You are the one who is in control of your health- take charge and be proactive about it! Enough for now. I will step down from my soapbox for now :)

Much love-

Jamie

Happy

25

HAPPY HALLOWEEN

November 1, 2007

Happy Halloween!

The last couple of weeks have been busy around here as usual. Aaron's mom and her friend came up to Bowling Green to visit. Then my mom came up to play with me in a doubles tennis tournament here called the Hope Tournament. It was put on to help raise awareness/funds for breast cancer and research. It also happened to fall on the weekend of my one year diagnosis anniversary. It was a fun time. We won three out of our four matches. I haven't seen the final results yet to see where we placed yet, I will let you know! Mom ended up staying for the week because I came down with strep throat after all the weekend activities. I was pretty wiped out and in a lot of pain from my throat. She helped out with Miss Kayden- and even went with me when we ended up in the emergency room again with another ear infection. So we are both on antibiotics now and getting better each day. I am still tired, but feel much better then I did last week.

We ended up making a quick trip back to KS last weekend for an unexpected funeral. A friend of ours step father passed away after a long battle with cancer. It was really sad for all of us, and hit home for Aaron and I. We also received some more bad news yesterday that Aaron's co-worker had passed away after a hard battle with prostate cancer. Aaron and I had been trying to lend our support to him throughout his battle. He was diagnosed shortly after we moved here. Today as I sit here writing about this my heart hurts for these individuals and their families. I almost feel guilty. I want to be mad- who gets to decide who beats cancer and who doesn't? Is it that easy for us to have kicked this cancer or do I have more to overcome in my future? Just when you think you have gotten past the hard part something changes and you are fighting it all over again. I guess all I can do is keep my head up and think the positive thoughts and be thankful for what we have right now. I have often given advice to people I meet along the way of my cancer treatments-people that are in the same situation as I am. "Don't stress over what you cannot change, the future won't change due to you worrying about it, so in the long run it is a waste of energy." Guess I need to take my own advice and stop stressing over what I can't control. Please keep Bill and John's families in your thoughts and prayers as they deal with the loss of their loved ones. They will be missed dearly.

On to happier talk from the Pursley house....

We had a blast doing halloween here with Kayden. She is finally old enough to enjoy it. She got to dress up as Snow White at her daycare open house on Monday. Last night she was dressed up as a Rock Star! I worked on saying trick or treat with her all day and she still couldn't quite get it.

We were invited by our neighbors the Armstrong's to go to their church's Trunk or Treat- they all decorated their car trunks and had treats for the kids to walk around and receive. Kayden was a little apprehensive at first but soon walked up on her own behind all the big kids and held our her open bag for treats. I finally got her to at least say thank you before she was off to the next spot. She turned into a candy monster as soon as she got back in the car and had to have some of everything. She was so sticky neither of us wanted to carry her :) We ran around town visiting friends and other kids and made a fun night of it. She was definitely hopped up on sugar when we finally got her to bed. She kept screaming "I need the bag!" meaning her bag she had used to trick or treat. We finally had to make the candy bag disappear for her to go upstairs and go to bed. Mom and dad were right behind her to go to sleep! We were all tired.

I have saved the best for last......I had my 6 month mammogram check up this past Monday (also had chemo). It came back NORMAL!!!!! No sign of any lumps or unusual spots. This is great news! I will not have to go back for my next one for another year!!! Yeah! All of your thoughts and prayers are working! Keep 'em coming! Better go for now, I need to go be productive since Kayden is at daycare working off the last of her sugar high.

Much love to everyone!

Jamie

Encourager

26

MERRY CHRISTMAS FROM THE PURSLEYS

December 17, 2007

Merry Christmas from the Pursleys

Whew- it has been a busy last two months. Sorry to be so out of touch. I am in Indy today getting my chemo and finally decided to get my update done and sent out. By the way...consider yourself "Christmas carded" from the Pursleys. Every year I vow to shop throughout the year for presents so it isn't such a strain on the ol' pocketbook, and to send out super cool picture cards with a letter, and to relax and enjoy the season. And every year I continue to do none of the above! Ugh!!! I have yet to get an actual christmas card list together with updated addresses for everyone. So the task becomes daunting and I put it off and declare that next year is the year! Oh well.....guess we have a lot on our plate with all of the traveling back and forth to KS to see our loved ones in person. That is my excuse this year. Next year I vow to do better :)

So we have been very busy the past month. I spent 12 days in Honolulu, HI in November, without Kayden. My dad did a couple of remodels on some Payless stores on the island and I got to go and "work" with him while he was down there. It was a much needed mommy vacation for me. My parents were there and my brother and Aaron joined us for almost a week right before Thanksgiving. I have updated some pictures from the trip on my picture page. We had lots of fun hitting the beaches and shopping in Waikiki. I even got to visit my friend Leigh who lived on the island. We played tennis several times with some locals and the boys rode dad's moped that he purchased while he was there :) We also went to see Pearl Harbor- which was very cool. We stayed in a house that my dad rented while he was there for the job. It had an incredible view of the city and also of Diamond Head crater. It was hard to come home to the bleak cold weather- but I missed my baby girl! 12 days is a long time to be away from her. It took me a few days to get back in the swing of things and win her back after she got to stay with Grandma Kitty for so long. I think she is still worried I am going to leave her again. We have had a bit of separation anxiety since I got home. That mixed with her terrible two stage in full effect- she has been quite a handful lately.

We had a good Thanksgiving with Aaron's family coming to Bowling Green to visit. We also headed back to KS last week to celebrate Kayden's 2nd birthday and my 32nd birthday. She was quite the princess at her party. She now sings "Happy Burfday" before she opens presents and may be in for a surprise when Christmas comes and we don't sing before opening presents :) She is starting to potty train and it is going to be interesting. We recently purchased a video called Potty Time- which is hilarious! She is super into it and sits on the potty chair with her pants around her ankles tapping her fingers to the music as they sing about going potty. It is a riot and I have some videos that will most definitely be grounds for embarrassment in the future!

I have been feeling pretty good lately. I have still been tired overall and we have all been battling a cold since Thanksgiving which doesn't help. Hopefully we will kick it by Christmas time so we aren't spreading germs in Kansas again. I have been pretty anxious lately for some reason. I think that my mind is racing a hundred different directions like it always has....but I can't seem to keep up with it as well as I used to. I can't really put my finger on what it is that is so frustrating. I just can't seem to get it together like I used to on a day to day basis. It is really hard to accept that I might still have some cognitive effects from the chemo and radiation that are impairing my ability to stay on task and focused so I can be productive. I feel like I am constantly making excuses when I forget things and run around like a crazy person without really accomplishing much. It is frustrating for Aaron and I know that Kayden probably feels my frustration too. I wish I could just snap my fingers and start with a clear slate with no to do list or anything I need to complete or take care of....but life doesn't offer that pause button or restart that would take care of my problems. So I struggle to keep up the positive attitude and do what I can do as well as I can. I don't like to feel incompetent or incomplete....but those are the two words I would probably use to explain myself lately. I recently wrote in an email to a friend who was commending me on my journey the past year..."Thanks for the positive words! It is always helpful to have people remind me that what I am doing is for a reason! Some days I feel just plain tired of doing it." I guess is is only natural after such an experience to want to make the best of everything. I want to make the most of what I have worked so hard to save- my family, my friends, my work, etc. I just need to find that happy medium where I don't feel so out of control and out of whack. I can't do that constantly worrying about how much I am doing wrong or not accomplishing- but rather what I have accomplished and am doing right. I want to get out of this rut and get back to happy Jamie sometime soon. It has been awhile since I have used my site for venting frustrations, I hope you don"t mind me speaking with my heart as I work through things on my end.

Enough of that talk....I want to wish you all a very Merry Christmas and safe New Year! Hopefully we will see you while we are in town over the holidays. Enjoy your families and friends and spoil your kids if you have them! It has been a long year and we intend to send it out with a bang! Let 2008 bring you all joy and prosperity in both love and life!

Much love to each of you from my chemo chair-

Jamie

Promising

27

LONG TIME NO BLOG...

June 17, 2008

Long time no blog...

Hey everyone. To those of you that have faithfully checked my site to see new news...thanks! Sorry to disappoint you in the past 6 months, but honestly there was nothing to report other then the fact that we had returned back to our normal lives pre-cancer. We have been traveling lots and making new friends in Bowling Green. I can't believe it has been a year since we moved here! Miss Kayden has grown up so much! And speaking of growing- my hair has done quite a bit of growing as well! We have been to Florida, Kansas, and Arkansas all in the last three months. We have a trip to Kansas planned over the forth. I will be headed to San Diego for a girl's trip at the end of July, and then we will hopefully turn around and go to Austin for Labor Day weekend. Whew.... it makes me tired just thinking about all the packing that requires!

Just to catch you up on my health. As most of you know I took part in a clinical trail for a drug called Avastin over the past year. I was driving to Indy once every 3 weeks to get my infusion. It was not a bad drug to be getting. No terrible side affects other then some sinus issues and minor headaches. No hair loss, nausea or neuropathy so I was happy to partake! In March my Dr. noticed my left arm was slightly swollen and it turned out that I had a blood clot in a vein in my chest. They immediately stopped the Avastin and made the decision to take my port out. I started taking a shot called Lovenox (blood thinner) for several weeks and then started on Coumadin (another blood thinner). I am still currently taking Coumadin and will be on it for a couple more months. So as of March I have been done with my treatments. It was weird to go from actively being treated to not being treated. I guess you could label me as a treatment junkie! I almost prefer to be actively kicking cancer butt rather then sitting back and waiting. I had my first cancer free anniversary on March 20th. It was a bittersweet day. I almost feel like I tiptoed through it. I have been feeling great lately. I have been able to start playing a lot more tennis here- I found a couple leagues that I enjoy during the week. I have started working out more and we are all really beginning to eat better as a family. It is such a lifestyle change to treat your body right. Isn"t that sad!? I have gotten a lot more involved with Juice Plus+ (I am a distributor of the product now) in the past several months and it has opened a lot of doors for me to learn more about nutrition and overall wellness. I am happy to share information with anyone that is interested.

I could go on and on since it has been 6 months since I last blogged.... but I should get to the point of my choosing to blog again today. I called my doctor a few weeks ago because the area where they did my original lumpectomy felt different to me during my monthly exam. There is a lot of scar tissue at the site from my surgery and my original biopsy so it is very hard to tell what is normal and what isn't. He told me to come in and Aaron and I met with him yesterday. After his exam he agreed that it was worth taking a better look at and sent me for an MRI of the breast that evening before we left Indy. He called back today to say that there is an area of concern and they want to do some more tests. So here we are northbound on I 65 (again) to stay the night in Indy and go in bright and early for an ultra sound and biopsy. Talk about speedy service! It pays to be a returning customer I guess :) Just kidding. It could very well be scar tissue but they want to be proactive and make sure we know exactly what it is. So here I am again.... holding my breath for another test result that could totally change our lives again. Part of me is mad, part sad and all these other emotions- but most of all I feel like the other shoe may have just dropped. I am struggling to listen to my own advice and not stress things I cannot change- but in all honestly this SUCKS! Anyways. I will keep you all posted. I know this is the first time that most of you have heard this- and I am sorry to send this mass information out.... but it has happened pretty fast and we are trying just to keep calm ourselves- so stay tuned and I will let you know what we find out as soon as I possibly can. Meanwhile, say a few extra prayers for us and cross your fingers and toes that this is not a reoccurrence.

Much love from I-65 North

Jamie and Aaron

Devastating

28

ROUND TWO...

July 3, 2008

Round Two...

As most of you already know, the biopsy came back positive for cancer. The cancer has recurred in the same location as my first tumor. We had a CAT and Bone scan done later that week of my biopsy to verify the cancer has not spread. Thank goodness it has stayed in the breast and has not traveled anywhere else at this point. There is no way to know why it has returned- the Avastin chemotherapy I had for the last year most likely kept it at bay during that time. When I stopped taking that chemo (due to my blood clot that formed) then my body decided to feed into this tumor. It is truly frustrating to have to be at this point again. Fortunately we are better prepared for this go round. We have a great team that we feel very comfortable with at IU and the unknowns we had the first time around are no longer there. We know what questions to ask the doctors and we know better how to deal with the waiting for results. Not that it is any easier just because you have been there done that. We met with my doctors to discuss options and have come to an agreement on the best plan of action. I will undergo a bilateral mastectomy, which means have both breasts removed. The right side (tumor) will be done with a Latisimus Dorsi Flap (click on the word to see an in-depth explanation- it's pretty graphic so beware). In a nutshell this procedure involved taking the skin/nipple/areola/tissue of my breast and transplanting skin/tissue taken from my back (lat area). Then they will put an expander (temporary implant) under my chest muscle before closing up. The left side will be what is called a prophylactic mastectomy. This is called that because we are removing the breast tissue even though there is no sign of disease at this time. This was my choice to do this breast as well. I don't want to take the chance of a tumor popping up in that breast down the road. The surgeon will remove only the breast tissue and will put an expander under the muscle on this side as well. My skin/nipple/areola will be spared on this side. Post surgery I will visit the plastic surgeon and he will gradually fill my expanders through a port in the expander itself. This will stretch the muscle and skin over time. It's kind of nice because I get to go home and try the size out for a week and then go back and tell him to keep going or that I am happy with the size. That will be nice. Hopefully it makes it easier to get used to the new girls size too since it will be gradual. The surgeon will also be checking the lymph nodes left on the right side to make sure there aren't any other nodes that be removed, not that I have that many left from the last surgery.

The surgery is scheduled for 7:30am on Monday, July 7th at Indianapolis University Medical Hospital. I am in KS currently with Aaron and Kayden and we are going to just drive on Sunday straight to Indiana. My brother and Aunt Cindy will be hopping in with us to be there for the surgery. They are expecting it to be around 10 hrs. long and I will most likely be in the hospital for approximately 5 days depending on how well I do after surgery. After they release me I will head back to KY to recover from the surgery. It will be 4-6 weeks to recover from surgery. I will head back in to see the plastic surgeon and have the expanders filled up over the next couple of months. I get to wear the new girls around for a few months as they get pumped up and then I get to choose when to say stop. Kind of a nice perk if you ask me! I will have someone do a posting to keep you updated on how the surgery goes on Monday. It was great to see those of you that we saw in KS. It definitely helped keep me distracted from thinking about the surgery! Better go for now. I will check back in before the surgery hopefully.

Much love from KS-

Jamie

Loved.

29
THE FINAL COUNTDOWN

July 6, 2008

The final countdown....

We shipped Roxy (our dog) and Kayden off to Grandma and Grandpa Pursley's this morning. They are troupers for taking on that kid for a whole week, but I feel so much better knowing she is surrounded by so much love and fun there. She has been riding horses with Kitty twice a day. It is too cute when she is screaming Giddy-Up. Part of me is sad that she has no idea what is going on and the other part of me is super glad that she doesn't understand. I tried to tell her last night at bed time that I would be going to the doctor this week- she got all excited and wanted to go too because she had a boo boo that she needed to show him. I have done good up until now but I am finally feeling that pit welling up in my stomach. Once we got checked into our hotel we went to PF Chang's in Downtown Indy to have a good dinner and topped it off with some ice cream at DQ! Aaron thought we needed to eat at Hooters for dinner. Hardy Har!

On a different note- to those of you that are saying prayers for me- I have a favor to ask. My friend Lisa had a baby boy, Austin, yesterday in Richmond where we used to live. He has been having trouble breathing on his own and is being transported from Richmond to St. Vincent's in Indianapolis to be taken care of. He needs some extra prayers so he can get better and go home with his family soon. Also, Nate, my brother in law, is in Illinois with his father who is in hospice care due to cancer. It doesn't look like he will be with us much longer so keep him in your thoughts as well.

As far as surgery news, my dad will be putting an update on the web site tomorrow after the surgery is over. I have to be there at 5:30 am (eastern time) and the actual surgery is set for 7:30 am. It is expected to take around 10 hours. So don't expect to see anything until late afternoon. I hope I am able to get some sleep tonight, if I don't- I have all day tomorrow to catch up on it! Bye for now...wish me luck! I hope to be able to do my own update be the end of the week. Thank you so much for your continued support. It has been such a help in keeping my spirits up as we come to this next challenge. Talk w/ you soon hopefully!

Much love from the "girls"-

Jamie and Aaron

Unbreakable

30

SURGERY UPDATE...

July 7, 2008

Surgery update...

Dad reporting in on Jamie, she's out of surgery and doing well. I'm not as good at writing these as Jamie is but here we go...

No More Cancer! Out with "The Girls", and in with the "New and Improved Girls"!

We (Kathy, Scott and Cindy) met Jamie and Aaron at the hospital this morning around 7am they had already been there since 5:30 am for pre-op. We were able to be in the room with her up until they took her away for surgery. The doctor was the only one allowed to sign "the girls"; the rest of us had to just wave bye bye. She went off to surgery around 8:40 and Dr. Goulet came out around 11:30 and said all had gone well with his portion and Dr. Cacioppo took over for the reconstruction procedure. He came out around 4:45 saying everything went well. After she was brought up to the 5th floor recovery room we were told to wait until the nurses said we could come in, Aaron did not seem to want to wait and was chasing after her bed down the hall. I waited a couple of minutes and had to go see for myself how she was doing. She was mumbling something to Aaron about "where's my mom?" and something about everything is itching. She is pretty heavily sedated with pain meds, which cause her to be a bit confused. It was nice to see her after waiting not so patiently in the very cold waiting room. Aaron plans on staying in the room with her tonight for when she wakes up. Hopefully I can have Jamie talk me through the next update so you won't have to stumble through another one of these. We can feel the love all the way out here in Indy and it is feels wonderful. Thanks for the support.

Dave, Kathy, Scott, Cindy, Aaron and Jamie with the "new and improved girls"

Dedicated

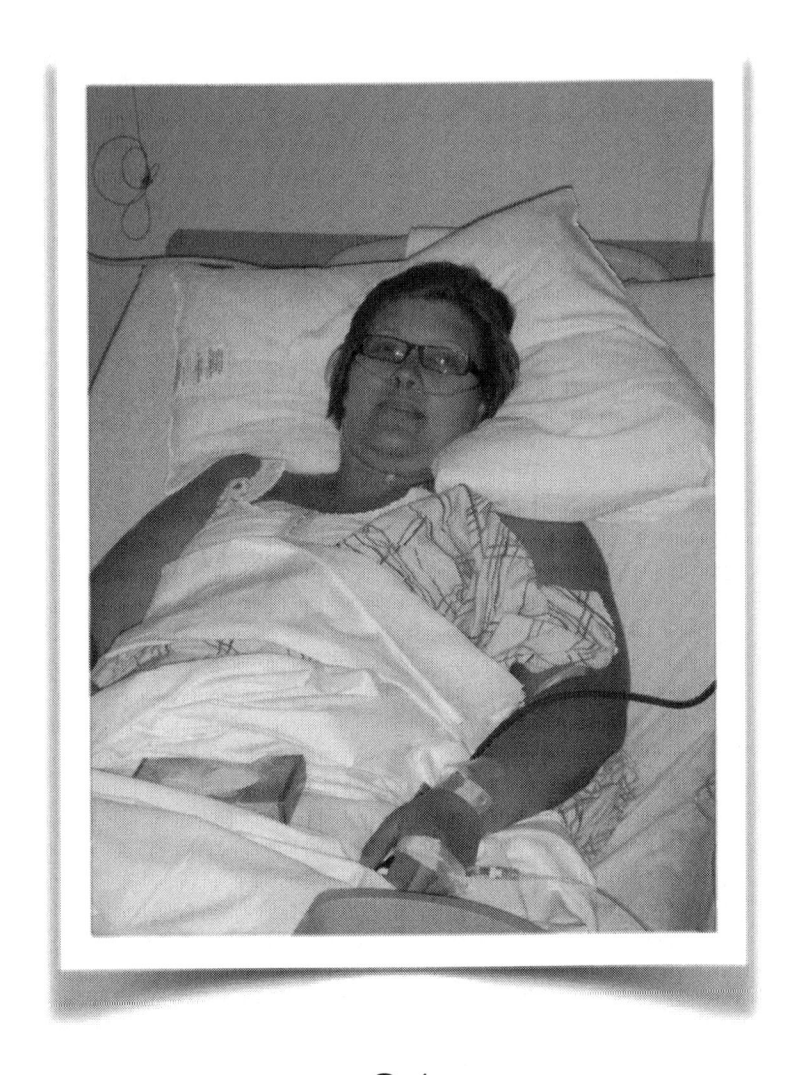

31

RECOVERY UPDATE

July 9, 2008

Recovery update...

Sorry, it's dad again. Aaron spent the night (Monday) at the hospital with Jamie. She was pretty restless so both of them went without much sleep. Yesterday (day 1 recovery) was a good day, Jamie was able to get out of bed several times with some assistance to use the bathroom. She is still on the morphine drip and is not bashful about pushing the button for another hit. Dr. Goulet came by late in the day and was very pleased with the plastic surgeons work. Everything looked good and he thought she might be able to head home on Thursday. Jamie showed all of us her new girls and she appears to be pleased with the reconstruction work so far. I was surprised at how small the skin graft on the right breast was, I was expecting something much larger. Kathy has been hovering over Jamie and fulfilling her every request. Jamie was able to get a call into Kayden for some much needed mommy/daughter conversation. My sister Cindy and Scott caught a flight back to Kansas yesterday afternoon and their support and love was very, very much appreciated. Jamie requested Aaron to sleep at the motel last night so he could get some sleep, he resisted but went along with her request since she was in good hands with the nursing staff at this hospital. The night nurse informed us this morning that she had a rough night, one of her drains was giving her some problems and she was feeling sick most of the night. They were able to get the drain corrected and she got some sleep from 10-2. Just so you know, we have been reading the comments everyone is leaving to Jamie and they lift her spirit, thanks. Day 2 of recovery is underway and Jamie is very strong in her determination to keep moving forward with her "kickin cancer" campaign.

Everyone in room 5744 says thanks for the support.

Gentle

32

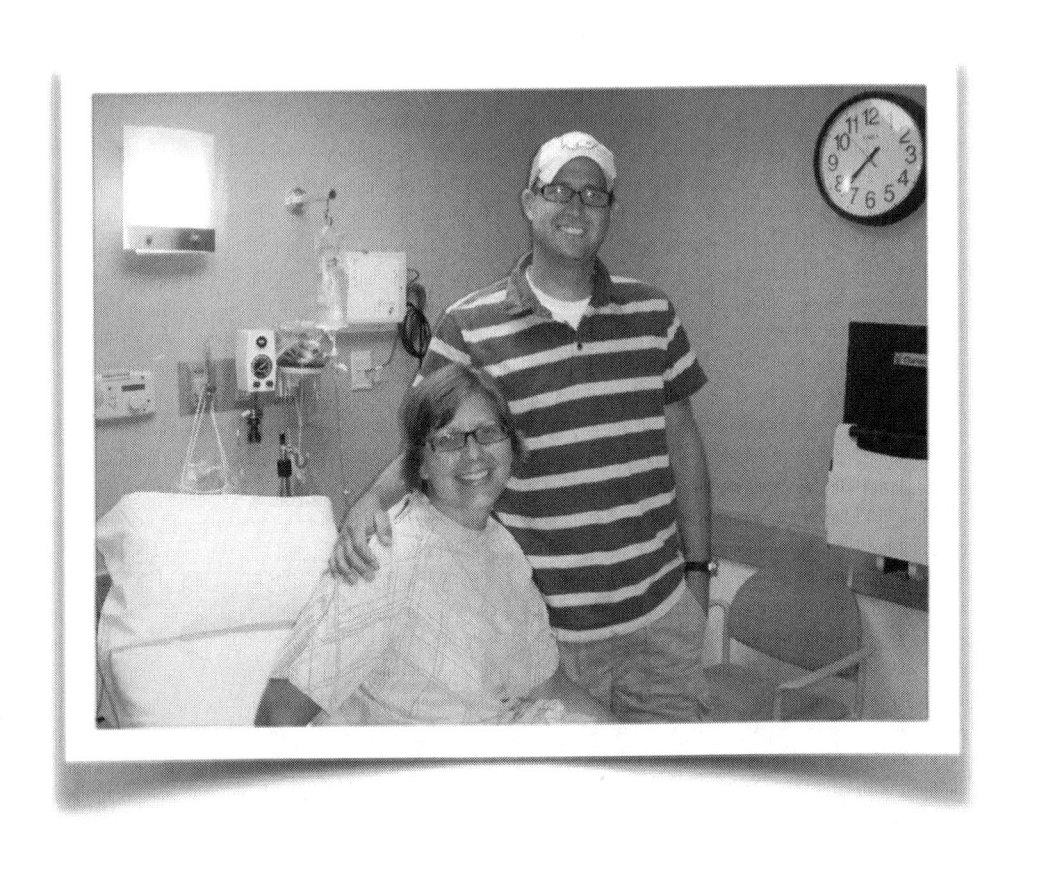

BACK WITH THE LIVING...

July 10, 2008

Back with the living...

I got my 4:30 am visit from the nurse wanting to do my vitals. I couldn't go back to sleep so thought I would do a quick update. Thanks to everyone that has stayed up to date on my progress this week. It has been slow going. I had a rough Tuesday night, vomited several times and then got a severe morphine headache. It took till about 11:00 am to come out of that horrible place. I finally had a real meal yesterday- peanut butter and jelly! Can't go wrong there. I also got an edible arrangement from the Kembles (friends of our family) that had delicious strawberries and pineapple and grapes on it. Yummy. They truly hit the spot! Thanks guys!

As far as how I am doing-my back is really hurting when I get up and down to move around. I have been pretty nauseous so they keep giving me Zofran to help with that. My chest is fairly numb for now so it isn't giving me direct pain. I have a Morphine drip that I get to push every 10 minutes so that helps a lot. Overall I'm just really uncomfortable and very stiff and woozy when I stand up. I have 5 JP drains that come out of different surgery areas. They are all still producing quite a bit of drainage so it looks like I will go home with all 5 of those. Lucky mom gets to strip and drain those puppies! I passed out cold once when she was draining one of my jp drains back during my lumpectomy surgery. Hopefully there is no replay of that! My breasts are all out of shape right now because there is just external skin with no tissue behind it to shape it. They are kind of rectangle shaped due to the expander that is now in place under the muscle. As I go back in to get the expanders filed up they will begin to take better shape. The transplant patch from my back to my front is smaller than I had expected and looks great according to both surgeons. I will have to trust them on this one because it is hard to know what is good and what is bad to me. Plastic surgeon says it's his best one yet, but I'm sure he tells all the girls that though :)

It looks like they will send me home either Friday or Saturday. Won't know for sure until we see the docs again today. I had better go for now. Too much typing is not good on my back incision. Plus I am getting a case of the sleepy eyes...finally. Talk w/you all soon!

Much love from my hospital bed-

Jamie

Transparent

33

PATHOLOGY REPORT IS IN...

July 10, 2008

Pathology report is in...

I am happy to report a very good day here in room 5744. I was able to get off the morphine drip and start my oral pain meds. I was also able to take off my compression on my legs that helped with circulation while I was on my back. So I can now get up to go to the bathroom without dragging a huge IV tree behind me. My pain is much better today. My back is giving me a lot of flare ups but nothing unbearable. I am able to do lots of walking around the hospital ward to get my joints back in action.

Dr. Goulet's nurse, Carol, reported back that the pathology report came back. My left breast was completely clear of cancer (which is what we expected), and that the right side had no new lymph node involvement. The tumor itself was 3 cm this time (my original tumor during my first diagnosis was 6 cm). It is very good news that the tumor was restricted to only the right breast and it wasn't able to move anywhere else. Very good news for the day! I am going to be released tomorrow (Friday) morning. I am waiting to see Dr. Cacioppo, the plastic surgeon, this evening so we can go over the final details before I am released. I don't know when this guys sleeps?! I also got to do a sponge bath and wash my hair today. Man it is amazing how much better that can make you feel after feeling so grimy yesterday. Now if I could just take care of the other two s's I would be nice and satisfied. Well- better sign off for now. The hospital is having major problems with their internet service today so I haven't been able to get this posted in a timely manner. You will probably get to read several of them all at once if I can get it to publish tonight. Ta Ta for now.

Much love from my chair and not the bed!

Jamie

Optimistic

34

HOME TO KENTUCKY

July 12, 2008

Home to Kentucky

Well I made the trip home to Kentucky yesterday. It was pretty uncomfortable, but I slept through most of it. I got to see my Dr. Cacioppo (that is him in the picture) on Thursday night late (he had a case he was busy with all day) so he came bearing a milkshake at 10:30pm. Now that is my kind of doctor! He gave me the OK to leave on Friday. He said that the incisions were looking great and he suggested we come back to see him on Tuesday July 22nd. By then I will hopefully be able remove all 5 drains and do my first fill on the expanders. The drains are the worst part so far. I have two coming out of my back from where he tunneled the transplant skin/tissue/muscle around to the breast area. Then I have two drains from my left breast and one from my right. They have to be drained twice a day and it is a pretty uncomfortable lengthy process. So I am going to go ahead and admit that part SUCKS! I am sure everyone else will agree with me since they have to be the ones draining it for me. It is a tedious process and one wrong pull puts me in major pain. I do my lamaze breathing to get through it usually. That way I am not sitting there anticipating the tug. Today has been a pretty quite day of laying around and napping. Kayden has been taking total advantage of having both sets of grandparents here. She has been very good with me so far- understanding when I tell her I can't pick her up. I got to shower today too- a real shower! Kayden decided she needed to get in on the action and got to get her shower before me....I had to sit there on my shower seat naked waiting for her. The things we do to make these kids happy! I will try to write more later. We are having a lot of trouble with getting these blogs updated due to the high level of activity on the Mac web site. They just released their new Iphone yesterday and everyone is online trying to get their phones activated. So if you can't leave a comment or there is an entire blog missing when you click on to read it then know that's what is wrong. Hopefully we will be back up and running as usual by the end of the weekend. Talk to you all soon!

Much love from my kitchen table-

Jamie

ps: I am apologizing now for my awful pictures that have been posted on the past couple blogs. Guess it is kind of hard to look good when you are on drugs and haven't showered for three days!

Humorous

35
LAYING LOW

July 15, 2008

Laying low...

It has been a slow start to the week for us here. Kayden had a play date yesterday with her friend Kaitlyn. It sounds like she had a ball. I am desperately trying to get things back on a semi schedule here so she can have some stability. She is definitely showing signs of over stimulation with all of the activity from the past several weeks. She is such a trouper as far as adapting to all the changes but I can't help but wonder if we aren't unintentionally creating some separation anxiety with all of these people coming and going in her life including Aaron and I while we were gone for surgery. She's been really good overall- with a few meltdowns along the way. It breaks my heart when she calls out for me in the middle of the night after a bad dream and I can't get up and go cuddle with her in her "princess bed" as she calls it. I got to read her a bed time book in my bed the other night after a particularly bad breakdown. It was so sweet to have her leaning on my pillow with Aaron on the other side of her doing the snuggling. Daddy's deserve cuddles too I guess I can share for now :) She is starting back to part time day care today which is two full days a week. Hopefully this will be a big help in getting her back on track.

Have I told you the story about our household name for breasts/nipples? Well I will tell it again for those of you that may not be up to date with the Pursley terminology. A while back Kayden was rubbing Roxy's belly and asked me what the nubby things were on her tummy. I took a minute to explain that they were nipples and that Uno our cat also had them, and mommy and daddy had them, and that she also had them. She was fascinated and proceeded to flash her chest around and talk about her...pickles, which apparently is what she heard me say instead of nipples. Pickles are a now a favorite topic in our household such as... we don't show our pickles to other people (put down your dress), pat my pickles mom (rub my belly) etc. It has been quite amusing and I am sure the term will last well into her high school days- kidding! Anyways....I explained to her that my boo boo's were on my pickles and she followed that with a very lengthy ohhhhhhhhh. She still asks to see my pickle boo boo's from time to time and she is very interested in all of my medicine and my drains. But overall- she doesn't miss a beat when it comes to her mommy- with or without hair, in bed or out of bed, with my alien babies (drains under my shirt) in my belly or anything else. Isn't it nice to just be appreciated for who you are? Kids are certainly good for that- at least at this age they are!!

I was able to go in to the Coumadin clinic here in town yesterday to get my coagulation level tested. I am unfortunately at a level of 1.0 (thick blood) when I need to be between 2.0 and 3.0 (therapy level or thin blood). So I had to double up my dose last night and tonight to try to thin my blood out a little more or get within therapy levels. Being within the right levels of coagulation will alleviate any worries that I may produce another clot in my body. There is no danger with me being this low for now because I have continued my Lovenox shots (which acts as a back up to the Coumadin). I know it all sounds confusing- it is and I am slowing learning more than I probably ever wanted to know about thinners/clotting and all other things blood related. I will try to explain the best I can when talking about the medical stuff. I am going to make another attempt with my dad this morning at figuring out why the site won't let people leave comments on my last few posts and to figure out why some of the blogs won't show up after you click on them. Hopefully we can get it figured out between the two of us. I'll catch up again soon!

Much love from my cocoon of pillows-

Jamie

ps: If you ever see a word or phrase written in a different color or in bold on one of my blogs- click on it for more information. For example Coumadin and Lovenox above.

pss: Did I mention how horrible I am at laying low? My mom is about to tie me down to something- she probably would if I could actually do it comfortably- but it takes me 20 minutes of situating to even come close to getting comfortable. I am like a dog circling around and around before I can find the exact right spot to lay. Not surprising with these drain tubes coming out of my lower back! Yeouch!

Kind

36

SO DONE WITH THESE DRAINS

July 16, 2008

So done with these drains...

I am so over these drains. I woke up this morning and one of the ones from my back was "leaking" ...ewwww! Apparently it is either clogged and/or infected and needs to be looked at. So I am headed in to see my local doctor here (I just saw him yesterday) to make sure we don't need to be doing something special with it. I heard back from my plastic surgeon and he said I could come up on Friday to get the drains out. I told him (or more so whined) that I wanted them OUT before the weekend. I will feel like a million bucks once I am drainless! Anyways...I thought I would dedicate this blog to all the awesome friends/ family I have helping me out. It always amazes me how much my support system helps me get through these times where I am not able to be 100%. I am so lucky to have a system that stretches from one coast line to the other and everyone is so awesome about thinking of their own special ways to show their support. I get cards in the mail throughout the week. I get calls and emails and comments on the web site (when it is working!). I have friends and neighbors here bringing food and trashy magazines :) It just makes me feel so good to know we are surrounded by such awesome people. And of course I can't leave out my mom who has been a trooper this week between Kayden and I she is hopping all the time. She has showered us both, fed us both, patched up our boo boo's....I can't even begin to say thank you to her for all of her time and efforts to make me feel better. It is something I know I would do for my own daughter in a heartbeat- but I know that it is not an easy task and I couldn't have a better person by my side. Mom you have and continue to be my best friend and confidant and I guess this type of experience only brings us closer. Let's make this our last though OK? And Dad- thank you for being her rock and my biggest fan- you know how much I love you. We will have the changing of the guards on Thursday and Aaron's mom will take over and give my mom a break. How lucky can I be to have two family's that love me enough to put up with me even in the worst of circumstances. And of course there is my husband. The rock in our house that keeps me in line and helps me look past all of the yuck of today towards the fun of the future. He has been so good putting up with my moodiness and my restlessness and sleeping on only a quarter of the bed since I take up the rest with my pillow cocoon. I know that you are working hard at work all day and then coming home to a house full of women that have had their own long day. Hang in there honey- we will get through this whether the house is clean when someone stops by or not :) Just kidding! I hate that we have to put our lives on hold again to deal with my cancer. It sucks and I wish it wasn't this way- but I guess we don't get to always choose how and when things are going to happen in our lives. I love you for helping me stay sane through this experience and I love you for loving me in whatever shape he may have me in- hairless, scarred up, boob-less hopefully we are done with all of the negative stuff and we can look forward to the full chest and cancer free Jamie soon!

Anyways. I just want to say that I can't say thank you enough to my friends and my family and don't forget my doctors for all that you have done to make this as easy as possible for us. You are appreciated and know that I would jump to get a chance to repay you down the road anyway I can. Off to the doctor to see about this icky drain. Check back in with you soon.

Much love-

Jamie

Unfair

37

OUT WITH THE DRAINS!!!

July 18, 2008

Out with the drains!!!

Can you believe how tolerant our cat is with her? He was lucky enough to get the princess headband and believe it or not actually wore it for a bit!

OK- so I was relieved of 4 out of 5 of the drains. I still have the one in my back. Ugh!!! I even took Dr. Cacioppo lunch from Jimmy Johns to try to bribe him into taking it out today while I was in Indy. But to no avail....he wants to keep it in till at least next Tuesday- possibly longer. The reason is that this particular drain is coming from the back area where they took the tissue/muscle and skin and it tends to put out more fluid for a longer time then the other locations, especially after taking out the other drains. He was pretty insistent that I keep it in so the fluid had somewhere to go for now. We don't want it to stay inside where it can cause another infection. No sireee! By the way...my antibiotic has cleared up the previous infection quite nicely so at least that part is better. So he told me the bad news with a sheepish smile and then bolted with my lunch I brought him! What a punk!! Just kidding of course! I got him to promise that if it is still draining less then 30 ccs by Tuesday then I can come up and get my first fill and he will take it out. If it is draining more than 30 ccs on Tuesday then he wants me to wait until the next Tuesday to come back. Let's cross our fingers cause this puppy is not fun! I wouldn't want to have to get violent or anything over a silly little painful pain in my back drain.

Aaron's mom is now here and taking care of us this week. She drove me up to the appt. and back. It is always such an exhausting day by yourself so I was glad to have someone with me. Not to mention I couldn't keep my eyes awake for most of the trip. I guess these pain pills are good for something :) Anyways...just wanted to let you all know that I am feeling much much better and it should only get better from here! Aaron is off to play some poker with the guys tonight...he gets the punk #2 award today. I guess he is entitled to a bit of fun too. Just wait. Once I am drainless and off these pain meds I am so taking part in a big fat margarita!

Much love from our house to yours-

Jamie

Warm

38

ROOM TO RELAX

July 20, 2008

Room to relax...

I have finally complained enough and taken enough room up at night in our bed. Aaron got us a king size bed yesterday! Yeah! I am one of those people who needs their space when sleeping or I wake up uncomfortable all the time. Nothing against you honey-I swear! I just like to have a little breathing space after a day full of being treated like a human jungle gym it is nice to have that extra space to spread out. Between the dog the cat, Aaron and sometimes Kayden, I haven't had a good night's sleep in forever so this is a true treat for me! Unfortunately, I won't get to enjoy it quite yet because I am still stuck sleeping in the pillow cocoon which consists of 6-7 pillows and requires that I sleep on my back (I am a side sleeper so this is killing me to sleep like this!). I have to put a pillow on both sides of me to keep me from rolling over in my sleep. My chest is still sore enough that I wouldn't want to put any undue pressure on it. Good thing these pain meds make me sleepy enough to forget how uncomfortable I am. I am just glad I wore him down enough to finally splurge! I will be sprawled out soon enough and when I do- I am so going to take full advantage of the new real estate!

It was a quiet hot day here at our house. Aaron headed out to the lake with some friends today to take advantage of the heat. Kayden and I were both sad to have to stay home. She made me promise we would go on the boat soon, now I know how she feels when we leave her out of the fun stuff we do sometimes. She loves it on the water as much as her daddy and I do! I went to run some errands with Kitty and kind of over did it. I felt pretty light headed and nauseous when we got home so I spent the rest of the afternoon in bed. It's so hard to not take advantage of the time when I am feeling good. The second I do I end up overdoing it and in bed. Ugh. It pretty much sucks. I don't want to lose all my stamina like I did last time I went through this. It took so long to get it back after all my chemo/radiation/surgery. But there is not much I can do at this point. I guess I will give myself till the drains are out and they let me lift my arms above my shoulders. Then hopefully I will be in a better position to get moving again and start working on the uphill battle of recovering from the surgery. It is going to take a while before I can even get back to tennis I am guessing :(

On a positive note my drain was only 10 cc's tonight (it was 20 cc's this morning) so far so good. If I can keep this pace up and stay under 30 cc for a 24 hr period by Tuesday then I get this drain out and get on with the filling of the boobies! I'm pretty sure Aaron is going to start sending subliminal messages to me while I sleep about how "bigger is better" the excitement is starting to build! Woo Hoo! Well, that's all the action going on here at our house. Hopefully tomorrow I will wake up in a better mood and less frustrated that I am stuck in this rut. This update is starting to sound pretty bitter I definitely need an attitude adjustment on my end here. I'll work on that. Don't let the bed bugs bite.

Much love from my rut-

Jamie

Creative

39

PUMP, PUMP, PUMP IT UP!!!

July 24, 2008

Pump, pump, pump it up!!!

Welcome to the cocoon...I counted and we have 8 pillows on our bed and 2 body pillows! No wonder Aaron bought me a bigger bed :) Kayden thinks it is awesome for jumping on.

So I got the final drain out Tuesday! Yeah! They were also able to do my first fill. For those of you that don't understand what I am talking about. My reconstruction of the new girls will require that I get saline injected into my expanders that they placed under my chest muscle during my surgery. Each expander has an inverted port in it that they poke with a needle and inject saline into the expander. Think of the expander as a temporary breast implant. It has the capacity to stretch. I will get an injection of saline each week for 4-5 weeks. By doing it over time it allows my muscle/skin/tissue to expand slowly rather then all at once. Now that being said- you should have seen the size of the needle they had to use to get to the port on the expander. Aaron took one look and pulled the curtain so he didn't have to look. He's quite queasy when it comes to needles. I was pretty collected when they injected the needle...but once she started to push the saline in I got a little queasy myself. It was a crazy feeling. Then when they were done my poor boobs were tight as a drum. You could have bounced a quarter across the room off of them. I was pretty sore on the ride home- mainly on my left side for some reason. I took my pain pills and went on with our normal night once we got home. When I woke up yesterday morning I got up to go to the bathroom and made it about 4 steps before I collapsed on the bed. OMG ! That means oh my goodness for those of you that don't know text shortcuts. I got all sweaty and lightheaded and was sure I was going to pass out on the spot. Turns out I maybe should have set an alarm to take some pain meds during the night because I woke up in EXTREME PAIN! I was pretty sure I was dying. My whole right side was tight and hard. My stomach was turning and I was seeing stars. I guess I let my pain get ahead of me and my body was shutting down. It was quite a rough moment. I made it back to bed and stayed put all day. I continued to be in pain and nauseous all day. That I was not expecting. Holy crap is what I texted my plastic surgeon. What have you done to me??? So needless to say- stay ahead of the pain with the pain meds is the lesson for the day. I have woke up in a better place today. I am still very sore but not in pain. I was able to get up and walk around without the room spinning. I wonder if this is what I have to look forward to for the rest of my fills? These boobs might not get as big as Aaron had hoped if that is the case. I am no woos about pain either. So for the record- pumping up the boobs HURTS LIKE H!@#!!!!! Now you know.

I will try to check in tomorrow to let you know where the pain level is at. I have to go back and get my blood level checked by the Coumadin clinic today. My coagulation level shot up to 4.1 on Monday so we need to get it back between 2-3. Hopefully I am within range today so I can stop these painful Lovenox shots I have to give myself twice a day. I'll let you know. Off to the showers since it has been a couple of days :) My teeth are feeling a bit furry. OK- TMI (that means too much information!)

Much love from my Hydrocodone haze-

Jamie

Honorary

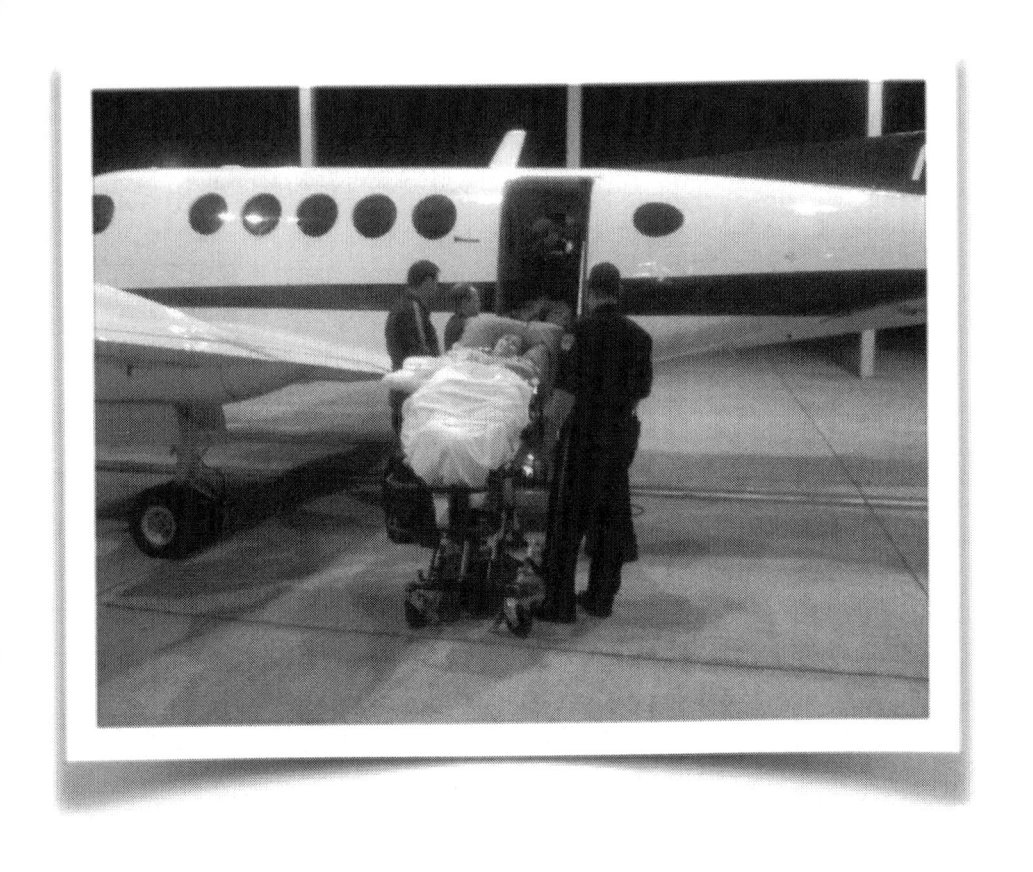

40

ICU KENTUCKY/INDIANAPOLIS

July 25, 2008

ICU Kentucky/Indianapolis

Jamie's update Thursday morning sounded like she was making some headway in her recovery but that was far from the truth. I'll try to keep this short, it's been a long 36 hrs for everyone, Jamie having the worst of it. Thursday afternoon she was having her blood levels checked at the doctors office, she became lightheaded and fainted. Kitty, Aaron's Mom, was with her at this time. They admitted her to the ICU at the Bowling Green Medical Center. Her blood pressure was very low. After running several tests, they determined that she was bleeding internally. At that time the doctors decided to give her a blood transfusion.

Sometime after midnight arrangements were made to fly her and Aaron to IUPUI. That trip was made around 3:30 in the morning and they admitted her to the ICU there. She had several more units of blood and plasma during the day to get her stable enough to operate. They took her into the operating room around 5:30 pm. They relieved the pressure and irrigated the area. Everything looked good, no infection and the reconstruction area was not damaged. She was back in her ICU room around 8:30 pm looking much better and experiencing a lot less pain. It's 12 midnight here and everyone is heading to bed to get some rest. I'll try to give a few more details tomorrow but just wanted everyone to know that she's doing well and we thank you for your support.

Dave

Supporting

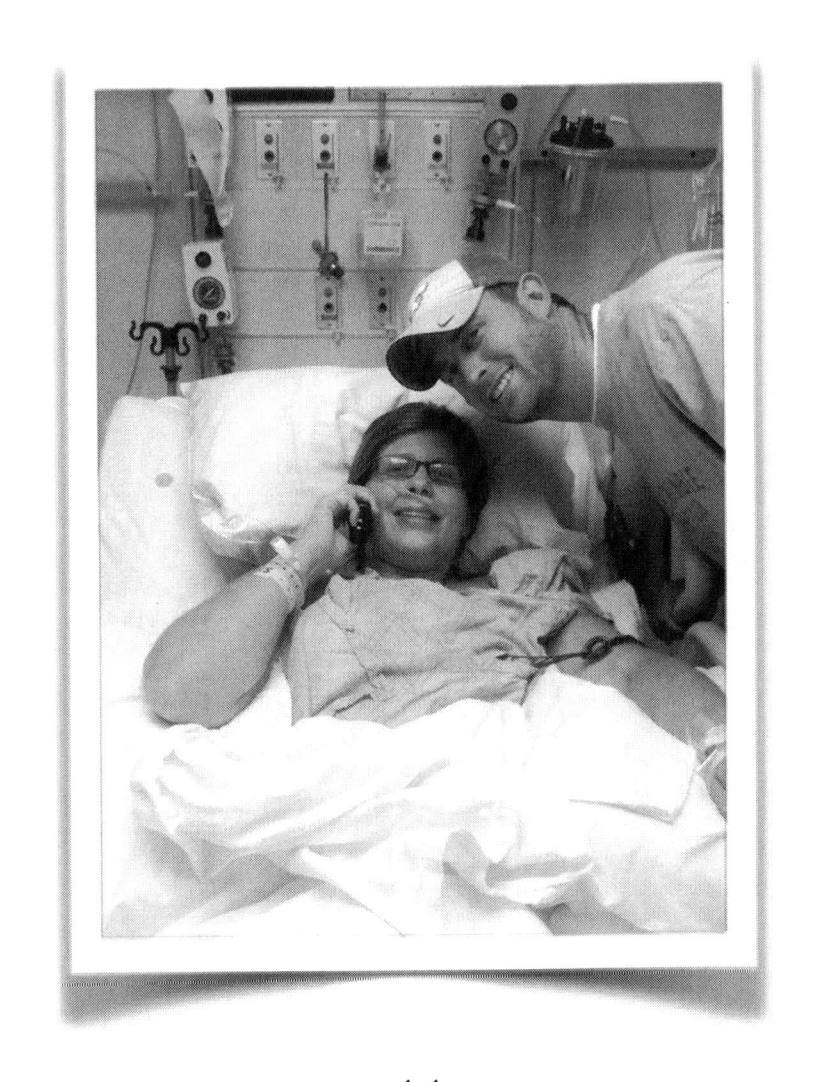

41

BACK AMONG THE LIVING

July 26, 2008

Back among the living

Same place different floor, ICU is located on the 3rd floor. Believe it or not, this picture was taken today around 2 pm, as she was talking with Kayden. It's hard to believe this is the same person that looked close to death less than 24 hrs ago. She is on bed rest today and I'm sure she doesn't feel like getting out of bed yet but she sure looks strong enough to. I said I would fill in a few details today about her time leading up to the surgery. I got a first hand narrative from her this morning when she woke up. After listening to her recount I am impressed with her ability to know when something is not right with her body and she knows she needs immediate medical attention. Her visit to have her blood checked started out as a regular trip but quickly escalated to a medical emergency. She began feeling like "her world was crashing in on her" while the tech was attempting to draw blood for the INR test. Each failed attempt to draw blood for this test put her closer to blacking out (hind sight, it's difficult to draw blood when 2-3 quarts of your blood has pooled around your body). After demanding to talk with her doctor to see what was wrong with her she was taken to an office to wait for him. He was on rounds and was not going to be there for 45 min. or so, this was not quick enough for her so she asked for the on call doctor ASAP. By this time she was in extreme pain and her body felt like concrete. A doctor came in soon and took some vitals and quickly decided to have her admitted to the hospital. While being admitted (paper work) she had a seizure type episode while sitting in the wheel chair. Kitty kept her from sliding out of the chair when she went rigid for 20 - 40 seconds. A nurse passing by her door called the First Responder Team and they admitted her to ICU. It was less than two hrs from the time she walked in for a blood draw to being admitted to ICU. Very glad this happened close to the hospital. The remainder of the day was spent taking numerous tests to determine what was wrong with her. She said that this was the worst pain she has had in her life (can't even imagine) and with each test she was taken from gurney to table or rolled around to have another doctor look at her back. At this point Jamie was in tears and very angry/frustrated with everything and everyone. Jamie said Aaron was not happy about so many different people coming in and doing the same painful thing over and over. He requested (not really a request) the medical personnel to be more efficient by having everyone come in that needed to look at her back so she would only be rolled over one more time. Aaron, it gives Kathy and I peace of mind knowing you're always watching out for her well being. The ultrasound test showed she may be bleeding internally and a sample of the fluid taken from the football size pocket on her back revealed only blood. This was considered good news, if there had been an infection it would not have been only blood. One transfusion later they considered her strong enough to make the flight to IU (Indiana University) Hospital (early Fri. morning). The decision to move her to Indy was a difficult one to make but Aaron and Jamie believed her having the doctor that operated on her the first time around would be better prepared to deal with this. There was not an operating room available to her on arrival at IUPUI and her vitals were too low to attempt the operation anyway. They gave her another transfusion in Indy to replace the blood she lost during the flight. The rest of the day was spent waiting on her vitals to improve enough for surgery. The waiting part was difficult for the family and friends that were aware of her latest attempt to give her dad more gray hair but the waiting for Jamie was on another level none of us could even imagine. She felt like her body was incased in concrete and the pain level she described was a 15 on a scale of 1-10. Thankfully she inched her way back to surgery level health and the plan came together with Dr. Cacioppo giving Jamie his best surgery skills. I can't say enough about this guy, he has been there for her anytime of the day or night to answer her questions or concerns. He may never again give out his cell number to a patient but I am grateful he let Jamie have it. While I have been writing this they have moved her to a room on the 6th floor (moving on up) so we are out of the ICU and looking forward to her getting back to her keyboard with her amazing writing skills that touch the heart and soul of so many people.

A special thank you goes out to everyone that helped her get through this with prayers, emails, text messages and comments on her blog. My sister Cindy showed up in Jamie's ICU room without us even knowing she was coming, she just left her husband a voicemail saying she was catching a flight and left without even a change of clothes. Aaron"s sister Jen thought she was going to assist in watching Kayden this weekend but ended up getting some great one on one time with "I'm so cute, Kayden" (well she really is cute). You can't find any sisters better than ours. Kitty and Bill, you're always there when Jamie, Aaron, Kathy and I need you the most.

Later, from the 6th floor this time,

Dave

Infectious

42

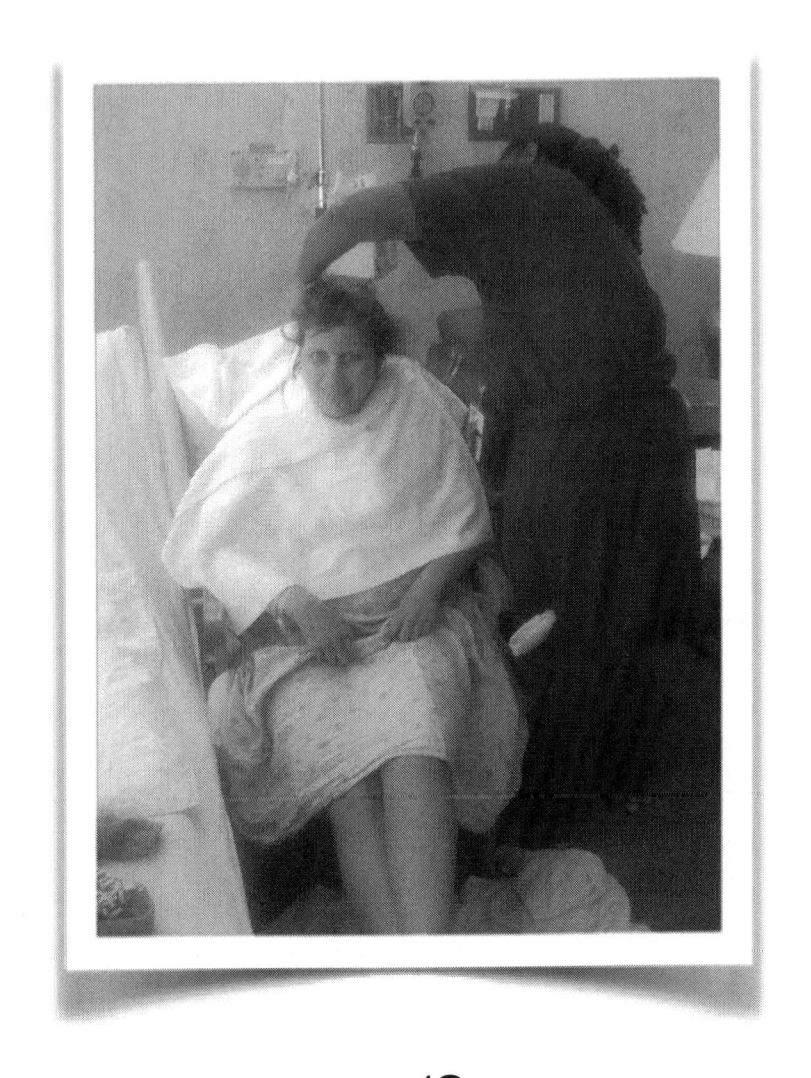

BACK IN THE SADDLE...

July 28, 2008

Back in the saddle...

Happy to report that this is me checking in to let you know how things have progressed over the weekend. As good as my dad is at filling in for me it stresses him out to be the one to tell the story :) You did good dad. Thanks for keeping the troops updated- you guys tend to get restless when there is a lack of information coming from my end, but that just makes me realize how much you love me of course! Anyways...on with my report. I got my hair washed today (picture above) and man it felt good!!! I am definitely feeling 100 % better then I was on Saturday when they moved me from ICU to my private room. This place is a palace compared to my ICU room. It is even on the top floor! We have a couch that Aaron stretched out on as soon as we got there- I thought I was going to have start setting up a schedule so my parents were not stuck sitting in the oh so comfy plastic chairs that were left. He and my dad spent the time by competing in how much they could win/lose on the new black jack game they downloaded on our Iphones. I had to practically drag my phone from him when I wanted to use it. I guess it is easy to get a little looney sitting around for so many days with nothing to do. I'm afraid to try the game out for fear I may have to call 1-800 bets off, kidding of course, you don't actually play with real money. But they definitely were addicted to the challenge of beating each other.

On to my TMI (too much information) section. I got my Foley catheter (the thing that pees for you so you don't have to get up to go to the bathroom) out this afternoon and am able to get up and move around a lot easier now. I wasn't quite ready to do that yesterday. My body was extremely worn out from the swelling caused by the hematoma, and of course from them reopening the incision on my back again to remove the hematoma. The anesthesia was finally out of my system by Sunday and I was really feeling the strain of the weekend so I stayed put in bed most of yesterday. I did get up and sit on the side of my bed for a bit in the afternoon and graduated to sitting in a chair by evening, but even doing that took all the effort I have to give. I am plain tired and worn out bottom line. I got some sleep last night and felt much better today from it.

Aaron headed home to relieve his sister of Kayden duty last night. It sounds like baby girl was extremely happy to have him back in the house. Although I believe she had a ball with Aunt

Jen from the sounds of their time together. I was so happy that they had a good time. Poor Jen does not have kids yet so I am sure she learned a bit by just being with the kid for several days straight. Most people without kids would run for the hills in the same situation. She went swimming on Sunday afternoon with Jen and then came home and napped. Jen promised that daddy would be home when she woke up and he was. She got up from her nap and came out in the hall from her room and announced that she was upstairs. He went up to get her and she just wanted to lay on his chest forever- I guess there is something to be said about getting that one on one physical touch to make you really feel good. She is a very touchy feely kid so she likes to be able to tangibly touch us not just talk to us. When I first talked to her she was slightly irritated that I had the gall to get ANOTHER boo boo that required me to be gone for so long again. I hated that I hadn't been able to prepare her for this situation. I didn't even get to give her a hug that Thursday morning. She just went off to daycare with Kitty while I was still asleep so she had no idea. You could hear it in her voice when I talked to her on Saturday that she was not quite believing my story?! I am going to have to have something really good for her to get a visual on because the only boo boo's she understands are ones worthy of a band aid and she has already taken inventory of all of my previous incidents. Apparently internal boo boo's definitely do not count in a 2 yr. old's world.

I have a lot to report on as far as what the doctors say and where we go from here so I am going to probably post again tomorrow morning after I get a chance to speak with the blood specialist here at IU. He is the know all on bleeding issues from what I hear. I don't quite have the energy to tell you all at once and I know everyone wants to know that I am feeling better. So for now this is all you are going to get. I am going to take a nap and write more in a bit, or maybe tomorrow depending on how great the nap is. I will post this portion for those of you that are resisting calling because you don't want to bug me. By the way it is ok to call me if you want. I just won't answer if I am sleeping or with a doctor, so leave me a message and I will get back to you as soon as I can. Hopefully this posting will at least let you know that I am on the mend! Talk with you soon!

Much love from the Penthouse-

Jamie

Hopeful

43

HOME AGAIN

July 31, 2008

Home Again

I know I know...I am about two days late on this update. I promised one the other day and didn't come through. I'm sorry! I was just plain TIRED!!! Plus the wifi was sketchy in my room so I was having trouble getting my info to update to the site properly- hence you not being able to leave comments at times. Hopefully since I am home those problems will go away. The picture above is of the needle/syringe my plastic surgeon uses to do the second fill on my expanders (temporary implants) with saline. He is filling the syringe in the pic and then he sticks that in my breast and it goes into the built in port in my expander. He uses a magnet to find the port and then marks my skin and pokes the needle on the marked spot. It is a bit crazy to watch and it amazingly enough doesn't hurt per say. I can feel the pressure of him adding the saline- but the needle poke itself doesn't hurt. Guess that is because I have lost most of the skin sensation on the surface of the breast since they severed the nerve endings when taking the breast tissue during the mastectomy.

I checked out of the Penthouse on Wednesday night. I did find out that the floor/wing (not the specific room) I stayed on was the same place Lance Armstrong stayed when he had his cancer surgery at IU. Pretty cool eh? They have some rooms that are like mine but have an attached room that the family can stay in. I assume this is where the VIP's like him stay. I feel so important to just have shuffled the halls! And only $55 more a night then a room with a roommate! I laughed when they asked me which I would prefer- room with a roommate or a privet room for $55 more a night....hmmmmm let me think....PRIVATE ROOM!!!

The doctors were very happy with my progress from Monday to Wednesday when I left. My hemoglobin stabilized around 9.3 (still low from the normal level of 12-13). I was climbing every day as far as numbers in general. My pain was better controlled overall and seems to be more of an ache then a sharp shooting pain that it was at times in my incision. Got my second fill before leaving- he did it Wednesday morning. I was a bit anxious about what to expect afterwards since that is what I thought made me such a mess the previous Wednesday pain wise. I asked to get the fill and be able to stick around the hospital for some time to make sure I didn't have any freak things happen to me afterwards. I was fine of course and felt nothing other then the expected pressure of the extra fluid in my chest. It wasn't bad today either, and they had told me to expect the 2nd day to be the most uncomfortable. I guess anything can be better then last time when I spent all day in bed nauseous and lightheaded. it is good to know that it is going to be a bearable process. I was second guessing how big these babies were going to get if I had to go through a second day like last week's every time. Happy to report that Aaron will still get his dream rack :) and mine too of course! Mom drove me home and tried to avoid most of the pot holes between Louisville and Bowling Green (which there seem to be many for some reason). I am sure it was nerve racking for her- but she did a good job. She is set to be here for another week or so. I cannot imagine being here so much in the last month. I would go insane that is for sure. Props to you mom! You are appreciated!

I am lucky enough to qualify for home care through my insurance (which is awesome- Thank you Hill's) and they sent a nurse to check on us today. She looks at my drains and my sutures to make sure everything looks good. She also takes my blood pressure and vitals which makes me feel better too. After last time and not knowing what to do when I was feeling so crappy- I now have someone I can contact that will come to me to check things out. This would have been a lifesaver last week when I was barely able to get out of bed. These home care nurses will come on Monday and Thursday for a couple of weeks to monitor my progress. A much needed safety net that we will appreciate having.

It is so good to be in my own bed and surrounded by Roxy, Uno (neither have left the bed since I got in it) and of course able to be with my honey and my girl. She was sooooo excited when I got home last night. We walked in and she was standing in the living room with no lights on and in a TV daze- naked from the waste down and scratching her butt. It was such a pleasant sight to walk into. My mom and I laughed and snuck up on her. Once she came out of her TV glaze her face lit up and she looked around to see grandma Kathy too. She had a hard time not squeezing me with her huge hug. I tried hard to enjoy it and not shrink away since she was kind of hurting me. It was awesome to see and hear her chattering on about stuff. She seems to have grown up so much in just the week I was gone. Her potty training has even continued to get better. She went to school and came home today in the same panties! Big steps for a potty trainer! She is so smart and constantly surprises us with her insight. Just tonight- she was going on and on at the dinner table while standing in her chair eating watermelon. I casually mentioned that they must have given her crack at daycare (just joking of course since she was wired from the time she got home) to Aaron. She looked at me and said "I have crack!" and proceeded to turn around and present her butt to the table. She pointed over her shoulder and said "see that's my crack- it's down there." Aaron and I about died trying not to laugh. Where in the world did she pick that up? Who knows. The things they say and miss with a video camera. That would have been a AFV (America's Funniest Video) winner for sure! Well, I am getting tired of typing for now. My left arm is still super sore from all the poking they did trying to get blood draws. It kind of hurts to put pressure on it for so long on my laptop, so I promise to post again soon and let you know how things are going as I ride the recovery train again. Till then...

Much love from the Pursley pad-

Jamie

ps: Robin- I am the worst best friend ever! I forgot your birthday yesterday- no excuses! So here goes-

Happy late bday to you, cha cha cha...happy late bday to you, cha cha cha...happy late birthday dear ROOBBIIIINN...happy late bday to you...CHA CHA CHA (envision a little boogie on my end)! And many moooorrre!

Comforting

44

FIGURED OUT THE ERROR MESSAGE

August 2, 2008

Figured out the error message...

Guess who's turn it is to wear the blue Barbie headband?? What a good sport daddies can be!

Dad and I finally figured out the error message you keep getting when trying to leave a comment. It stems back to the changes Apple has made on their end. Without boring you with the details here is what needs to happen. You need to discard the bookmark you have for my website. We believe that replacing the mac with me will take care of all of the error messages. So delete your previous bookmark and go to the new site (they will look exactly the same) and make a new bookmark.

I am definitely feeling good today. I have a lot more energy compared to the past two days since I got home. If I am up to it I think we are even going to hit the farmer's market to pick up some fruit today- if not we will catch it on Tuesday hopefully. If you have the opportunity to buy what is called a Sugar Baby- it is a type of watermelon that is more round in shape and the rind is dark green. It is so perfect to eat right now. It is a bit sweeter then a regular watermelon. OMG. I couldn't wait to get home from the hospital and have some. I emailed my friend Jen here in Bowling Green to go last Tuesday and get me some melon and cantaloupe to have this week. Yum Yum!!

I have been able to lengthen my time between pain meds which was a goal of mine. The last thing I need out of this experience is an addiction to pain killers. I am not taking ANY chances that's for sure. I hope to be able to be off them by the time I get my drains out (in 2 weeks on the 12th). I am looking forward to that! I can't complain this time about the drains like last time. I know now that it is there for a special purpose- to allow any collected fluids a place to escape to. Had I had it in last week then I would have known that I was bleeding internally sooner then we did, Although had I had the drain it would not have stopped what happened. So NO complaining this time. Maybe just a little griping for good measure :) So that's it for today. We are going to enjoy our weekend and try to stay cool. It is hot hot hot here. Wish I could take part in some good pool time- but not with the drains.....uh oh there I go again. Positive thoughts Jamie- positive thoughts! Hopefully if we can find my ice cream maker we are going to try to make some homemade ice cream tonight! That is something to definitely look forward to. Mom is headed to pick up some pizza for us for lunch (thanks for the gift card Goering)- she is such a good sport running here and there to satisfy my cravings :) More later this weekend....

Much love from the land of positive thoughts-

Jamie

Persistent

45

"ROCK" N CHEST......

August 6, 2008

"Rock"n chest...

10:00am- My chest is ROCK HARD. That is all I can say. If you were to squeeze my breast it would not give when you squeeze. It is the craziest feeling. They are like two rocks glued on my body. I am a little obsessed with their state right now so you will have to bear with my discussing it. They are currently not exactly 'normal' looking. My right side is still extremely swollen under my arm- this is where he tunneled (for lack of a better word) the tissue/skin/muscle from my back to my front. This makes my breast look like it goes clear under my arm, hard to describe in words. There is no definition where it stops and my side starts. If I could take a picture to show you without it being considered pornographic I would....but I don't think Aaron would appreciate me sharing my new ta ta's with the public so I will spare you- you'll have to use your imagination. Maybe I will draw a picture and post it for you :) Stay tuned and I will work on the masterpiece. It is my understanding that my expanders are quite a bit sturdier than what the implant will be that they eventually put in place. I guess it has to be since it is stretching the muscle and skin in my chest. I can't wait until I can look in the mirror and see a real rack staring back at me- well a one eyed rack that is...at least for awhile. Boy I bet I really have your imagination going now :)

Enough about my rack- I really have to stop writing after I take a pain pill- it brings out chatty Jamie just like 2 beers does! I am definitely feeling better this morning. I had to cut out my 3-4 hour afternoon naps finally because I would wake up at 3am and lay there unable to go back to sleep because I wasn't tired anymore. I hate to give it up- man Kayden doesn't know how lucky she is to get that afternoon nap and still be able to sleep at night! I am still doing the pain meds unfortunately. My drains ache a lot and my left breast is still causing me some pain. Hopefully once I get the drains out next week I can move to Tylenol so I can finally drive again. My mom is leaving late this week. I think my dad is beyond bored without her there. He tallied up how many days she has been gone in the last month and it was 23 days. Wow dad- you have a lot of time on your hands :) I couldn't have recovered without here though. It has been such a help for her to step in and take over with Kayden. Aaron has had a super busy month at work and with trying to catch up and deal with the day to day stuff- he has been really tied up. So Kayden has stopped hollering mommy and started hollering grandma instead. I'm sure my mom will be happy to get back home and get a full nights sleep. We have been having a tough time with Miss Kayden and sleeping since I got home. Her little mind just won't stop at night. She is like the energizer bunny when it comes to slowing down and getting into bedtime mode. She usually has some trouble getting to sleep but will sleep all night once she is down. That hasn't been the case this week at all. She even fell out of bed the other night. Poor thing. She will hopefully get back on track in another week or so after being back in full time daycare and us being home. I have to leave to run some errands so I will get back to this later this afternoon.

8:30pm-After taking a short trip to the mall for lunch I came home feeling really sick. My stomach was super queasy and I felt really hot. Once we got home and I laid down for a minute I ended up getting sick and losing my lunch. I have come to the conclusion that it was the Wendy's I ate that made me sick. But man....what a scare. I think I am going to have some anxiety for a long time whenever I start feeling weird or queasy. Thank goodness it was a false alarm today...but it was enough to get my mind running. I ended up popping some nausea medicine they sent me home with and taking a nap (so much for cutting out the naps). I felt much better after waking up and having some dinner. I guess I have to stop taking for granted that I feel better as I have learned that it can change in the drop of a hat. Well- my mom is headed home tomorrow. I am glad she is able to get back to dad but I am a little nervous to not have her here....I have to branch out on my own sooner or later. Aaron's parents will head down here next week because his dad is speaking in Louisville on Wednesday. That will help next week. Aaron and I had a date night last night just the two of us at dinner and we talked about our long term plans for getting our lives back on track. We are both ready to be back to normal after this last month- I've asked to leave Kayden in the full time daycare at least for the time being so I can not be stressed with making sure she has the stability she needs. My overall feeling is so up and down still I think it is everyone's best interest. I am getting back to work slowly but surely. So hopefully tomorrow is a better day.

Better head up to get Kayden in her jammies and start bedtime. Cross your fingers for another full night of sleep for our household. Talk with you soon!

Much love from us all to you-

Jamie

Educator

46

NA NAN A NAHHHH....HEY HEY HEY....GOODBYE

August 12, 2008

Na nan a Nahhh...Hey Hey Hey ...GOODBYE

6:30 am- We are headed north on 65 now, back to Indy for an appointment with Dr. Cacioppo (plastic surgeon). It's time to get these drains out! In the last month and a half I have had drains in all but 3 days. I am not going to jinx it by celebrating until I get there and he actually takes them out. I am also going to get fill #3. Fun Fun! Aaron's parents are here this week to spend some time with Kayden so we don't have to rush home tonight which is nice. I had a rough end of the week last week. I threw up my lunch three days in a row and then Friday afternoon I spent most of the day in bed because I felt so bad. I tried nausea medicine and it still didn't settle my stomach. By Saturday I was starting to panic that there was something else wrong again. Just what I needed. My face felt numb and tingly and my stomach was still not back to normal. I had no appetite and my head was pounding. By process of elimination I decided I was having withdrawl from my hydrocodone. I hadn"t been eating much so I wasn't taking my pain meds because they make me sick on an empty stomach. So I broke down and called the home care nurse on call for the weekend to see what I should do. After hearing my symptoms she said that my problem didn't sound wound related so there was not much they could do for me. She recommended that head to the ER if I was truly concerned, that was enough to put me in tears. That was the last thing I wanted to do. So I pumped myself full of gatorade and ate some chicken soup and saltine crackers. Low and behold I was a new woman by the end of the day. Man was I glad to get past that. Better sign off for now- we are pulling in to Indy so I have to pack up to go into the hospital.

9:01 pm- Got my drains out!!! Yeah!!! I couldn't be happier. I also got a 60 cc fill on my left side only. He wanted to give my right side a rest since we had filled it quite a bit last time. Now my left side has finally caught up to the right side which has been bigger since the beginning. In fact the left one is looking pretty good other then my nipple pointing down and to the left, better then it's neighbor with no nipple though! That will eventually be taken care of when we are all said and done if it is still out of alignment- so no worries- or so he tells me :) It is kind of creepy looking though. I couldn't make a drawing that was worthy of posting so you will have to use your imagination. I bought a C bra this afternoon during a timed 15 minute stop at the outlet malls on the way to Indy (seriously he timed me so we wouldn't be late- we ended up being 30 minutes early and the doctor was running 45 minutes late on top of that). After trying it on tonight my left one fits nicely- righty is a little oddly shaped with the bulge under my armpit so it doesn't really fit the bra cup properly yet, but give it another fill and it should be good. By the way, I found out today that that bulge is not swelling as I had been told by the nurses. It is actually the muscle he brought around from my back. I guess I didn't realize that he left the muscle attached to it's original spot- he truly stretched it around under my arm and made a boob out of it. Holy cow- pretty amazing what your body can be manipulated to do. Supposedly that muscle will soften up over time and not be so noticeable but it will take time. Kind of disappointing but I can live with it. Hopefully people will be looking at my chest and not my armpit after all is said and done! Anyways...I also got to talk w/ Dr. Schneider (oncologist) and my general surgeon today. It was a good day when we are able to see all 3 of my doctors in one trip. I will fill you in on my next blog about what came out of those appointments. I am super tired after starting so early today so I am going to hit the hay for now. I promise to post again in the next day or two. I have to take some new pics because I am running out of ones to use! The one I used tonight was of Kayden and her friend Kaitlyn- they had a ball in a box of peanuts. Would have been nice if Kayden was wearing a shirt but oh well...it's better then her birthday suit which is what she prefers half the time! More later...

Sing a little bon voyage to those pesky drains with me!

Na Na Na Nah...Na Na Na Nah.....hey hey hey....GOODBYE!!!

Much love on this day of celebration!

Jamie

Pure

47

FEELING GOOD!!!!!

August 20, 2008

Feeling good!!!!

Ok Ok- so I am going to stop making promises I can't keep. I owe everyone a run down on what the doctor's said last week. First off, I am FINALLY feeling really good again. Got some energy back. Off the pain meds pretty much. I just feel more like myself. It has been a good last week. We have been able to get out and enjoy the summer at the dog park and the playground, and even went swimming yesterday. I am not going to jinx it by saying anything about what is to come...but hopefully it is all good!

As far as my doctor's appointment's last week all is well on the recovery front. My surgeon Dr. Goulet said he is happy with the final appearance and that Dr. Cacioppo did a great job finishing up. He is going to have me go through some physical therapy here in BG for my left arm that is bigger then my right arm due to that pesky blood clot earlier this year. I am still waiting to hear from the PT people here...but I am guessing they might put me in a compression garment for awhile to help get the fluids up and out of that arm. Nothing like wearing a hot tight wrap on my arm in the middle of August. Oh well....better then a fat arm which I DO NOT want! As far as my meeting with my oncologist Dr. Schneider, he started me on my Aromatase Inhibitors (click here to learn about what this is) called Arimidex. I take one pill a day for at least the next 5 years and possibly longer. This pill is replacing the Tamoxifen that I was on prior to my second diagnosis. It was decided that the Tamoxifen was not doing its job in my body since the cancer came back and that is why we are switching gears and trying a different method. In addition to that we have decided it is time to take my ovaries out. I know a lot of you have asked yourself why didn't she do this before? Well....to be honest. It was a choice that I made the first time around with the possibility that I could maybe have another baby in the future. After my second tumor showed up it has become painfully obvious that estrogen is not my friend and that another child (naturally at least) will not be in our future. A pregnancy raises the levels of estrogen in your body and that would create a tumor growing atmosphere in my body. We are in a totally different ball game now that we have dealt with this recurrance. I am ok with having the ovaries out. They will not do a hysterectomy (taking both uterus and ovaries and the stuff in between). My uterus will stay in tact and it will just be a matter of clipping the ovaries and taking them out. This will help reduce the estrogen present in my body even more then the Aromatase Inhibitors will. I will be able to stop the Lupron shots once the ovaries are removed as well. We will remove them at the same time I go in for my final implant switch out- hopefully in early November. As far as my fill's on my expanders...I had one last Tuesday and another this past Tuesday. My friend Amberly drove me to my appointment this past Tuesday. We had a lot of fun chatting all the way down and hitting the outlet malls in Edinburgh on the way home. I was exhausted from talking and laughing all day once we finally made it home! Aaron wanted to know why it's not like that when we drive down together (I usually sleep, read or work on my laptop)...sorry honey- it's a girl thing you wouldn't understand. The girls are really starting to look good! I am sitting between a full B and a C right now....they actually look more like C's. Aaron (and I) says we aren't quite done :) He's trying so hard to let me be the decision maker on the final product but he can't help but ask me all the time..."so how big do you think you want to go? or how many more fills do you want?" It is funny. Just when I thought they couldn't get any more tight and firm they did. They actually tried to float in the pool yesterday but it is so tight it was like my implants were defying gravity. It was a weird sensation that I was truly surprised about. The other bonus to my upcoming surgery in November is that there is some discussion of maybe doing a tummy tuck since we will already be in that area for the ovaries. No decisions have been made. We have to get a quote from some of the hospitals to find out what it will cost us. But I am pretty excited at the prospect. Might as well get something positive out of this situation. Let's just say we are making lemonade out of my lemons. Anyways...wanted to check in and say hi to everyone. Thank you for the continued support from each of you and the get well cards and gift cards have truly kept my spirits up! I am desperately trying to get my thank you cards out in the mail- so fair warning they will be fashionably late in true Jamie style :) Talk with you all soon!

I almost forgot to explain the picture I used for this posting. I have had many people walk or run in my honor for different races that involve breast cancer. Be sure to send me a pic of you and I will post it. This particular pic is of a great group of girl friends (and a fellow survivor!) that started a Team Jamie for the Susan G Komen Race for the Cure that they do in KC every August. I was able to partake last year which was the first time they participated. I was sad to not be able to travel there to partake this year but my drains were still in and I couldn't fly with them in. The team was even bigger this year. Next year I intend to be there and actually run the 5K portion. It's a goal to work towards. Better go for now....

Much love from me to u-

Jamie

Traveler

48

RECOVERY REBELLION.....

September 18, 2008

Recovery Rebellion...

Where to start...it's been awhile. As most of you know I tend to jump back into life after I feel better and our family is off and running to all ends of the earth, almost as if we are making up for lost time. This time is no different. In addition to our trips to Indy for my fills (I am on my home from one now), I have been back to KS for a short trip and also spent a weekend in Austin at Lake Travis with Aaron and a group of friends from college. We have been out on Lake Nolan here in Kentucky, we have been to a hot air balloon event in Bowling Green, we are headed to the KSU vs. Louisville game tomorrow and the list goes on. We have already filled up the rest of our calendars for the rest of the year with trips here and there. I will be headed back to KS at the end of this month to attend a breast cancer awareness event with my mom at the racquet club they belong to. Mom has been helping on the committee to put the event on and I am excited to be able to attend! That trip back will just be Kayden and I because Aaron has work here in Bowling Green to take care of. There are also some Harley Drags in town that weekend so I think he had hoped to attend those all weekend without us anyways :) I will stay on into the first week of Oct. to hopefully work some with my dad and then help my brother work on his new house he bought in KC, MO. Go Scott! He is very excited to have his own place finally. It is a fixer upper and dad has already dove in to help him take care of some of the major issues so he can get moved in and start on the aesthetic details. I owe him quite bit of work from the days when I bought my house and he helped out on my repairs. Then we will be in Nashville the weekend of Oct. 4th for the Komen Race where my mom and Aaron will run in my honor. Kayden, Dad and I will most likely do the family walk. The race is also the same day as Aaron and I's 5 yr. anniversary. Hard to believe it has been that long already. Had I known how crazy things were going to get after we had Kayden I might have partied it up a bit more the first two years of our marriage :) Just kidding. Looking back it is amazing what this family has been through in the past 5 years. I am proud to say that although adding a child to the mix and being diagnosed has brought both expected and unexpected obstacles and changes to our lives as husband and wife we have weathered the storm- and what a storm it was at times. But I can honestly say I respect Aaron for sticking it out with me throughout this mess. Going through tough times so early in your marriage can truly bring out a person's true colors. I am happy to celebrate our 5th anniversary cancer free and look forward to many many more to come.

As far as recovery goes, I have been feeling better every day. I am completely off the pain meds and have been for almost a month. I even used just regular aspirin for my fill today. Today was my last fill until the surgery where he takes the expanders out and puts in the actual implants. We are hoping to have that scheduled some time in November. Yeah! Looking forward to that areola tattoo and new nubbin'. I have donned my right breast with the skin patch my "Barbie boob" since it is currently lacking any nipple or areola. I will hopefully have a nipple by the end of the year if all goes well. Now that is something to celebrate on New Year's!

I have been in a bit of a rut for the past few weeks, even with all the activity. I vaguely remember this being the case last time I went through surgery in 2007. Even thought I am feeling better- I feel a lack of energy or drive to do much on a personal matter. It's almost like I don't want to do anything that is not easy or fun. I call this my recovery rebellion phase. Aaron pointed out seeing some trends in my actions- lazy days, spending more money then necessary, and overall lethargic attitude. It's almost like I don't want to be responsible for anything. I just want to be me and not answer to anyone. Well that is all fine and dandy- but I have a family to be with and take care of too. So the selfishness, though to be expected after all I have been through in the last two months, is not an attitude that can stay. So it is back to the real world I am headed. Back to bills, laundry, eating right, exercising, and all that stuff we deal with every day. I feel myself looking over my shoulder and wishing I could just stay a little while longer in Jamie-ville. But it's not fair to Aaron or Kayden. I think Aaron is trying to be patient but there is only so many days he can go with out a clean white t-shirt. It is a weird state to be in this Jamie-ville. I love it and yet I hate it because it reminds me a bit of the pain of the process that got me there.

It is time to leave the comfort of my world and start looking forward so you could call it a bittersweet good bye.

I am still feeling a bit out of sorts- more so lately for some reason as far as feeling on the ball. I am still having some memory issues as well as reduced retention of information. I just plain don't feel as sharp as I would like to feel. It is frustrating and I do let it get to me sometimes. Aaron has pointed out that if I stopped procrastinating things maybe I wouldn't forget them. Boy- wish I had thought of that.

I have started seeing a physical therapist for my left arm. It is still slightly swollen due to the blood clot I had earlier this year. They are treating me as if it were lymphedema, although it is technically not. We are trying to flush the fluid that has settled in that arm due to the blockage from the clot. The clot is still there, although broken down a bit from its original form. It will take quite a while for my body to flush it from my system. We are doing some massaging, wrapping and using a pneumatic pump to help the process along. It is a tiring process, as I have to go in every weekday for about 1 1/2-2 hrs. for my session. I have to keep my arm wrapped (like a soft cast) from my knuckles to my armpit all day every day until the swelling has diminished. It is hard to know what the long-term situation is going to be at this point. I hope that it doesn't leave me wearing a compression garment every day to keep my arm size in check, but that is a possibility. We'll just have to wait and see. Hopefully since I have not had any lymph node dissection on that side then once the clot is reduced then I will not have the flare up in size like I have so far. I know this is a bit over most people's head so I won't bore you with more of the details. Let's just say I will keep you updated. If you see me with a big wrap on my arm- don't ask me if I had an accident :) It is amazing how many strangers feel the need to ask me what I did to my arm. I usually ask them if they want the long version or the short. That stops a few people from pursuing the topic. I posted some pics in the photo album so you can see what it looks like.

Better go for now. It is pretty hard to type with this thing on my arm. I will check back in soon!

Much love from the real world-

Jamie

ps. I added quite a few pictures from our trip to Lake Travis and some other fun ones.

Social

49
SUSAN G KOMEN RACE - NASHVILLE

September 22, 2008

Susan G Komen Race- Nashville

I forgot to mention last posting that you can log into Aaron's web page for his upcoming Komen Race on October 4th. I just wanted to include a link so it was easier for you to see the page. I am lucky that there are so many different fundraisers for our cause....but this particular race is the one event we try to reach out to friends and family for donations every year....that way we are not constantly hitting up friends and relatives for every little event we take part in =)! Please do not feel obligated to donate.

Thank you so much to those of you that have supported us so far this year! We continue to work towards the cure in what ever way we can!

We are doing good here. Had a good weekend together as a family. I am STILL wearing the wrap on my arm 24/7. There has been a 10% drop in size from when we started before Labor Day. Kayden and I am headed back to KS this week for all of next week to help uncle scott out with his house and attend a Breast Cancer event at Wood Valley Racquet Club in Topeka. We will be back in KY in time to attend the race with Aaron. Hope to see some of you in KS next week!

Much love on the first day of fall!

Jamie

Mommy

50
CRAZY BUSY IN KANSAS

October 1, 2008

Crazy busy in Kansas...

Holy Moley- don't know if I need a nap or just a vacation from my vacation. Kayden and I have been in KS since late last Thursday. We have packed our schedules to the point where she asks me where we are at every time she wakes up in her car seat. She has been to the KSU game last weekend. She got to ride HER pony Marlin. How many 2 yr. olds do you know that have their very own horse? She is having a blast with all the kids we have been able to visit with and mommy loves all the girl time gossiping we have gotten in. I even got to enjoy some "mommy juice" (wine/beer) on Friday night with a few friends at Barley"s Brewhaus. It was great to see everyone. Especially Benson who was in town from San Diego.

I was able to have a play date with some Pi Phi (my sorority from college) and their kids on Monday. It was a lot of fun! One of the little boys, Nicholas, looks like he could be Kayden's twin brother. They are only about a week apart in age and are too cute together. I couldn't help but document their day in case they get married later...ha ha! We can wish can't we Kristin?! My friend Kelli's sweet baby girl Cambell got to play a little Barbie with Kayden- for the few minutes she would share her toys with her. She has two older brothers so it was cute to see them play together. In fact...she got a huge dose of cars, dinosaurs, and boy toys while we were there. She kept up most of the afternoon and it was so fun to watch them all play. She is at a great age where she isn't clingy and after a few minutes of warming up will join right in to play with about anyone. We topped off our day with dinner at a place called Beach Bum's in Overland Park with all of my old roommates from my freshman year at KSU. It's this great pizza place with all kinds of games and things to keep them busy. This was the first time in a LONG time that we had all been able to get together in one place...with all of the kids. It was a fun evening. I hadn't met several of the kids so we were lucky enough to visit and have the kids play all over dinner. I can't believe that this Boyd Hall group has finally grown up! It was so surreal. It was a blast to see everyone. The kids did great together and I can't wait to do it again! By the way...Josh- you are a true trooper to be the solo guy in the group with all those chatty women and crazy kids. Kudos! Aaron would have run for the closest door! Good to see everyone and I am so sorry it has taken so long to make these meetings happen. We will do it again soon!

I was also able to catch up with our close friends the Goertzen's. Aaron and Scott work together at Hill's and they have recently moved to Lawrence from Richmond, Indiana where we used to live. It was a rowdy fun time at their house as the boys showed off their skills and shared their toys and just plain loved on my little girl. She loves that family and I was happy to be able to be together again. I miss that dearly. I just wish Aaron could have been there and it would have been like old times...except I had hair! Ha Ha!

We were lucky enough to have some family visiting from Arizona while were in town. Jess and Connie McMahan stayed at mom and dad's house with us over the weekend. They were in town for a wedding and it was great to see them. I wish Ivy and Scott and the kids had been here too so we could see the kids all play together! Maybe next time.

Oh yes- and I played tennis for the first time since my surgery on Saturday. Mom had the Wood Valley Rally for the Cure tennis event on Saturday and I was able to partake! It was a great event and I was so glad we came home for it. It was a bit scary at first to get out there and take some hits...but I got back in the swing pretty quickly. I definitely don't have the same power I had before...but that is to be expected since my muscle has been relocated. My right arm was sore for several days...but it felt good to play again!

Anyways.. I won't drone on and on any more- you are all probably tired from just reading about our adventures! No moss grows below these feet! I am exhausted- we are both missing Aaron and Roxy and Uno- but it has been a great trip. We can't wait to be home at Christmas so we can do it all over again. To those of you we missed- I am so sorry we didn't make it happen this time, but hopefully next time! Us footloose and fancy-free girls have to wind this trip down and get ready to head home tomorrow. Talk to you soon! Be sure to check out the photo album so you can see the week's pics.

Much love from the Flinthills corporate office-

Jamie

ps. sorry to all of you that I made touch my boobs :) Can't help but share these rocks of Gibraltar!

Sweet

51

FALL IS HERE!

October 28, 2008

Fall is here!

I can't believe October has almost come and gone already. I love this month for some reason- it always seems to bring good moods and great weather. We have been doing great here. Since I last blogged lots has happened. Aaron, my mom and I participated in the race in Nashville. We were able to run about 1/2 of it. I decided at the last minute to stop and try to score some free t-shirts they were throwing out to the crowd- so we ended up getting stuck behind the crowd of walkers/strollers. We eventually were able to run around all those people and finish the race at a jog. It was fun. Kayden ended up sleeping through the whole race in her stroller. She woke up as we were getting into the car and wanted to know when we were going to do the race? It was cute. Aaron and I also celebrated our 5-year anniversary in Indianapolis. We went up on a Sunday night and stayed at the train station hotel and went out for dinner. It was fun! We even stayed up late enough to go to a late movie :) Not a Disney or cartoon movie for once! I had an appointment to meet the OBGYN surgeon from IU that we are going to use to do the female portion of my surgery on Monday morning. We ended up having a very productive meeting with her. Aaron and I both really like how down to earth she was and she didn't ho hum around about the details. It was her opinion that we should think about doing a full hysterectomy instead of just removing the ovaries. There are not enough negative side effects that will come of taking the uterus to not go ahead and do it at the same time. I took some time to read up on it and speak with people that have had the same procedure. In all honesty when they take the ovaries the uterus has no function at that point anyways- it is like a big bat cave hanging out with no importance. So we have decided to take her advice and do the full hysterectomy. So that being said- I decided to go through all of Kayden's old clothes and stuff and have a big garage sale. There is no sense to continue to store all this stuff if we are obviously not going to have another baby. Even if we adopt down the road (big if) then we would most likely try to adopt a boy if possible. So as hard as it was- I cleaned out the attic and passed it on to some other little girl that can use it more then we can. It was harder then I thought it would be- my heart felt kind of tight as I was going through things and even the day of the sale. I know that they are material items- but each item seem to have a little silly memory that went along with it. I hope I don't regret down the road doing this...but it seemed like the right thing to do now. I kept a few special things and passed some items on to friends. I always thought I would be able to pass stuff on to my brothers kids- but obviously that isn't happening any time soon is it Scott??? Kidding! On to happier stuff.

I went to West Virginia this past weekend with my friend Jenn (who is also pregnant) for our friend Amberly's baby shower. It was a fun quick trip for the girls to get away. Both girls are due right around Kayden's birthday and mine so we are excited to have the babies join us for the holidays! Jenn has a daughter the same age as Kayden. The dad's worked out a deal that Jenn's husband watched the girls on Saturday and Aaron got them Sunday. Needless to say they all got a good dose of the girls. It was fun to hear the stories of what they had to deal with and how they made it work. They made cookies and played in the mud at Kaitlyn's house and Aaron made pancakes with them on Sunday. It sounded like lots of fun. Kayden ended up sick Sunday evening with an ear infection and fever. We got her on antibiotics yesterday to get her feeling better. Now Kaitlyn woke up today sick. Oh well. Guess it was maybe too much fun this weekend :)

I have been waiting in suspense to hear when they are scheduling my final surgery and I finally got a date last week. It will be scheduled for December 10th. Just one day before I turn 33. Guess I will have to eat my birthday cake in the hospital this year. Figures! At least I will be OK for Kayden's birthday on Dec. 7th for once. It seems like I am always sick or recuperating from something on her birthday. So the party is on this year!!!

Well- I plan to post again later this week with some Halloween pics so I will sign off for now. Hope all is well with everyone and have a safe happy Halloween!

Much love from our spooky house to yours!

Jamie

Unforgettable

52

HAPPY HALLOWEEN!

November 2, 2008

Happy Halloween!

Can you believe we are already changing the clocks back? Of course Kayden doesn't care what the clock says...she had me out of bed at 6 am and we've been watching some Toy Story this morning. I downloaded some of our Halloween pics so be sure to check out the ones I added to the 2008 Picture page. We had a great time trick or treating in our neighborhood. She went with her friend Megan that lives around the corner- she is a year older then Kayden. The two were hilarious running from one place to the other- Kayden kept saying Happy Halloween or Trick or Treating when they answered the door. About half way through she decided she needed to be carried and shortly after that she declared she wanted to go home. Then we got to go through the loot- while she and daddy talked Mommy weened the pile down to a manageable amount of candy (hid the rest for Aaron) and we have been fighting over when she can eat it ever since. I kept telling myself we would trow it all out on Saturday after letting her eat it on Friday- but of course I felt bad and didn't do it. Now we have all had toooooo much candy and it's been a bit of a whiney weekend for us all. Oh well.

I played tennis on Friday morning as a sub for a different women's league and ended up having some pain in my right shoulder. It only hurt when I served so I played through the game and just had terrible serves throughout. After talking to a trainer at the fitness place (they have a physical therapy business there too) I found out it seems to be my rotator cuff. After the quick screen he said it is definitely something we need to address now before it gets worse and I end up tearing something and requiring surgery. I will know more on Monday- but he thinks with my lat muscle being moved my rotator cuff (stabilizes your arm) is a bit confused on its job and is not functioning properly when I raise my arm overhead- this in turn pinches muscles creating pain. The pinching can actually over time sever tendons and cause some major damage. So now that we have caught it in what he refers to as a vulnerable state- we can hopefully retrain my muscles to function properly with all the changes we made from the mastectomy surgery. I guess all the tennis I have played in the last month and a half has finally had an effect- it just took a while for the pain to present itself. Figures. Just when I get back on the wagon of being active life throws me another curveball and I have to ween back again. Ugh. I meet with the Physical Therapist (different place then where I did my lymphedema treatment) on Monday morning. I am not restricted from doing anything at this point- he just wants to check it out more thoroughly.

I also got to get my baby fix in this weekend. I have several friends that are pregnant or have had babies recently (hence my baby envy). It has really made me miss having a little tiny one around. Had this cancer thing not happened to us I know we would have been already working on #2 around here about this time. It makes me sad- but then again- having just one has been quite the challenge around here. So I get my fixes by using other people's babies. Looking on the positive side of things- it is nice to be able to hand them back over when the going gets rough. I hope this longing wears off soon though- I don't want to always have this hole in my heart where having a bigger family fits into it. It just seems weird to think of it just being the three of us. It is what it is I guess. No need to ponder on it.

I have been setting an alarm so I can get up early this last week- usually I let Kayden wake me up at 7 when she gets up. But in an effort to get the house organized and keep a better laundry and house cleaning schedule- I have added some duties to my morning and night time routine. You would be amazed how much it helps to just do one load of laundry at night, clean up the kitchen and living room and run the dishwasher before I got to bed. Then I get up and fold the laundry and empty the dishwasher- and the house is already somewhat presentable for the day. It starts the day off with two things already checked off my list and a clean sink because the dishes can go in the empty dishwasher - I feel so liberated! My life does not revolve around folding and putting away clothes or cleaning up the kitchen! Just another of my self-bettering things I have been focusing on. My three goals for this last week were to get up at 6:30 every day which I pretty much did, I had to do weights three times that week, and also I had to make a conscious effort to eat more vegetables for the week. It was a success. Small goals lead to better results for me. I tend to go overboard and then I burn out early and cannot complete any of my grand ideas :) So I hope to add one more goal to those for this week and continue to do so till some of these things become a habit and I can move on to bigger and better things. I have really been trying to better our lives inside and out lately and if I do it for myself first I think it will flow into my home and family life in turn. We'll see. I just really want to raise Kayden to make good choices in food and health- better than the choices I have made for myself growing up. It is something that might eventually save her from having to face breast cancer. And that is a one hell of a motivator for me. So you will probably hear me venting/sharing my self help trials and tribulations in the upcoming months. Bear with me- I am sure you all probably think I am a big weird-o but hey- I am not ashamed to share my world with you so you can't judge me on what I do :) Feel free to share any tips you have that work for you! I am a healthy sponge just waiting to soak up some good habits! On that note- I am going to go and unload the dishwasher and fold the laundry I did last night! Talk to you all soon!

Much love from my house of health-

Jamie

Frightened

53

MY 3-MONTH CHECK UP...

November 9, 2008

My 3-month check up...

Tomorrow is my 3 month check up with Dr. Schneider (oncologist). I am sitting here in my bed thinking about it and decided to share my thoughts on it. For some reason this weekend has left me feeling a little blue. I don't know if it is the weather changing or what...but I just feel out of sorts. I am sitting here reflecting on it tonight and I can't put my finger on it. I know I have to get up early tomorrow and head to Indianapolis for my appointment- and I don't mind the drive or getting up early- but I am resentful for some reason. I guess sometimes I just get frustrated that I have to stop what I am doing in life and revert back to thinking about the cancer- just when I am doing everything I can to forget about it. To tell you the truth- I pretty much hate that I have to do that- and there is no one I can take that anger out on because it isn't anyone's fault. For those of you that make me out to be a trooper with my positive attitude about things- I'm not. I am angry and resentful and annoyed that I have to get up and go to Indy tomorrow and talk about cancer and all the little aches and pains I have that pop up and "could" or "could not" be something important. I am tired of counting down the days that I have till surgery gets here. I am frustrated that no matter what I do in my life I will always have to make sure I am making the right choices so that I can evade this stinking black cloud that hangs over me. I can be pretty positive most of the time....but on days like today- I guess I have to resign to the fact that no matter what I do to get past this beast it is always going to be there trying to drag me back to that frustrating place that cancer takes you. I sit here typing and frowning and just want to pull the covers over my head and fast forward to a better day. So I guess that is what I am going to do. I just wanted you to know that I am having one of those days. And it isn't really fair to only show you my positive side all the time if you really want to be a part of this journey with me. You deserve to see all the sides to my life. So here's to throwing out the negative attitude tonight and hopefully waking up on a better side of the bed tomorrow! Sleep tight.

Much love from my glum day-

Jamie

ps. This picture of Roxy is the closest pic I could find to represent my mood.

Thought-Provoking

54

SURGERY TIME AGAIN...

December 9, 2008

Surgery time again.

I can't believe it's finally here! It seems like I have been waiting for this forever- even though it has only been 5 months since my double mastectomy. I am writing this in the car on our way up to Indy this afternoon. My surgery is tomorrow Dec. 10th at 11:00 am. They anticipate it to be 5 hours long. I will be having my temporary breast expanders (used to stretch my muscle and skin) taken out and my silicone implants put in. I will also have a full hysterectomy (in hopes of eliminating estrogen as much as possible from my body), and to round things out I am having a little cosmetic surgery while I am in there- a tummy tuck. Yeah for me! It is what I have been referring to as my surgical overhaul :) I can't wait to get theses rocks off my chest- It would be nice to be able to hug someone without stabbing them in the chest with my two camel humps. They anticipate that I will be in the hospital for 2 days assuming all goes well (which it will). I should be home by this weekend. My recovery time is expected to be around 4-6 weeks give or take. I will come home with 2 drains in my lower abdomen, which need to stay in for approximately 10 days post surgery. Hopefully not jinxing our plans- we would like to be able to drive home to KS on Christmas Eve if I am able. Now that being said...I am realistic in the fact that I realize that may not happen- but who knows! I am one tough cookie when I need to be- it may happen. If not, Santa sure knows his way to Bowling Green if necessary.

As far as mental preparation for this time around- I am anxious, excited, worried- all of the above. I have had a lot of time to prepare for this surgery unlike my others and it has left me with lots of little worries in the back of my brain. My biggest being that the surgeon will find something we don't know about in my body while he has me open. So it is a good and bad thing that I will once again be open on the surgical table. Dr. Cacioppo will get a free peek inside my whole trunk to see what may or may not have shown up since my surgery in July. Don't get me wrong...I do not think that the cancer is back for any reason. I just worry that it could be and we may find a new tumor unexpectedly while in surgery. So that thought weighs on my mind right now. But overall- I am excited to have all these positive things happen and look forward to my new and improved look. I would post the before and after pics but I don't want to scare anyone... maybe just the after :) More later...

I am now sitting in our hotel room after dinner with my parents (who flew into Indy's new airport today to be here for the surgery). Aaron and I are both sitting on our laptops wrapping up the loose ends so we can both be out of the loop for a few days. I will have my dad do a posting tomorrow to let you know how the surgery goes. Aaron will also be updating many of you by phone and text. Look to see/hear something later in the afternoon. I wish I could hit a fast forward button and be done with this all.... but that just wouldn't be fair would it? Although I did text my plastic surgeon today to tell him no drinking or partying tonight as I need him tip top for my reconstruction tomorrow.. I was kidding around with him in case any of you took that to be a literal concern of mine. That's what he gets for giving me his cell #! Let's hope this is the last surgery I have for a long time, with the exception of my new "pickle" in 2009. Kayden asked me just about a week ago when I was going to get my other pickle at the store? I had to laugh- if only it was that easy. Anyways... it is time for me to take care of a couple of pre-surgery things (those of you that are familiar with abdominal surgery may know what I mean). I can't even utter the word aloud as I am not looking forward to it. That got you wondering didn't it?? I really appreciate all of your good wishes and positive karma you have sent my way. My friend Deidre even gave me a set of karma beads that represent Happiness and Strength. Perfect timing- I am going to need them both in the next few weeks- although I thought I lost them on Monday and was worried I might have to cancel the surgery. Talk about a bad omen- but I found them and Aaron is going to take care of them while I am in surgery. Talk to you sooner then later hopefully!

Much love from the Residence Inn-

Jamie

Sparkle

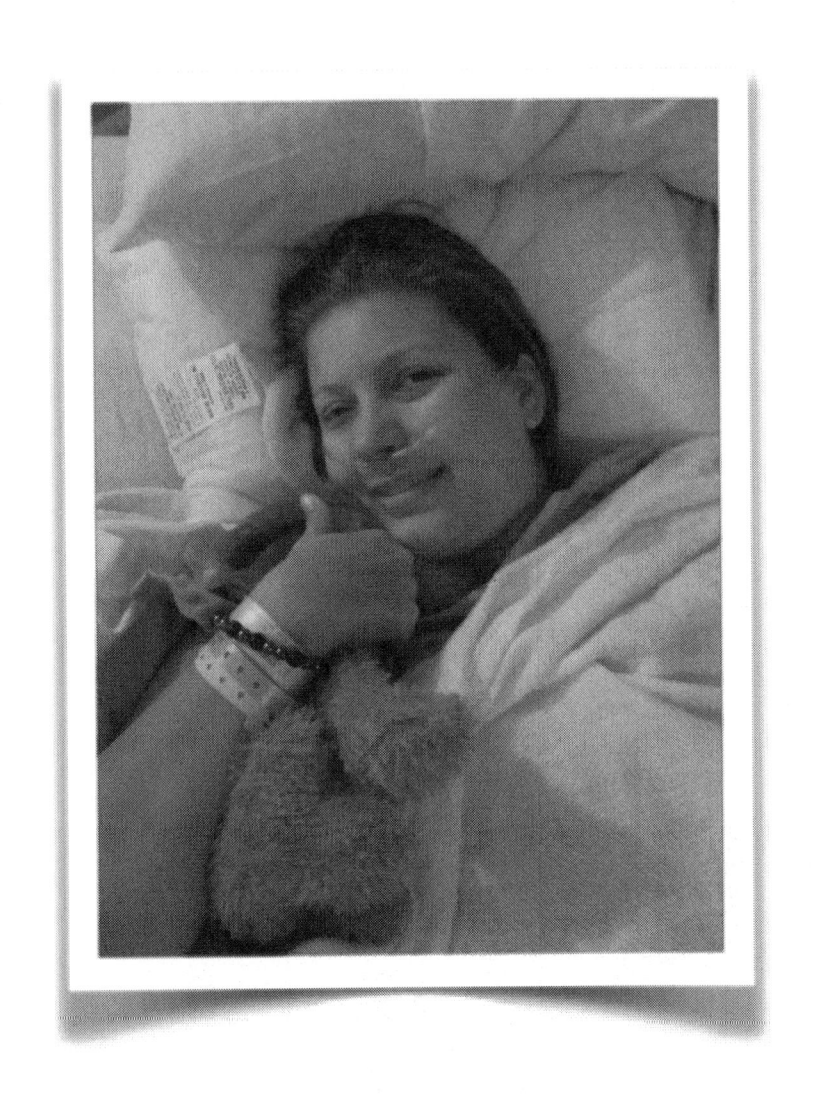

55

ONE LAST TIME

December 11, 2008

One last time

Dad here, I took this picture about 10 pm last night, she was holding onto dogdog II. Kayden has the original dogdog that is close to falling apart. Jamie thought she could substitute a new one without Kayden knowing the difference, so wrong. Looks like Jamie is getting the same comfort from II that Kayden gets from I. She came through 7 hrs of surgery very well. All of the doctors thought their part of the operation went as well as possible. She hung out in recovery 2-3 hours before we were able to see her, that was a very long day for her and us. She has had some tingling in her left hand and this seemed to concern her last night but after an ultrasound the doctor has assured her that it was probably from the position her arm was strapped down during surgery. Aaron stayed with her overnight and Kathy and I stayed at a good friends house. Jamie had a pretty rough night, she had some severe nausea around 3:30 am. It was bad enough that the hospital decided to do a CT scan around 4 am to make sure everything was OK. Doctors confirmed everything was fine and she began to feel better by early morning. I'm certain she will be feeling much better by Fri. and will probably do her next update herself. Thanks for all of your support.

Much love from the 3rd floor of the newly remodeled cancer wing.

Dave, Kathy and Aaron

Insightful

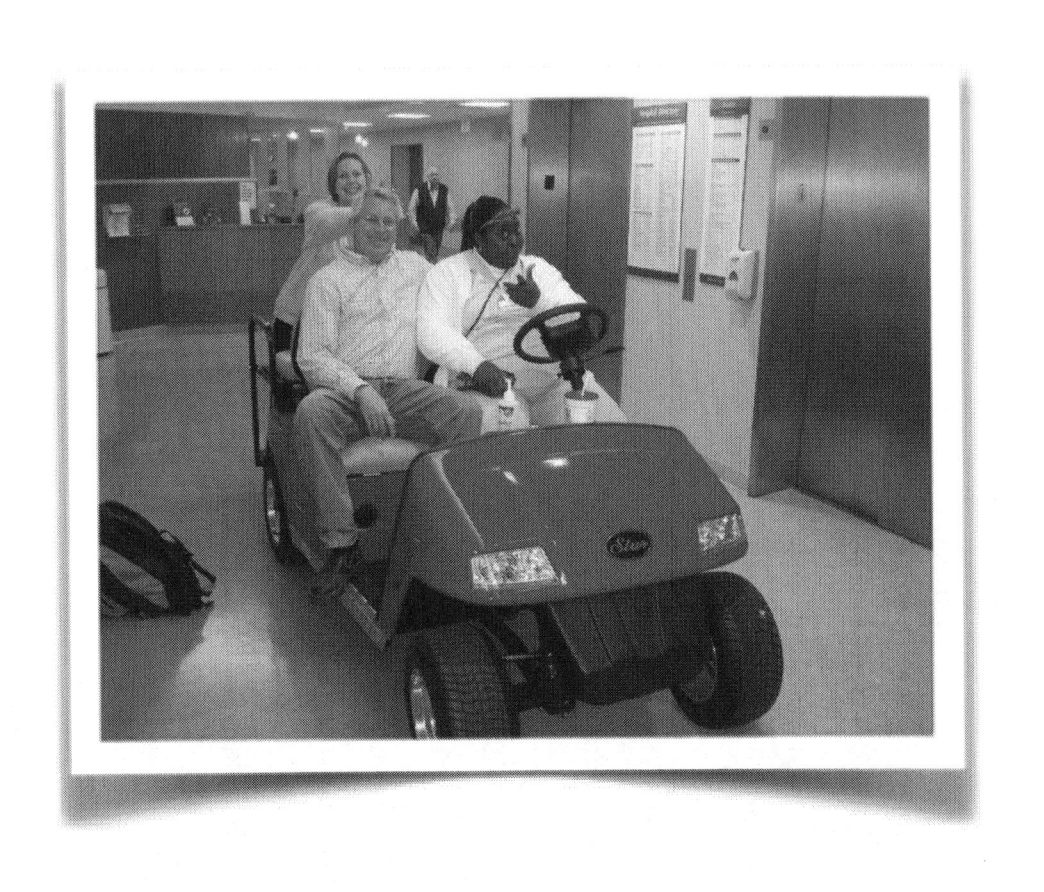

56

HEADING HOME TO HEAL...

December 14, 2008

Heading home to heal...

It's me. I'm back after a few days off to lay around in bed and sleep. They released me on Saturday morning. We got home around 4:00pm. I have to admit, I am feeling much better today then I thought I could feel after the past few days. It has been a tough couple of days. My body is just not bouncing back like it usually does- mostly from the anesthesia more than anything. I seem to be pretty sensitive to it and it takes a while to get out of my body. I have stitches in both breasts where they took out the expanders and put in my silicone implants. Also I have an incision where the hysterectomy and cosmetic surgery was done. There are two JP drains coming from this area to help remove any excess blood around the surgical cuts. Everything looks great now and I am still pretty swollen and puffy. I also have very soft realistic breasts now! Finally! Maybe once the pain has gotten better then I can get a little more excited about the results. I guess I am a little distracted at the moment to say the least.

I had a pretty tough go round of it on the night of surgery. Aaron woke up from the couch in my room to the nurses trying to get me to wake up and me not really responding. I guess I got over sedated after switching drugs in the middle of the night (morphine drip was making me itchy), then my O2 levels dropped down around 60 for a bit. Aaron was a champ-his voice is the only thing I remember from that whole time telling me to wake up and that everything was going to be ok. They had to give me a drug that reversed the effects of the painkillers. I came out of it groggy, confused and throwing up. A lot. It was pretty scary actually. I felt like my body was being ripped apart from the inside out. I ended up in the fetal position, which was not nice on my stitches across my waist. Ouch. I am glad to have that behind me. I have taken it very slow today at home. Kayden and I have put a few Disney shows under out belt. She is a pretty crappy couch partner if I am going to be honest. It's always about her...more this more that...I dropped this...turn it louder....come on...can't I have the spotlight for just a minute? Just kidding- she is having trouble not touching me in my surgical zones, especially my waist. She is either kicking me while laying with me or leaning on me with her bony elbows. She keeps looking at me with the big eyes telling me she's just trying to make it feel better. Sweet- but that doesn't take the pain away pumpkin. So get BACK!

Hopefully I will get some more energy as soon as my appetite returns. It has been pretty weak so far, we had some homemade chicken noodle soup from our friend the Ferrel's yesterday and my friend Diedra brought some homemade Lasagna that I plan to eat tonight. Yum Yum. Well, I will check back in tomorrow to give you another progress update. Thank you to everyone for your messages and cards. I appreciate it all so much! I hope to have more energy to communicate in the next day, so I apologize if you have called and I haven't been able to talk. Also, many of you have mentioned that you cannot get the web site to let you leave a comment. This is most likely still from the same issue with the web site name that we changed earlier in the year. Check your web address you use to get to my site.

I'm off for a nap. Aaron is taking Kayden to the Hill's Children's Holiday party. My mom is here and she gets to go to the grocery store to stock us up. I forgot to say thanks to my dad for taking over for me while I was down and doing a posting. As usual he found the most "flattering" picture he could to post :) Thanks Dad. Bye for now.

Much love from my haze of painkillers that cause crazy dreams-

Jamie

ps: The picture at the top of the page is me BEFORE surgery...I am no where near that spry now :)

Listener

57

THINGS ARE GOOD!

February 26, 2009

Things are good!

It's been too long as usual, but as I have said before....no news is good news on my end! I have been feeling great ever since my surgery in Dec. We were able to go home to Kansas for Christmas and New Year's. It was a good place to be while getting better. I pushed myself more then I would have sitting at home and that always allows me to bounce back better and faster. I was lucky and didn't have any problems with the healing process. Since the beginning of the year I have been slowly adding exercise and weights back into my daily routine and I am glad to say I am finally back to normal. I still have twinges from time to time in places to remind me that I can overdo it still. I try to listen to my body as best I can. I had appointments in Indianapolis in early February. I met with the surgeon that did my hysterectomy- she said everything looks great. For those of you that didn't know- she did remove two polyps from the rectal area and had them sent in for biopsy just to be safe at the time of my hysterectomy. The biopsy came back fine and this is not anything I will need to worry about in the future. I had already gotten the results a while back but it was good to have her reaffirm that things were normal. Also she told me that she went back to my scans and realized that I still have splenetic matter in my body- a surprise since I had an emergency splenectomy in 1998 from a car accident that shattered my spleen. So apparently I have a few pieces that have gotten together and are functioning on some small level still. Pretty interesting stuff!

I then had my 3-month check in with my Oncologist. This was also a thumbs up appointment. There are no signs (persistent pains or skin marks that last longer then 2 weeks) that I have any need for scans and we are now 7 months out from the surgery that removed the cancer in July. We will continue to do the 3 month check ins for now. That will move to 6-month check ups eventually. It was good to see Dr. Schneider. I kind of miss his smiling face when we don't get to see him for a while. He's more like a big brother to me now after all we have been through than my doctor. That may sound weird but it's hard not to see him as more then just my doctor. I have trusted him with my life after all.

After this appointment my plastic surgeon stopped in to take a look at how my scars were healing. Great work I did there! he said :) You can hardly tell the left breast is an implant except for the scar. My right one is still a bit more solid and unnatural compared to the left...but it is because of the radiation I had on that side. It has affected the skin and tissue on this side and caused it to be harder for lack of a better word. My scars are still pink but beginning to even out. Everything looks great and I am feeling like a new woman! All this positive change is good for the soul that's for sure.

So overall- it was a busy day full of good news. As usual Aaron and I have jumped back into life and are busy busy busy. We are still enjoying Bowling Green and love traveling as much as possible. We recently took a trip with Aaron's family to Belize in Central America. IT WAS AMAZING! Kayden came with us too! I have downloaded a new picture album so you can share in our pics. It is a whole separate entry and I will save it for next time. We intend to keep adding stamps to our passports in the near future if we can. It's always good to be able to expose Kayden to all these new things- mom and dad are enjoying themselves as well. I had better sign off for now. I just wanted you to know how great things are here for us right now. I hope all is well in your homes. Be sure to do your monthly exams- mark it on your calendars and set yourself and alarm to remind you. Say a prayer for my pink pals Amy Tyler and Kristen Worden- they have recently had surgery for their own breast cancer situations and will need help getting better as quickly as I did!

Much love from our happy household to yours...

Jamie

Fun

58

ONE LAST SURGERY

April 20, 2009

One last surgery...

Oh where to start... it's been a busy last few months as usual. Like most of you, we have been riding the roller coaster of crazy weather here in KY as well. When it's nice we are headed outside for play dates and time in the park. I myself am playing on a USTA women's 3.0 tennis team. I love the sport and am so happy to be back in physical shape and able to play now! I have also been working out and trying to get rid of some of this extra weight that seems to have crept on in the last few years. I have been using an app on my iphone called LoseIt. So far it has been very helpful by tracking my calorie intake and exercise- it is great to start seeing the results of this hard work as swimsuit season is fast approaching!

We spent Easter in St. Augustine, Florida with my parents and brother. It was a full weekend of eating, shopping, and relaxing and of course keeping up with Kayden. The constant "tell me why..." request had everyone about to pull their hair out. She kept us on our toes with her constant motion and exploration. She kept referring to the beach as 'summer' and had an Easter egg hunt going about every 10 minutes. Uncle Scott was pretty impressed with her ability to talk and talk and talk about nothing. You'd think he would have been used to it after growing up with me =) She is growing up so fast. She talks a mile a minute and has an amazing imagination. I have cut back to doing daycare only one day a week. Because of this I think, she is really craving attention right now and is willing to do about anything to get it. She is such a social child and thrives on being around people. I hope being an only child isn't going to be too hard on her. She is constantly singing songs about what ever is on her mind at that moment. We have new addition to our household, Grandma Kathy got her a Beta fish when they were here earlier this month. Its name is GiGi. It is currently co-habitating with a minnow she got from some fishermen at a local lake, its name is Dory. She also got a big girl bike with training wheels this past weekend. She rode it out of the store with a big grin on her face. She has already taken a couple of good falls- while wearing a helmet of course! She's a trouper and after some negotiations got back on it again. Her hair is finally growing out a little from her personal haircut. She is in that shaggy stage currently and it is driving me crazy. I want to get it cut to clean it up so bad and Aaron stands firm that we are not touching it- it will grow out eventually.

Aaron has kept busy with work. He has done some mountain biking with friends and works in a guys night when he can, of course I make sure to get my girls night too so we are even! This past weekend he had the boat out getting it ready for the water. Hopefully it will be warm enough to go out soon! We are all looking forward to it.

OK- I am boring even myself as I read back over this...onto my health. First of all, I have been feeling great lately! That is the question I am asked the most so I wanted to be sure to answer it for those of you I may not talk to as often. Today is a big day. I am headed to Indianapolis for my "pickle" reconstruction! For those of you that may not remember- this is what Kayden calls nipples- I said nipple she heard pickle- who am I to correct her? Seriously how do you explain to a three year old why you have to go to the doctor to get a new pickle? She responded to my explanation by exclaiming that she wanted to go to the pickle store and get new pickles too. Ohhhh if it had only been that easy....

Say good-bye to my Barbie boob (that would be the right breast currently living with no nipple at all hence the Barbie boob nickname). From what I understand he will be taking some skin from another area on my body, TBD, and using it to build up a faux nipple or nubbin as I like to refer to it. I will then have the areola tattooed on later this fall. The surgery is scheduled to start at 1:00 pm. I have to go under IV sedation and am scheduled to be on the table for 2 1/2 hours. I get to head home shortly after surgery so it is considered an outpatient procedure. Now I am sure you are all a bit curious- but no- I will not be posting pictures of the finished product. Feel free to google 'nipple reconstruction' and look at other women's boobs... as Aaron has told me he would like to leave a little to the general public's imagination, wink wink.

I have a few other minor issues that weigh on my mind as I write this. I have a red spot about 1 inch in diameter on the right side of my chest just below my collarbone. It looks like it is a mark from scratching the area- but it doesn't go away. I have been keeping an eye on it since late February. As a rule of thumb if a pain or in this case an unusual skin area does not change after 2 weeks then it is worthy of mentioning to the doctor. After discussing with Dr. Schneider, my oncologist, he wants to have my plastic surgeon take a look and then biopsy it if necessary while I am on his table today. I also have a place on my back where I found a tick over a month ago after hiking at Mammoth Cave. The spot has not healed yet and continues to itch if I touch it so I am going to have him take a look at that too. I also have a weird bulge under my right armpit. I would like to think it is a developing muscle from all that working out....but since that underarm is very different looking then my other underarm (they took most of my lymph nodes out 2 years ago and it is now caved in if you can picture that) I want to have him look at it as well. I am not going to claim that I am sure it is nothing...because as we all know that is not always the case, but I have to pay attention to this type of thing. That is the down side of having had the big C. I have to notice everything and ignore nothing. So as I sit here on the morning of my final phase of reconstruction...I am not really worried about going under the knife once again....I am more worried about the other spots and lumps and bumps on my body. Aggh! It always leaves me with a heavy heart and scattered mind when I am worried about these things. I am just glad that I can get them out of the way today. If it is something then let's take care of whatever it is. If it is nothing then I can stop wasting my energy worrying about it. I will keep you updated! Since it is an outpatient surgery and we will be heading back to KY early this evening. Kayden stayed last night and possibly tonight with some friends of ours who have a daughter her age. Having her stay there is a huge help and I am so grateful to my friend Deidre for offering to do this so I can focus on myself today.

To end on a good note...Dr. Schneider has been a very busy man, now that he is done saving my life and all...JK! He has recently received a $6 million + grant from the Susan G. Komen Foundation to study Avastin in breast cancer patients. This is an AMAZING opportunity for him to continue his research. This is a very big honor, especially for a doctor as young as he is. I am very proud of him and am glad that I was able to participate in some of the research on this drug! It is so great to know that donations made by my friends and family have essentially ended up right back in the very hospital that helped heal me.

I am sitting in the car on the way to Indy writing this-my stomach is growling since I cannot eat or drink before surgery. My nerves are a little on edge with the anticipation of another surgery...but this also is a significant day because this is essentially the end of the reconstruction road minus the tattoo this fall. What a long journey this has been this second time around. We are so ready to be done! Thank you for all your thoughts and prayers. We will keep you updated on how today goes.

Much love from my lonely headlight-

Jamie

Faith

59
SURGERY UPDATE

April 21, 2009

Surgery update

We are back in the car on our way home to BGKY. I am doing great thanks to a couple of percocet they gave me before I left! My surgery lasted about 2 hours. I had Dr. Cacioppo take a look at the red spot on my chest. His decision was that it was not worth a biopsy at this point, but we did take a picture of it close up to keep on file so we can keep an eye on it. The bulge under my arm was another story though. He felt that it was not a muscle from feeling it...and told me he didn't feel comfortable discounting it as nothing. He wanted me to talk with Dr. Schneider and possibly do an ultrasound to see what it is. He thought it could possibly be the end of the area where they removed my lymph nodes and therefore there is a small shelf where the scar tissue meets muscle. It is hard to guess until we have a better look at the area. At least I have less to mull over and worry about now.

The surgery was successful! He ended up using a peaked area at the end of my scar on my back. It had healed with a small pucker at the end of the scar. It was not quite enough skin to use for the nubbin so he ended up extending the scar line a bit to collect the proper amount of skin for the job. He seemed happy with how my scars were healing from my December surgery. He claimed he could tell I have been working out =) Positive reinforcement works for me! He wants to see me for a follow up on May 5th. I will hopefully be able to get an ultrasound at that time on my underarm. I will let you know.

In the meantime I am restricted from any heaving lifting and cannot get my breast area wet at all. He surgically attached a bolster (?) bandage/gauze to the new nipple area so I cannot see what it looks like at all. I assume this is to help allow the new skin graft to heal properly. My back incision has some type of clear coverage over it and I am able to be a little less protective of it. I think it is some sort of Derma bond or something like that. It looks like plastic wrap glued to the area. My foot is pretty sore right now, as they had to put my IV there. I have both right and left arm precautions, which means that I cannot be stuck with a needle, or have my blood pressure taken in either arm since my lymphatic system has been compromised (my blood clot on the left side and my lymph node dissection on the right). If that were to happen it could flare up my lymphedema and I am certainly not interested in having elephant arms that are constantly swollen. My foot was the next best option, but it is very painful, especially for a narrow thin foot like mine. The anesthesiologist is who I usually prefer to place the IV and that is who did it today. Most nurses tend to not be comfortable sticking the foot since it is a harder stick. Fun Fun! It makes it a pain to walk anywhere once it is placed and of course I always end up having to go to the bathroom soon after they get it placed. I am full of surprises once I get into the OR =)

I sent my surgeon a text prior to surgery telling him to lay off the sauce at lunch because he had a nubbin to create! I am sure he thinks I am a goofball- but I like to keep him on his toes! He apparently came in after I was in the recovery room to check on me and I gave him a big hug and thanked him for healing not only my body but also my soul. It was apparently a touching moment and he blushed....I on the other hand have absolutely no recollection of this happening. Must have truly come from my heart, eh?!

One last thing and I will sign off so I can take a nap in the car. Aaron's aunt Ginny put a quote on my Facebook page yesterday after reading my status update telling everyone about my upcoming surgery. It made me smile and I thought it would be good share it with you all too....

"All the kings horses and all the kings men PUT Jamie back together again!"

How true that simple statement is. I finally feel whole again and look forward to having this healing process done and over with. I will see Dr. Cacioppo for a follow up on May 5th. I plan to schedule an ultrasound at that time on my underarm so we can get some answers on that situation. I will let you know as we get more info. Well, it's been a long day and I am bushed. I will let you know how the rest of the week goes. I am scheduled to come back to KS this Saturday for a week so hopefully I will be able to connect with many of you in person soon! Bye for now...

Much love from my new headlight!

Jamie

Realism

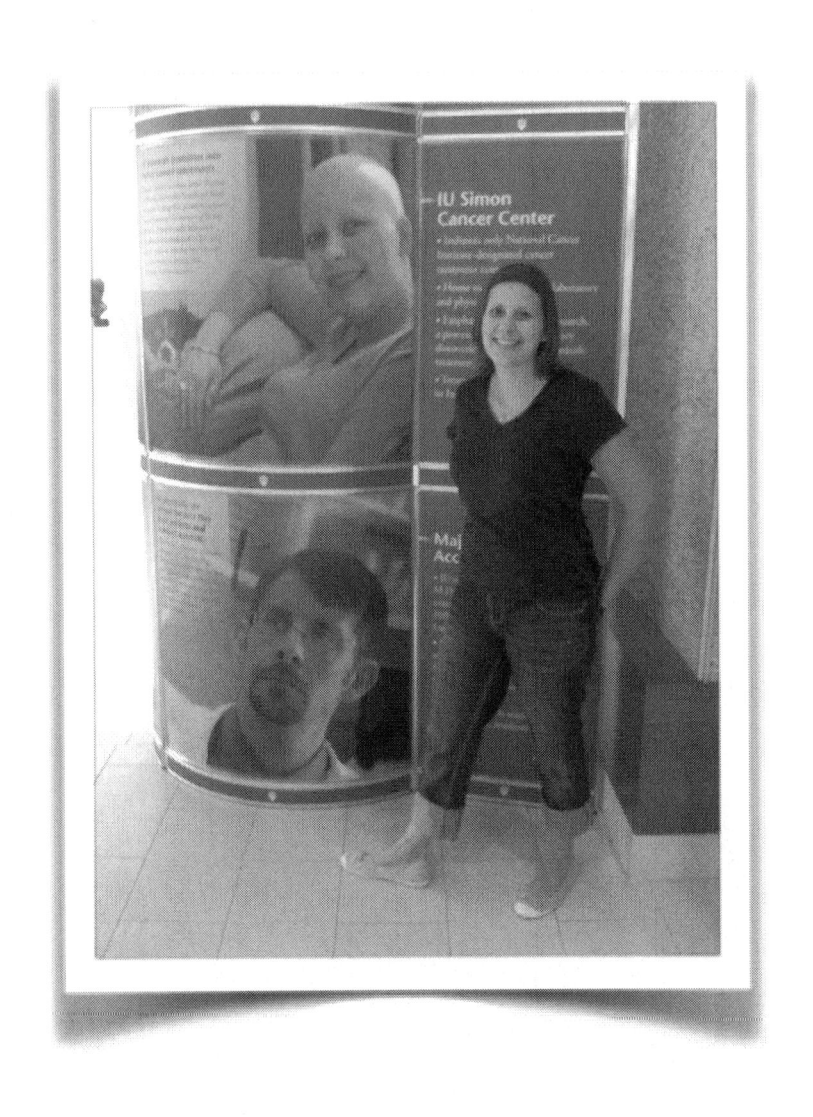

60
CHECK ME OUT!

May 6, 2009

Check me out!

So I wake up today with another of those gray clouds hanging over my head. I have an appointment with my general surgeon Dr. Goulet so he can have a look at my armpit "bulge" (for lack of a better word). Ugh again with the potential for bad news. As always I hate the unknown.

This day could go from a quick easy appointment to an all day testing and biopsy day in a matter of seconds. Luckily Carol his nurse coordinated me being able to see Dr. Cacioppo at the same time so he could take this bandage off of my nipple skin graft. Oooooo-now that is something to get excited about! The big unveiling! Kind of like when they unwrap the gauze from the patient that got the new face only not quite that dramatic. Although there could have been a small drum roll and it would have seemed completely appropriate for the moment =) So I tried to focus on the nipple thing and not the bulge thing so I could drive and not have my mind wander to the gray places. Which ended up not being a problem since it rained cats and dogs the whole way to Indy and I had to be super focused on driving.

I should add that I am a totally paranoid driver as my personal driving record has been a bit marred this past month. A ticket for not stopping at a stop sign in Bowling Green a few weeks ago and then a speeding ticket in KS on I70 in the construction zone at the East Lawrence exit while I was home last week. Grrrrrr......what can I say? I've sat around long enough! This girl has places to be and not enough time to get there!

OK- so back to my day. As you can tell I am writing this on my way home so I keep switching tenses in my writing. Grammar was never my strong suit; neither was spelling if you couldn't tell. Sorry Mrs. Judd- I should have paid attention better. Off track again- I am a bit spacey today to say the least. We got to Indy with a bit of time to spare thanks to the extra time I planned into our trip since I had to drive the speed limit- kidding of course. I texted my plastic surgeon to see if he wanted some Jimmy John's for lunch and Kitty (who came with me for the trip) and I grabbed a quick lunch. How cool is it that I can have such an awesome relationship with my doctors? I feel pretty lucky. I wonder what they would think if they knew I went on and on about them on this site? There I go again- scatter brain- off subject. Back to the topic at hand.

When I got to the cancer center I ran into the gift shop to get some gum and as we were walking out I was stopped in my tracks by a giant picture of none other than myself! I was floored! A while back they asked if they could use my picture on a traveling display for the Elks Club conventions. If you remember a while back I spoke at one of their conventions thanking them for their ongoing generous donations to the IU cancer center. That was almost 2 years ago. Anyways- my picture they used for the brochure for that event was blown up huge. There was a picture of Dr. Schneider (my oncologist) below mine and I was just so proud. It was a really really cool moment. I couldn't wait to share that with you all!

While basking in my newfound celebrity glow I headed up to wait for my turn to see the docs. Dr. Cacioppo was the first to show. He missed out on my text till it was too late and he hadn't eaten lunch. I now know his top two picks and can fulfill his lunch requests in the future :) He went right to work and took that dang bandage off. Drum roll please.....the nipple looked absolutely marvelous! Not that I expected anything less of course. I am so happy he chose to go the skin graft option for me rather then some of the standard ways you can do nipple reconstruction. It is so real looking even though it is still very early in the healing process. It was well worth all the effort that it took to get me to this point in my reconstruction. I am truly looking forward to have such a realistic new set of boobs. I couldn't have asked for a better final product.

As for my appt. with Dr. Goulet- it was a pleasure as always to see him and his entourage (that's what I call all the students that get to stand in on my appointments while they shadow the doctors). He came in today wearing the greatest yellow bow tie. You can't help but smile when that walks through the door. He always calls me Pursley instead of Jamie which is funny too as I am so used to being called Barkes from my maiden days. We chatted about this and that while he did my examination and within a couple of minutes and lot of hard probing in my armpits he declared that my bulge was indeed.....drum roll please.....a

MUSCLE! Whoo Hooo all those sculpting classes have finally paid off! He explained that my node dissection on that side has created a shelf like area where he removed tissue. It has left the muscle exposed much more on that side so it bulges out rather than looking smooth as on the other side. There is no tissue for the muscle to nestle behind/beneath so it looks un-natural. Sheww!!!! That was how Aaron replied to my text telling him what the diagnosis was. Talk about a weight lifted off my shoulders. I felt a thousand times lighter walking out of that building. Kitty and I celebrated with a several hours of shopping at the outlet mall on our way home. My kind of day! A clean bill of health and a little shopping! Not a bad ending to what started out as a gloomy day. I am happy to go home and take my shower and redress my new nipple and get some good restful sleep tonight. To tell you the truth, it has been awhile since I have had a restful sleep. Hopefully my good karma will stay around for a while this time. I have another follow up appt. in two weeks to look at the nipple progress. That will also coincide with my next 3 month check up with my oncologist. I don't anticipate this to be too eventful but I will keep you updated. Better go for now. We are pulling into Bowling Green now. Will touch base soon! Check out the new pics I added.

Much love from clear skies, a clear head and a clear heart-

Jamie

Up for Anything

61

FALL IS HERE....

October 12, 2009

Fall is here....

I can't believe it's been so long since I last posted. It just seems like yesterday we were in our swimsuits out on the boat....now it's already time to drag out the coats. It's been a busy time for us around here. So much has happened since my last post. I always have trouble starting these postings as I don't know where to start. Oh well....I'll give you all the short long story :) You all know I am incapable of telling a short story anyways....I had a scare this summer where I was having weird twinges and aches in my right breast area. I made an appointment to see my oncologist and he scheduled a breast MRI for me. It was an extremely stressful time for me waiting to hear about the test results. But in the end the MRI came back clear of anything in the breast. It is hard to know why I am having these pains, but it could be many things that are not cancer related. As usual we have to rule that out first though. I hate that. It is sooooo hard to first acknowledge that there is something out of the ordinary and then to make the drive and go through the test, not to mention wait for the results. Agh.....it is enough to give me heart palpitations and cause me to freak out internally. The more worried I am the more forgetful I get, and spacey. It is just so hard to concentrate when you have this black cloud sitting over you. I was so happy to have a clear scan but it still doesn't stop that feeling of dread. It takes me some time to get back to not thinking about the cancer or dreading that I am missing some sign that could mean it is back. We all let out our grateful sighs of relief that we jumped this hurdle and went on to enjoy our summer.

We decided halfway through the summer to trade our boat we had in for a wakeboarding boat. This allowed us to do more of the wake surfing- our new all time favorite water sport. I also learned to wakeboard and was doing pretty good at both by the end of the summer. Kayden was even able to partake while standing up with her daddy. She is such a daredevil. Definitely gets that from her dad and not me! We got a lot of fun video and pics of the lake time. I will work on getting those all added to the albums on this site after I get this posting up. We have spent a lot of time with friends this past summer. I forget how nice it is to have a social outlet. We haven't really had a steady group of friends that have kids Kayden's age. That makes it so much fun to get together. I will be sad when we have to leave this group some day. I have been really trying hard to get Kayden and I on track to be home while I am working- I decided to put her in a morning out program this last month to help give me more time alone at home to work and clean and all that fun stuff. She already had two friends in the class that meets on Mon and Wed. They are quite the trio. The teacher said they are "figuring it out" as far as making sure they are all good in class. My guess is that they are quite a handful when they are all together. But it has been good for us both so I'm glad we made the choice to do it. I'm keeping busy trying to find new projects for my dad's business. The economy has been rough on our construction company and we are trying all sorts of new avenues to get new projects on the books for the last quarter of the year.

I have been playing a ton of tennis this summer and I have recently started doing a spin class a couple of times a week...now if I could just get that running thing down so it didn't feel like I was about to keel over and die :) Then I would be happy....but no seriously. I am more active now then I have been in a long time. I have a lot of making up to do from the last few years of non-activity. It feels so good to be getting active and I am looking forward to the benefits of choosing this healthier lifestyle. My hope is to set an example for baby girl so she doesn't have to struggle with the repercussions of not being an active kid. If she sees me doing it then it is only natural for her to want to take part.

It seems like there have been a lot of sadness in fellow cancer fighters lately. I want to be sure that you all say prayers for some of my friends that are struggling with their own battles right now. Amy, Tory and Chase are all people that are not cancer free currently and I want to send them positive thoughts, prayers and courage to deal with their decisions and treatments they are going through right now. We all have different roads we travel with cancer...but the pain and suffering are all the same. They can use some extra support to get them through their struggles now.

I don't feel like I have filled you in on all that is on my mind , but I'm tired and I promised myself I would get this posting out before I went to bed tonight. No more procrastination just because I have so much to say. So I am signing off, bye for now...more l8tr.

Much love and a big fat yawn-

Jamie

Believe

62

THIRD TIME'S THE CHARM

NOVEMBER 21, 2009

Third time's the charm....

Well unfortunately this posting is not to tell you how great things are going, I am sad to tell you that my breast cancer has returned. I wish with all my heart that I wasn't forced to have to share this kind of news yet again, but I guess this little disease of mine has decided to rear its ugly head for one more battle. I'm sure you are all asking how, what, where. It's come back on my right side (original cancer side) in the form of a spot (not a palpable lump) on my skin. It is a flat smooth piece of skin that reminds me of an old scar or something. It is mainly flesh colored- although it turns red if you touch it. I have been watching this particular spot for the past 4-6 weeks since I hadn't noticed it before. It doesn't hurt or itch or even move if you try to pinch it or move the skin. It is just a raised smooth spot on my skin.

I had a regular 3-month appt. this past Monday with my oncologist. This appt. was meant to talk about any pains or concerns I may be having. After he looked at it and had another surgeon come in and take a look, we made the decision to do a punch biopsy in the office that day just to be safe. We got the results of that biopsy back yesterday afternoon and just like that- my cancer is back. Ugh. I was super pissed off when I first found out. I took my frustration out on the dashboard in Aaron's truck since we were driving. Then I kicked a fence at a gas station- a couple of times... I'm not one to act out my frustrations.... but I won't lie, the fence kicking helped and hurt all at the same time.

What now? Well, I have an appt. back in Indy first thing Monday morning to get a CAT scan and a bone scan. This will tell us if the disease has moved anywhere else in my body, which is a very very important piece of information. If it is localized (or only in my breast not in any of my organs) then we will have one plan of action. They will need to remove the spot and get clean margins. A general surgeon will do this. Then we will discuss radiation options and systemic options (chemo). If it has spread to other organs then that changes my original stage 3 diagnosis to stage 4 and we will deal with the metastasis first then the spot. This is all what if situations that we will be able to address after my scans on Monday. Aaron and I have decided on our end that it HAS NOT spread and we are going to go with the power of positive thinking from here on out so jump on the positive thinking train with us and think LOCALIZED not METASTISIZED.

So where do we go from here I am sure you are all asking.... my dr. hopes to have my scan results in time for us to discuss at that meeting. So for now... we wait and try not to worry. We will have a plan by Monday and I will let you all know then what we have decided. Keep us in your thoughts and prayers. I could use all that you can spare right now. We've done this twice already- I guess the third time is the charm. I am doing good mentally- a little more pissed off then I was the first two times I had to hear this news. Kayden is in KS with grandma and grandpa so we are able to get this figured out without worrying about putting her in the situation. I know this is hard to hear- trust me- but know that I will not go down without one hell of a fight and I am so glad to have such a great support system. I will be keeping you all updated through this website so stay tuned. I will post on Monday when we get home or at least by first thing Tuesday to let you know what we found out in Indy. Till then.... keep those prayers and positive thoughts coming our way!

Much love from a soon to be 3 time breast cancer survivor-

Jamie

Sunshine

63

THE WAITING GAME....

November 22, 2009

The waiting game...

We are on our way to Indy tonight since we have to be up early to make it to the hospital to get my contrast started for my CAT scan. 5:15am!! We stopped in Edinburgh IN to do some Christmas Shopping. Funny though- for once, I am not feeling the Christmas spirit. Those of you close to me know that I LOVE the holidays and live for shopping. It's just one more thing this stinking disease has taken from me; watch I'll bet that I end up being in the hospital on my birthday again at this rate. OK- enough venting.

After having a couple of days for the news to soak in I am still feeling a range of emotions. I definitely keep coming back to being just plain pissed off. It is not fair that we have to do this again. I know that I am strong and that we will beat it yet again... but seriously. I do have better things to do like living my life and making plans for the future. We had just this month booked our tickets to head to Florence, Italy on Dec. 26th. Who knows if my upcoming treatment plan will allow for this trip? Isn't that silly that that is what I am most worried about right now? Well that and the fact that I may have to do chemo and possibly lose my hair again. The thought of that just makes my stomach sink. It was such a hard and humbling thing to go through, and it took so long for it to grow back... I'd rather not do it again. I know it's vain and pretty unimportant when you really think about all the things I should be worrying about right now... but my brain is in Italy/don't want to be bald again mode and I just can't help that. Judge me if you want =). It's probably more my mind breaking down the feelings into more manageable thoughts then anything. If I sit here and worry about if I will be around to watch Kayden graduate high school and some day help her plan her wedding or have a baby- then I just might not be able to get out of bed in the morning. So I will continue to worry about hair and plane tickets and if we will be able to make it home to KS for Thanksgiving. Those are the things that allow me to get out of bed in the morning and function as a normal person.

A lot of you have commented on how well I am taking the news; don't let my positive attitude fool you for one minute. I am absolutely terrified to have to do this again- but the difference between me and someone else is that the terror fuels my desire to kick this cancer's ass- again and again and again if that is what I have to do. Because my baby girl is going to have me around to see her grow into the beautiful caring and charismatic woman that I know she will be. I am not missing that ride for anything.

As cliche as it sounds- I have to believe that there is a greater plan for me that involved these detours for a reason and I just have to strap in and hang on for dear life. I have the most wonderful husband and family and friends. I can do this as many times as I have to because I have an awesome team of doctors on my side and such a wonderful support system that is as seasoned as I am. I couldn't do any of this without all of you. So as I sit here another night not knowing what is in store for me, it is much easier knowing that I have so many others doing it with me in both mind and heart. Keep those positive thoughts and prayers coming because we will truly need them tomorrow. Remember- LOCALIZED not METASTIZED!! I will post something as soon as I can.

Much love from one anxious girl-

Jamie

who decides who BEATS CANCER & who doesn't?

—JAMIE

64

November 23, 2009

I am leaving the title of this entry blank tonight for a lack of words. There is no easy way to say this so I will get to the point. My CT scan showed that there is a small area on my right hip that indicates bone deterioration. It is a very concerning spot that my oncologist and the radiologist both agree is most likely metastatic disease. This will be confirmed with a bone biopsy that is scheduled for Monday 11/30/09 at 11 am in Indy. I know this is a lot to digest, trust me I am still numb.... but let me break this down. My breast cancer has most likely spread outside of the breast and is in my blood stream, which has in turn allowed it to take up residence in my bones. If this is the case and the biopsy confirms that it is cancer in my bones- then I will be considered to have Stage 4- metastatic breast cancer. I know many of you say what does that mean. Well it means that our attempts to keep the cancer from spreading outside of my breast tissue where it originated have failed. We are now dealing with a disease that is roaming free in my body and needs to be stopped or put into remission. Being Stage 4 means that I no longer will look to cure my disease but to stabilize it and keep it from continuing to grow or spread any further then it already has. We will do this through as many avenues as possible- most of which are drugs that can be taken in either pill form or infused, as was my chemo I did early on. I will not go into the details right now as it is just too much for me to really process. Just know that we have a plan ready for whatever the biopsy tells us.

There is room for a miracle in that this biopsy comes back negative for cancer- but I am not going to give myself the pleasure of even thinking that is a possibility. I just cannot bear to be disappointed once again. We discussed at length our options and what to expect. A lot of this I will share with you in the days to come after we have had some time to comprehend it all. When I asked how long do I have he gave me an honest answer. The average life expectancy of a woman that has metastatic breast cancer is 3 years. Now that means some make it longer then 3 years and some do not make it 3 years. It all depends on how my specific cancer behaves with the drugs we throw at it. This is very very hard to stomach, but please understand that the more they learn about the disease the more that life expectancy average goes up. I know that this may seem like I am being very matter of fact- but unfortunately there is no sugar coating these facts. The longer we can keep this cancer in check the longer I get to stick around. I cannot say that my mind has completely absorbed this information. I feel like I am writing a story about someone else's life right now. It is going to take me a while to really accept the reality of this news.

Looking back we have done everything we could possibly have done. I would have done nothing different and I don't know that anything would have changed our final outcome. So I will not waste my mental wellness over what ifs and I ask that you take the same advice. What I need right now is to focus on the present and work on doing what we can for the now. Please realize that the decisions we make are the ones that will be most beneficial for our family and its immediate future. I know it is a very helpless feeling to be a part of this situation and everyone wants to help as much as they can.... but for now we just need to be together as a family and take strength in the people that surrounds us. As we get the rest of the answers we will be better equipped to help you all understand the situation better.

For now we have to dig deep and find the courage to continue our lives in a way that will allow our daughter to get the most of the time I have with her. I have to take a step back and really focus on the present as that is what we have and what we can control right now. Please know that I wish I could call each of you and tell you this news and answer all your questions.... but I just do not have it in me to tackle that task right now after what might have been the longest day and most likely the worst day of my life. I love you all and I am sending you hugs and kisses as you continue my journey with me as your friend/sister/daughter. Know that I have not changed with this news it's just that I may not be able to stay for the long haul so let's make it the best we can and not dwell on what we cannot change. If that is what is to come then I will be ready and know that I have done what I set out to do-, which is to have lived my life with no regrets. I intend to leave my baby girl with a memory of a mommy that she can be proud of when she grows up and can better understand all of this, lets just pray that time comes not sooner but later. For now I am going to make sure that the best times are ahead of us and that we take every opportunity we can to make it as wonderful as possible. I love you all and will be in touch via website in the next couple of days. Pray hard for a miracle and call in on those favors if you don't mind. Bye for now...

Much love from the bottom of my aching heart-

Jamie

Role Model

65

GIVING THANKS.....

November 29, 2009

Giving thanks....

Ahhh.... what an awesome trip back to KS we had. We were able to see a lot of people and spend some much needed time with family giving thanks. It was really good to get my giant hug from Kayden and my parents once we got home late Tuesday night. She had been trying hard to stay awake for us and was so excited when we finally walked through the door. After catching up with everyone I headed down to read her a book so she could go to bed. She explained that we could read but then we needed to come back up to go to the airporch (airport). She truly thought we were taking her home THAT night. I explained that mommy and daddy wanted to stay in KS to visit with everyone, she literally melted down. She was sobbing and telling me that she missed her Calli (her kitty) and her house. It was enough to just break your heart. I know she was so tired and had been having such a fun week being in KS , but I am sure some part of her wanted to get back to her home and the routines we have there that make her days more stable. Aren't we all like that after vacations.... it's nice to be away but it's also nice to get back to your everyday life. I can only imagine what goes through her little mind, especially because she couldn't help but feel the stress and sadness with my metastasis news. Although we have not discussed it with her yet... she's a smart kid and she knows when something is wrong. She even delivered a couple of unsolicited hugs to my parents on the the night they got the news. She finally agreed to stay a "little bit" longer and as quickly as it had begun the fit was over. Overall, we were able to make our visit a positive one and really enjoy our time with family and friends. Mom and I went out at 3:30am on Black Friday with my cousin's daughter Courtney (our official line stander) to take advantage of the craziness and discounts. Talk about retail therapy!! I'm not sure if Courtney or my mom have recovered yet but it did wonders for me =) We also made it to Manhattan to spend time with Aaron's parents and sister. I got to drive his dad's new Polaris Ranger around their property. It was FUN! Look out crazy driver with some aggression to get out =).

Kayden wasn't quite sure she liked going as fast as mommy did. Aaron and I went out in Aggieville Friday night where I had a great time indulging in some (OK a lot) of adult beverages and socializing with our group of friends there. It was a short trip but it felt great to get back and see everyone- it was just what I needed to fuel myself for the weeks ahead. I think it made everyone else feel better to see me and hug me too. It sucks to be so far away sometimes.

We are now back on the road headed to Indianapolis for my bone biopsy that is scheduled for tomorrow at 11 am. I have had a lot of questions about what the biopsy involves so I thought I would better explain it. I won't be seeing my doctors at all tomorrow. This is done at the hospital at our scheduled time. I will be sedated and they will take a piece of the the bone from the area that showed up on my CT scan via a large needle they will insert into my right hip. That sample will allow them to see if there are indeed cancer cells present in my bone. It is a pretty painful procedure and I will be sore from it afterwards. I do not expect to hear results on the biopsy till the end of the week, although it could be earlier. I have prepared myself for another week of waiting for results. It's easier this go round as we are treating this as confirmation of what we already know. That may seem pessimistic to you but for us it is easier to move forward as if we already know the results of the biopsy. If we get news that it is not metastasis then that's awesome!! I refuse to wait on pins and needles and waste another week being afraid of what I might hear.

Once again we are reminded that time is precious and it's easy to get complacent in our lives and let the days slip by unappreciated. I will need to start taking my own advice and stop wasting energy over the things that I have no control over. I need to focus all of my energy on what we do from here on out. Our first few days of hearing this news was spent absorbing it and trying to sort out our feelings. Now we are moving on to the next step which is to put together a plan of action. Of course we need the biopsy results to finalize our treatment plan, but that doesn't mean we can't put the Pursley plan into play. We are still working on this plan of course but that is what we are focusing on for now. There is this fine balance of being realistic about my future yet living your life in a manner that is bearable and enjoyable at the same time. We want to know that we are taking advantage of all that we can do now while I am feeling great but not assume that I won't be feeling great for a REALLY long time. We have agreed to switch gears and stop looking at the average age of a survivor and talk more about how we are going to beat that average. I have been doing some research on women that are past that 3 year mark from their Stage IV diagnosis and there are a lot out there. I even heard from a fellow cancer survivor friend about a woman (who is currently treated by my oncologist) that is 14 years out from her Stage IV diagnosis. It's always positive to hear numbers like that! For right now my goal is to see my 40th birthday (which I turn 34 in two weeks) and hopefully many more past that. I ask that you help me focus on the positive and not get caught up in the doom and gloom of it all. This mindset will be a better long lasting plan. It's exhausting to constantly think about death and the what ifs and none of us should do that. Living life is a lot more rewarding than fearing death. I know we have so much ahead of us that will test my positiveness. But I will not try to do this on my own. There is a therapist at IU that we will be sitting down with soon. Ironically, she is also a Stage IV survivor. I can't wait to talk with her, possibly even tomorrow! We are also going to get set up with someone in Bowling Green that we can see as a family. This will help us work through the emotions and life changes we have ahead of us. I am grateful to have someone that can help involve Kayden in a positive way that will not allow my disease to scare or overwhelm her.

I am mentally doing pretty good right now. I have worked through a lot of my emotions, good and bad, and am ready to take action. I do feel this burning desire to take control of what I can- so that is what I will do, whether that means my kitchen is spotless or my pictures are organized by the month and day they were taken, or who knows what I will become obsessed with this time. I always come up with something to take my mind off things and it is usually some silly thing that I get started on and can't stop until it is done to the tenth degree. I will keep you updated on my latest projects. We are even going to start a bucket list of sorts, not because we have to... but because we can and want to. For us we want to plan out the things we want to do and it gives us something to look forward to. We have learned three times over now to try not to get too caught up in the tomorrow that you forget to enjoy today. Take the time to look at your own lives and make sure you are appreciating what you have because you never know what is in store for you around the next bend. No regrets. My motto of choice. With that said.... I will sign out for now. Stay tuned and I will update you all again later this week.

Much love from us to you-

Jamie

Vibrant

66

THE RESULTS.....

December 4, 2009

The results…..

I got the call Wednesday afternoon from my oncologist. As expected, there were cancer cells present in my bones. I apologize that I am just now sharing this news with you, but I needed a day or so to just absorb the magnitude of what this means. I now get to dedicate my life to controlling the disease in my body. I look ahead and know that treatment will be a part of my everyday life. I will learn to appreciate each day, month, year that we can stay in control of the disease. It is a life goal not a death sentence and that is how we will treat it. This news is devastating and freeing at the same time. I am just glad that we finally know and can move on with what we need to do.

I have been thinking about all of the things that this news changes in my life. I decided to make a pro con list that I am going to share with you. It helps me to put my fears on paper, or internet =) so I can grasp them and attack them head on.

Con-

1. Insane fear of thinking about the future - all the things that I could miss out on.

2. I will be on some type of drug treatment for the rest of my life.

3. Wondering if I could have done something different to keep this from happening.

4. Causes extreme stress in my personal relationships.

5. Creates financial strain on our family and co-supporters.

6. Potential for bodily pain and suffering.

7. Dying at an early age.

8. Kayden - enough said.

Pros-

1. Helping me realize how important it is to write down my experiences, organize my life, take pictures, travel, laugh, hug, cry, love, live, smile, enjoy, let go, learn, teach, live, try new things, enjoy old things, exercise, eat healthy, throw out the clutter, appreciate, love, live, pray, give thanks, believe, trust and never give up hope.

2. Enough said...

I have had so many people praying asking for a miracle and it is hard to not question God's plan for me, but I know in my heart that He is saving my miracle for later. It will come down the road when we find a drug that will stabilize my cancer and give me the long full life that I so desire. That my friends, is when we will get to see the miracle that we have prayed so hard for over the past few weeks. So we have to be patient and respect that there is a purpose for what is happening.

I know you all have so many questions about what is next and how can you help, but for now I am going to be selfish and end this posting. I have a 4 year old Princess and Pirate's party to throw tomorrow and that is what I am focusing on this weekend. Just know that I am doing well and not wallowing in my news. I am taking that first step in living with metastatic cancer which is put one foot in front of the other and make each day count. I will lay my head down at night and say thanks for another great day in my book of life - and you should too. I promise to post after the weekend and give you more information on what the next step will be. I love each of you and ask that you continue your prayers for our family and its journey to come.

Much love-

Jamie

P.S. That is me on the left in the picture, my cousin Kasie is in the middle and my brother Scott is on the right.

Tie That Binds

67

MY PLAN....

December 11, 2009

My plan...

It's been a pretty hectic week here at the Pursley household. We had a very successful Princess and Pirate party at our house on Saturday. Aaron's mom, sister and my parents were all able to attend. It was a full house for sure! I wouldn't have had it any other way! She was quite the princess that day- you could not wipe the grin off her face all day! She even had a couple of costume changes. It was great to see how much fun the kids had together this year compared to last year. I guess that one year of growing up really does make a difference. I had them all make their own glass bulb ornament to take home. It was a lot of fun. It has taken the rest of the week for me to get the house back in order though =) We have such a great group of friends here in Bowling Green- I can't believe how lucky we are to have so many friends with kids that are near the same age as Kayden. It was so comforting to just look around and realize that she/we were so loved even in the short time we have been here in Bowing Green (2 1/2 years). Be sure to check out the new pics in our photo album which I plan to post later this weekend.

I wasn't sure how I was going to hold up after all the commotion was gone- but I have been doing pretty good. I have my moments for sure, but I am learning to work through them as they come. It is weird the things that put me over the edge sometimes. Yesterday we got a new car and the guy asked us how we wanted the title to read- with one or both of our names? We both looked at one another and paused. Silly I know- but both of us had the same thought. Another example, I went to a MOPS meeting the other night with my friend Jennifer and they were talking about traditions that you can start for your children around the holidays. For some reason the thought of traditions and the fact that they are carried on for years to come just made my chest seize up. It's not a good feeling to have that anxiety overwhelm you. I am learning how to calm my nerves when that feeling hits. I saw a therapist here in town that is teaching me some techniques to stay calm if I get overwhelmed. I am sure over time that this reaction to thinking about the future will lessen- it is just very powerful right now. I have to admit I may be tough but I still get to claim fragile for now.

Aaron and I have talked a lot about this and it's just going to be something we have to accept. People around us go on living their lives and making plans for the future- I can't expect that to change just because my future has been challenged. We are going to just have to learn how to accept this change in our everyday lives and learn to not let it or the cancer cloud our decisions. I guess you could say we are learning to live a new norm. We must or we will wither away in fear of the future and that is not going to happen. So for now the tears have dried and we are working on moving forward one step at a time!

As far as treatment goes I have already started my first drug which is considered an aromatase inhibitor or AI which is a type of hormonal therapy. It is called Aromasin. There are minor side effects of this drug such as fatigue but nothing that should interfere with my day to day life too much. I have previously been on a different AI called Tamoxifin for 16 weeks, and then Arimidex for the past 1 1/2 years. There is also a clinical trial that I am going to be taking part in starting in January. It is called PTC299 (click on it for a full description). This trial drug will be done in conjunction with my Aromasin. I will be getting a new port put in on January 8th in Indy. This is a 4 hour procedure which is considered outpatient. Since I am right and left arm precaution, which means you can't stick me with a needle in either arm, ever, I will need the port for all of my blood draws the trial requires. They have been doing all of my blood draws from the top of my foot or ankle which hurts, a lot! The port will also be used for my Zometa infusions which help make my bones stronger. I will be getting it infused every 6 weeks. Once the port is in I will go through some pre-screening to prepare me for starting the trial drug. If all goes well I should start my first dose at the end of January. The PCT299 is pills that I take twice a day and the side effects are minimal compared to chemo. I won't lose my hair or be sick all of the time so that is a huge relief for now. If this works I will be on it for life, if it doesn't then we will go back to our bag of tricks and try a different route. I will be getting different scans throughout this trial to check for cancer progression. I believe it is every 6 weeks that I will have scans but don't quote me on that. So hopefully that clears you up on what our plan of action is for now. I have to hop in the shower so I can head to lunch with some friends to celebrate today- it's my 34th birthday! Oh, and I forgot to mention that I get to drive my new car, a 2007 Acura RDX to lunch too. Thanks to my wonderful hubby for his early birthday present!!! I can tell you one thing, today will be soooo much better than last year which I spent in the hospital recovering from my hysterectomy and breast reconstruction, talk about a crappy way to spend your birthday! So in honor of my new "norm"… I am going to enjoy my day and not look back or forward cause that's how I roll for now…

Much love from the birthday girl-

Jamie

ps. love you all for your positive thoughts, prayers, cards, hugs, emails, comments and all that jazz. It helps a lot and I can't possibly thank you enough.

pss. take notice that I made several words in the body of this posting links to outside sources where you can get more info on that particular word. Just click on the words that are a different color.

Whimsical

68

RINGING IN THE NEW YEAR....

January 17, 2010

Ringing in the New Year...

Depending on what order you read the last two postings in, it may not be in correct timeline. I decided it was too hard to jump from Italy to cancer. They should not have to share the same post :) Oh and by the way- consider this your Holiday card from the Pursleys. Happy Holiday's! We wish you a year full of wonderful! We just had too much going on this December so I apologize. But we loved getting all of your cards and letters and pictures! I promise we will do it someday! I am sure you are all wondering how our holidays were and of course our trip to Italy. Kayden and I traveled back to KS on Dec. 20. I woke up with the stomach flu on the 21st and was sick in bed at my parents for the next 3 1/2 days. Man that SUCKED! Aaron made it in to KS on Christmas Eve morning just before they shut down the airport from the snow. We actually ended up snowed into my parent's house for the rest of the day and all of Christmas day. It was kind of nice not to have to run around from here to there to see everyone. Aaron's parents dared the roads from Manhattan and joined us for part of the day. Kayden was so fun this year!! She got two Zhu Zhu pets and house and thought that was just the coolest. It was a great day to be with family and just plain hanging out. My brother headed back to his house that night in KC and ended up in a one-car accident that totaled his Pathfinder. He was not hurt, but it deployed both air bags and it was quite a pain for him to try to get it towed and all on a snowy Christmas night. It was quite the dramatic ending to our low-key day.

Aaron and I headed on our trip to Italy the next day. Kayden got to stay in Kansas with the grandparents. I know you are all waiting on pins and needles for my pictures (all 1250 of them- don't worry they are not all keepers!). We flew from to KC to Charlotte, NC- then on to Frankfurt, Germany. From there we took a small plane to Florence, Italy. It was a long overnight trip and we were exhausted! There is a 7-hour time difference (they are ahead) from Central time. We got there on a Sunday afternoon. There were 10 of us staying in an apartment in Florence. It was Aaron's aunt Sunny and his uncle Dan, their kids Emily and Taylor, a foreign exchange student Isak from Sweden, Emily's friend Elise, Aaron's uncle James and his sister Jen. It was a big group to travel with but it was a lot of fun to have all the different personalities there to make the trip interesting!

Emily has been studying in Florence through a program at Gonzaga where she is a junior. That lucky duck gets to spend her entire Jr. year in Italy! She goes to school Monday -Thursday and gets to travel and explore the other three days of the week. What an amazing experience she is having. I only hope that some day Kayden is able to do something so great! It rained off and on the entire trip so we learned to roll up our pants and bring umbrellas. It was a very wet trip I must say. We spent the first part of our week in Florence visiting local places that Emily had already scoped out during her first semester of classes. She played tour guide and interpreter for us, which was extremely helpful! It was a lot of fun to try to learn the Italian language. It is truly beautiful to listen to- but very hard to really pick up! I even had trouble ordering food at a McDonald's. How hard can that be?? Aaron's sister and I did our customary shopping while the others visited a museum to see the original Statue of David. I know we are terrible aren't we?!! There was leather to be bought I tell you- you couldn't hold me back 'til I got my leather fix! A girl has to have her priorities! We got to meet Emily's host parents that she will live with in Florence for her second semester. They were so sweet! They own an antique store where they restore things and sell them. They joined us for a dinner at the apartment one night for BBQ chicken and baked potatoes. It was so American to them! They loved it. We shared wine and some special cake dessert, which I can't remember the name of that is special for Christmas time there. We spent all of our other evening playing Skip-Bo and looking at Italian commercials and news on TV.

We took a day trip to Venice, which was absolutely amazing! The waterways and narrow alleys/sidewalk's were surreal. I never thought I would see such a place. We visited St. Mark's Basilica, which was very beautiful. Several of us decided we couldn't be in Venice and not ride in one of the gondola boats! It was so much fun! I can't even believe that they are able to maneuver those things through such narrow passages. Our guy was only 21 and he didn't speak a whole lot of English. He kept using his foot to kick off the buildings so we didn't scrape the side of the boat. Keep your fingers inside the boat on this ride for sure! We did learn an interesting fact. Most first floors of the buildings in the city are not inhabited due to the water. I guess it causes a lot of issues so the ones that are right at main water level are empty. We took the water taxi back to the rail station. It was over 3 hrs by train back to Florence. We had some local gyros for dinner that were very yummy! We had great weather finally and it was truly the perfect day!

We also made a half-day trip by rail to Pisa to see the leaning tower. It was about an hour and a half ride from Florence. Again- it was so worth it! You have no idea how much that thing is leaning until you walk up on it. Holy cow! Aaron and Jen and I were able to go up to the top around sunset and it was breathtaking. The pictures do not do it justice. Everything is so old and sturdy and big! I have never walked so much in my life as we did on this trip. And man this group walked fast! It was more like we jetted through Italy =) Aaron was always hollering at me to catch up cause I would fall behind taking pictures of anything and everything (hence the 1250 pics). My hip bothered me a little bit and I had to take painkillers throughout the trip but it was so worth it! The architecture of these places was so unbelievable. It is so different then here in the states.

Rome was our last stop. We left the apartment and took our luggage and stayed at Hotel Victoria for the last two nights of our trip. Let me tell you- this city deserves no less then 5-7 days to see everything there and we did it in two. We got there on New Year's Eve late morning. After running our luggage to the hotel we took a taxi to the Coliseum. That place is everything I expected it to be. It was huge! We didn't do the inside tour but just the outside was impressive in itself. Emily recommended we try to get over to see the Pope speak at noon so we all jumped on a jam-packed subway. Unfortunately after all of that effort we found out that he only comes out on Wed. and Saturdays, not Thursdays :(We also found out that a lot of the tourist type tours were all closing early due to it being a holiday. So we all made the decision to tour the Vatican and Sistine Chapel. It was a great decision! We got to see such amazing art and learned a lot of history on the different artists that contributed to the city's history. We spent New Years at the Trevi Fountain. That is going to be a hard one to top next year! I made three separate wishes- one before midnight, one of them at midnight and one afterwards. They were all the same wish but I won't ruin it by sharing it. I cannot even begin to list every place we were able to visit in Rome. It seemed like every time we turned a corner there was another amazing building. I wish we had had more time. We made the most of our trip and I can now say I have been to Italy! My only regret is that we were not able to visit anywhere close enough to get that beautiful view of the Mediterranean. I hear it is breathtaking. I will have to settle for Emily's pictures I guess. Well I could go on and on but my fingers are starting to tire and I need to get Kayden to bed soon. I will hopefully get my pictures up soon... well as soon as I can figure out why my iPhoto won't let me open it up. Dad is going to help me try to trouble shoot tomorrow so I can get to work on sharing our amazing trip and I am so thankful for everyone that helped make it happen. I can't thank Aaron's family enough for including us in this trip of a lifetime! I still can't believe we were able to go there. Ciao for now!

Much love from one lucky world traveler-

Jamie

ps. the picture is of the fountain where we made our wishes. Pretty amazing isn't it!?

Joy(ful)

69

FINDING THE WILL TO FIGHT...

January 17, 2010

Finding the will to fight...

We've had a busy month and I have much to share so I am going to do two posts. One dedicated to our holidays and our trip to Italy and this one filling you in on what is going on with me.

I can't believe it has been over a month since I have posted. I knew I was due for one but didn't realize how long I had procrastinated it. I'm not sure why I was having a hard time finding my inspiration to post. Maybe because I am still trying to figure it all out. How I feel about my life, my health, my family, my friends. It's like everything is all flipped upside down and inside out. I'm struggling to learn to live a life with metastatic cancer. Is it what I am? No definitely not, but how do I not let it become who I am? How do I live as ME not Cancer Jamie?

I have so much running through my mind that at times I'm more apt to just shut it down and not think about it at all. That is a dangerous place to be as well. That is when I disregard things and make bad decisions like stuffing skittles in my mouth or choosing to catch up on my DVR shows instead of head to the gym. It's one thing to have bad habits and be lax in your lifestyle. It's another to have cancer and know that your decisions can literally shorten your life. Sadly the cancer is already most likely going to take me at a younger age then most. It seems like a no brainer that I should be able to be disciplined enough to make my lifestyle as healthy as possible to help my long-term situation. DUH! I feel like I am having a de ja vu from a previous entry? Sorry if I am repeating me. Unfortunately, we are all creatures of habit (good and bad) and just cause I have cancer I don't get a bye that makes it easier for me to be healthy. I am now at a place where I have to admit I need help. I need knowledge. I need WILL POWER. I need to wire my jaw shut and drink veggies through a straw for the rest of my life. Aghhhhhh. How do I do it? How do I eat a cancer-diet, cut the sugar out, the processed foods? I've been online, and there is no myth to the fact that sugar feeds cancer. Whole foods help build your immune system to help rid your body of the awful things that lurk there like cancer cells waiting to gather and have a party at my expense. There is so much out there to weed through to find what will work best for me. It's not as easy as Just Do It like Aaron says (he could work for Nike as much as he says that to me). I am constantly making bad food decisions. I need help. That's the bottom line. The guilt is overwhelming me and causing anxiety, which is also bad for me. So 2010 becomes my year of health. There is no more time to waste. The goal is to make my body a temple that will reject the cancers attempts to grow and take over. It will take time and I will do it one step/decision at a time. The healthier my body is the better chance it has to fight and keep the cancer cells at bay. I need my body's main focus to be kick cancer ass! So now I just need to find the right person(s) to work with that can help me bring it all together in a manageable daily plan that I can follow. So I am on a mission to find my Yoda(s). Boy I am on a tangent here or what? Can you tell I woke up with things on my mind? I'll move on because I have so much to share still.

I lost a fellow breast cancer sister this past week. That has weighed heavy on my heart. Her name was Amy. She was a friend of my brother's in Kansas City. She has been battling since 2008. She was 30 and had a very young son she left behind. I had never actually met her but have followed her journey through my brother and it was not easy. I have included her Caringbridge link if you would like to learn about her journey. I'm so sad for her son Harrison. It is my worst fear that I leave Kayden while she is young and not able to really remember me. I also had a hard time hearing how painful it was for Amy as she passed. It is not a place I want to go in my mind. I have another friend Gayle that I have talked about before. She is also a patient of Dr. Schneider's. She is dealing with a lot of new challenges in her fight as a metastatic cancer survivor. She has been a big support for me as I join the metastatic club. It is hard to see her deal with all of these new issues that could happen to me. I have included her Caringbridge link as well if you would like to learn more about her. Please keep both of their families in your prayers.

http://www.caringbridge.org/visit/amytyler

http://www.caringbridge.org/visit/gayleroswarski

I've never held things back before so I guess I won't stop now. No sugar coating in this blog. I am hurting. I'm tired. I'm anxious. I'm happy. I feel guilty. I get angry. I get overwhelmed. I'm annoyed. I'm sad. I'm exhausted. I'm relieved. I feel loved. I feel lucky. I feel jinxed. I feel empty. This is my typical daily routine of emotions and this is even with my happy drugs I take. You can imagine how bad it would probably be if I wasn't on those. I just try to exist as if it isn't what it is sometimes, other times I pour over the internet researching (that's what I'm good at), it's instituting the process and things I research that I suck at. I've always been that way. I can research something to the end of the earth then the follow through is what screws it up for me. Call it a flaw. I say it's a personality trait. Aaron would just say it is plain annoying if you asked him. I am feeling very unsure of what is to come. That is so hard. I have my first Zometa treatment on Feb. 1st. I will also be getting my prescreening done for my clinical trial that day. I will stay in Indy over night and do a day of blood draws the next day. It's going to be a long day. But I am glad to finally get everything kick started. I got my port put in this past Monday. After some deliberation my surgeon (Dr. Goulet) decided to put it in my upper right thigh. He was concerned that my upper chest veins would be compromised from my previous DVT (Deep Vein Thrombosis- or blood clot). It is a power port placed on the outside of my leg. The small catheter is fed through to the inside of my thigh and up into my groin where he attaches it to my artery that runs through your groin area. The port is placed directly under the skin. It is a small disk shaped object that allows the medical people to punch a needle into it just like they would into your vein in your arm. The catheter attached to the port allows a path for the blood to be drawn directly from the main artery (which is faster than vein) and it also works as a path to put medicine directly into my artery. The port speeds up the process of all of the above, which is a benefit when you are getting poked and prodded all of the time. It also helps keep my veins from being too over worked, which can cause them to be damaged long term. It's been a week and I'm still a bit sore from the surgery and hobbling around a bit. I hope to be 100% by early next week.

I thought I would wrap this up and share a bit of good news with you. Ok- it's actually GREAT news! After almost 4 1/2 years of moving around for Aaron's job we are now following the yellow brick road back to Kansas. Yes- you read right. We're coming home!! It is a bittersweet move for us. We are so excited to move home and be closer to our family and friends, but we have made a pretty great life for ourselves in Bowling Green. It is a blessing that Aaron is able to take a position at his company's corporate office in Topeka. How lucky are we?!! His new job is a position where he is able to work from his computer if he has to. He will not have anyone reporting to him directly so he can be gone with me for treatments if necessary without leaving people in the lurch. He is excited for the opportunity to do something new, but I know he will miss the plant lifestyle so much. It will be a wonderful move for us and we already have the wheels in motion for it to happen. We hope to be there by the end of February / early March depending on how the house hunting goes. We hope to live in Lawrence if possible and already have a house-hunting trip set up for the week of the 25th. Our house will go on the market this next week. It's been busy here since we've been back from Italy getting the house ready to sell. My mom and Aaron's mom came up to help me knowing my surgery might put me out of commission. Thankfully they make a great team as Kayden would say and were able to really help me knock out a lot of what needed to be done. I am actually procrastinating the rest of what needs to be done by doing these posts! It's funny how I can do that so professionally. Anyways... I won't wait so long next time to do a post. I can't possibly try to keep you up to date and not have my fingers fall off from typing. I hope to be inspired in the next week or so to share more. I love you all and read on for a more upbeat post about our holidays and trip.

Sorry this posting was a bit unfocused. It's just how it came out of my brain and onto my keyboard. I'd rather not refine it because I want you to know me and what I am thinking- not an edited version. Hope you can follow along without getting lost or falling asleep!

Much love from my cluttered mind and uncluttered house-

Jamie

Beautiful

70

ANOTHER TWIST OF FATE....

February 4, 2010

Another twist of fate..

Well as many of you know we had a house-hunting trip in Lawrence, KS last week to find our new home. It went great. We found a house in the neighborhood/school district we wanted and were able to enter into a contract on it with the current owners. It is within walking distance to Langston Hughes Elementary School where Kayden will start in August of 2011. We were also able to sell our house in Bowling Green! Can you believe that? We didn't have high hopes as the average days on the market in our neighborhood was over 100 days. I think ours was on the market maybe 14 days. It was a huge relief for us. All that is left is to get through all the inspections on both houses and we will be closing the last week of February. Yeah! Kansas here we come!

I visited a couple of preschool programs while we were in town and found one that we all agree would be perfect for Kayden. She came and visited it with us and was extremely impressed with the classroom pets in each classroom and the basketball goal in their gym. What an easy sell she is! She told us several times later in the week when we drove by it that it was the school she wanted to go to.

Not that our week wasn't busy enough... I made the time to meet with an internal med doctor there in Lawrence that was recommended by a friend of a friend (thank you facebook!) His name was Dr. Kevin Stuever and I liked him right off the bat. First thing he said was that he had just got finished reading some of my blog so he already had a feel for my situation outside of the medical details. We had a great conversation and were able to establish a general plan for his role in my health. He was also able to get me in to see Dr. Sherri Soule, an oncologist I was looking into meeting with but hadn't gotten an appointment with yet. I was able to see her later that same afternoon. It turns out that she actually came from the IU program where I already go now. She started there and moved to Lawrence to be with her husband. My current oncologist took her position when he finished his fellowship and they already know each other. How small is our world? I met with her and we clicked immediately. So needless to say it was a productive week! Aaron and I can't be more thrilled to already have our medical team in place and have a preschool that can take Kayden right away- all before we even move.

Most of you also know that Aaron and I traveled from Topeka to Indianapolis to start the pre screening for my clinical trial. We arrived Sunday night and checked into our hotel. We were so lucky in that we stayed for free at the Westin downtown. My clinical trial nurse Anita helped arrange the rooms thanks to an American Cancer Society program. It was much appreciated on our end! It means everything to have a great room to go back and relax in after spending the day in the hospital.

I had a pelvic MRI first thing Monday morning and then met with Dr. Schneider afterwards. We went over the aches and pains I had been experiencing since our last visit. The one weighing most heavily on my mind was an area along the right outside edge of my right breast/under arm area. It had been sore all week and I had discovered there was a large knot if you pushed hard. He felt around and declared that I needed a breast MRI right away to identify what the mass was. So they got me into a nearby hospital for a last minute scan and we rode the people mover (a big above ground tram) over from his office. Afterwards we came back and I received my Zometa (bone strengthen medicine) infusion through my port in my leg. It was an uneventful 30 minutes. We headed back over to Dr. Schneider's office to wait for the MRI results. By this time it was close to 5 pm. He came in with Danni (his nurse) and just put it to us short and simple. There is a 3 1/2 cm new tumor in my breast. I still can't believe it. This means that the hormonal blocker (Aromasin) I have been on for the past two months has not worked. The cancer has progressed and it seems to have done so at a very fast rate. Folks, this is not good news. For whatever reason the cancer is no longer acting as if it is driven by hormones. Up until this point it has primarily been estrogen sensitive, meaning that it feeds on estrogen. We have focused on removing the estrogen from my body so there would be nothing to feed the mutant cancer cells running around in my body. If they don't get food then they can't multiply into new tumors. This news is quite surprising and disappointing to say the least.

So we had to regroup and decide how we were going to address this change in behavior. First off, I will no longer be able to participate in the trial drug I told you about. It involved a hormonal drug so I no longer will benefit from that type of treatment. Dr. Schneider and Dr. Soule (my new KS oncologist) both discussed the options and came to a decision to start me on a chemotherapy called Navelbine. It is a drug that will be given to me through my port in my leg once a week, for 3 weeks, and then I will have a week off and repeat the cycle for as long as it works. Luckily for now I will not lose my hair, nor will it wipe me out like the chemo I took at the beginning of my cancer journey. Overall it seems to be fairly tolerable compared to a lot of chemo. I will have to be mindful of being around people who are sick as my immune system will be suppressed, I have to go to the ER if I have a fever over 101.5, fatigue and muscle weakness can also be expected. It was scary to hear Dr. Schneider tell us that if the cancer continues to grow while I am on this that it is not good. There is a plan B in place with a couple of other chemotherapy drugs, but I hope with all of my heart that we never have to go there. I just can't imagine how it will feel to know that we are nearing the end of our options. Actually I can imagine it and I have to stop because it's going to do me no good to waste my energy on it. Easier said then done.

I had a chest/abdomen/pelvic CT scan first thing Tuesday morning to check the status of the rest of my organs. Afterwards I got my first round of the chemo. It was a quick infusion and I will be able to continue it in Lawrence once we move, which is a huge relief. Until then I will go back to Indy each week to receive the next two treatments. One good thing was that my new port worked great! I was pleased. Aaron even suggested I get some breakaway Adidas pants which I sported for two full days at the hospital. The snaps on the side allowed them to access my port without me striping down every time. Quite handy except if you forget to snap one and you walk around flashing everyone, oh well!! Snap patrol! On our way home Tuesday I was hit with a serious case of the chills. It was crazy... my teeth were chattering and my whole body felt like it was jittering out of control. It lasted an hour or so and I finally fell asleep. Good thing I had Kayden's snuggie in the car! It was small but it helped keep me warm! I'm not sure if this was a reaction to the Zometa infusion from the day before or if it was from the Navelbine. I guess I will find out next week when I have only chemo and no Zometa (I only get that once every 4-6 weeks). I have been feeling OK since I have been home. A little run down and tired, but some of that is mental exhaustion more then physical exhaustion. I got a call on Wednesday with the results of the lower CT. It was not what I expected to hear at all. The scan showed that I had a new right interior pubic bone non-displaced pathologic fracture. I have not had any pain in the area so I was really surprised to hear this. They had an orthopedic surgeon look at the scan and they decided it did not need to be addressed at this time. It is surrounded by soft tissue and they were not worried it would become displaced for now. In the future if I begin to have pain I will need to possibly have radiation done to the area (I'd rather not considering the area). The Zometa I'm on will also help coat the area and strengthen it. I have no specific restrictions other then be careful not to get kicked or hit in that area or it could become painful. There was also an 11 mm spot that showed up on my liver in the same scan. Dr. Schneider had prepared us for the fact that we would probably see some other organ involvement considering how aggressive the cancer was acting. For what ever reason they have not gotten the upper CT results yet. Hopefully by Monday we will have an answer as to how my lungs look. Needless to say this was all hard news to hear, but truthfully... it doesn't change our course of action at all. The Zometa and Navelbine will continue to still be our plan. We will meet with the Dr. after my 3 courses on my off week and see what he says. We need to get as much out of this chemo as we can as we are quickly going to run out of options. Even if it just stabilizes the tumor growth (easiest to tell in my breast tumor which you can actually feel) we will take it. We just do not want to see continued growth while on this drug. I need you to all understand that it is very important that this drug works. I am truly afraid to face the reality of what happens if there is growth while on this drug. So I will take specific prayers for the Navelbine to kill my cancer and stop this rampage it has been on.

I am sure you are all as shocked as we were. I have had a rough week trying to absorb this change of plans. I am trying to allow some room for tears and sadness, but there is a fine line between accepting and being depressed. So I am taking it minute by minute. My heart hurts and then I can laugh in the same thought. I am back on the emotional roller coaster that is cancer. I am feeling quite a bit of pain, especially in my hips and lower back and in the tumor in my breast. I am able to keep most of it at bay with Tylenol and a high tolerance for aches. I am limping a bit and favoring my right side. I hate feeling so brittle because it has everything to do with my outlook on things. I find myself with this panicky feeling that I am being eaten from the inside out. I am sure this will get better as I get more chemo treatments and we get things under control.

Aaron has been so supportive and understanding as I reel through the different emotions. I can't even imagine how he must feel from his end. Kayden is too young to understand being sick on the inside. We try to talk with her as much as necessary and she continues to be our sweet yet sassy diva of the house. Our families are waiting patiently for us to be home so they can literally surround us with their love. I will keep you updated as we get more information.

On a positive note I have decided to distract myself with a new creative project. I started a .com site. It is lovingpink.com. I'm not sure what all I am going to do with the site yet. It's just a starting point for now. I know we are trying to get some new Team Jamie shirts together here in the next week. There will be an order form on the site so keep an eye out. Also, it is easier to remember than this address. I have added a link on that site for you to get to this site. I'm tired and it's time to start dinner so stay tuned...

Much love from my achy breaky bones-

Jamie

Friend

71

MY UPS AND DOWNS....

February 10, 2010

My ups and downs..

So Tuesday was a rough day for me. It wasn't just the fact that it was a chemo day, or that it was snowing and icky out, or because I was having some pain. I think it was just a heavy heart day. I am realizing that I have to allow myself to have days like that. If I don't it will honestly eat me up inside. The reality of my situation is not an easy burden to bear. I will not get the luxury of growing old with Aaron. Or of watching my baby girl grow into a woman. I will not get the honorable title of grandma. Reality is that I will be lucky to see my baby off to her first day of kindergarten and I understand that. It doesn't mean I have to agree with it. My mind has been filled with visions of sadness in the past few weeks. I lie in bed in the darkness of our room and think about all of the things I have taken for granted, that I will eventually be forced to leave behind. It absolutely breaks my heart to realize that I will have the easy part. When I think about it it leaves me almost paralyzed with heartache. How do you recover from a reality like this? How do you crawl out of this pit of dark terrible thoughts and manage to continue to live life and not miss any more opportunities to make memories and enjoy the here and now? I am trying. That is my answer. I am putting one foot forward and taking my day hour by hour as I wait for this chemo to do what it is intended to do. Kill the cancer cells. I envision the chemo in there in true Harry Potter style with swords and armor hacking away at these evil monsters in my body. I envision the tumor dying and shriveling away to nothing. It is getting harder then it was and I hope that this is a sign of narcosis (death) of the malignancy. Doing this helps me feel more in power of my situation. I have been able to better watch what I put in my mouth with the understanding that each morsel will pose as food for the cancerous intruders or fuel for the body to fight off the evil invaders. How is that for a reason to eat healthy!! Hey- it has worked! So I am going to keep on keeping on as they say.

I wanted to give some credit to the people helping me set up my new lovingpink website. Aaron's sister Jen has been a huge part of it in acting as liaison with these individuals. They both work with her at the Augusta Chronical and are donating their time and skills to help me. Erin Erhardt has done the work on my logo. This poor girl has put up with my desire for perfection and endured my tons of changes to get the image JUST RIGHT! I am even driving myself crazy! Thanks for your patience Erin. It means a lot to me and I know you guys are probably ready to strangle me on your end... so I promise we are almost done =) And to Calin Coroban who has become my IT guru (outside of my dad of course!) and is answering all of my questions about what I can do with the new web site. I am sure you will feel Erin's pain soon my friend! I promise to try to keep my requests reasonable =) And to Jen and Kitty who have been patient as I try to figure out the shirts and all of the other details I just can't make a decision on... glad you guys already loved me before! My dad bought my domain name and I have had several offers of people wanting to help me get the shirts figured out. So thanks to everyone!

You all rock! Now if only I could make some final decisions so you guys could actually see the final product of all of the hard work! Soon I promise!

Well- I have much to do today and I have a little girl to wake up. More l8tr.

Much love from me to you-

Jamie

Spiritual

72

A TIME TO BELIEVE....

February 12, 2010

A time to believe...

I want to delve into a topic today that I have never really discussed with you my readers. It is the topic of religion. I am sure that many of you have wondered over the years where I stood in matters of faith. Was I a believer? Did I attend church? Did I pray? Well, in keeping with my honesty pledge to you I will tell you about my spiritual life. I have always been a believer that there is a greater power, but I was not raised in the church. We attended from time to time for holidays and I have been to services with friends over the years. If you asked me what church I attended I would have rattled off the church my mother attended when growing up because that is the one I could remember the name of. Some may see fault with this lack of spiritual guidance, but you are mistaken. I may not have attended church, but you had better believe I was raised in a loving home with boundaries and rules and a clear understanding of what is right and wrong. I was raised to be a good person and I have tried to walk that path throughout life. I have strayed from the path for selfish reasons over the years... but I have always found my way back because my moral compass is in tact thanks to my parents. I'll bet that many of you can say that this is a true statement for your own lives. I have grown up to be an empathetic, honorable, independent woman that is capable of living a full life. I thank my parents for the lessons that they taught me over the years, and believe me, I tested them and took them to the end of the parenting rope at times. What respectable independent woman wouldn't? But in truth, I can honestly say that my support system did not include a relationship with God. I would ask for things from time to time if I needed them. I would say the only prayer I knew by heart- Now I lay me down to sleep... when things were rough. But in all my years I never had a spiritual support system that I turned to in good times or in bad. In fact I know many of you are probably a little surprised that I am talking about this topic at all.

In the past, due to my lack of understanding, I tended to shy away from anything remotely religious. People would invite us to church and I would make excuses like I believe in a greater power, or I would tell people that they were in my prayers, or that I didn't need to go to church to show that I believe in God. I even blamed it on Aaron at times saying he was not comfortable going to church or that we had little time together on the weekends as it was... church was just another thing to take time away from "our" time. The truth was that I didn't feel comfortable. I didn't understand the bible nor had I ever read it. I was afraid to talk about the topic for fear that I would say something wrong or worse offend the person that I was talking to. Even after my original diagnosis I still did not turn to God in my time of need. That was the time I probably needed it most... I was afraid I would look like a bandwagon jumper, that I was being selfish and only reaching out because of my illness. It took me a long time and a lot of patient people to finally realize the truth. For so long I was hung up on looking selfish. Only recently did I come to understand that it is not the "why" that matters in pursuing a relationship with God. It is the fact that you want to open you heart, that you want to learn more about Christ and what he has sacrificed in order for us to live our lives free from worry. I had to stop being afraid to ask questions and when that happened a whole new understanding of life opened up for me.

There is something that I didn't share with you about the day I got my metastatic diagnosis. Aaron and I traveled home in a daze. When we got home that night I cannot explain the loss of perception I had. It was like I was walking around with no sense of sound or smell or touch. I walked outside and saw the porch light on of some friends in our neighborhood. I grabbed Aaron and I knew we needed to go to them. See that friend of ours is a youth pastor at a church in town. It took me at my absolute lowest point to look up and see the light. Literally. It was 9:30 at night and I marched up and knocked on their door. Them opening their door that night opened a door in my heart. I overcame my fears and pushed aside my misunderstandings and I allowed him to pray for us and they did. I cried and I shook and I closed my eyes and I listened. For the first time, I truly listened. That was the beginning of our spiritual relationship with God. Aaron and I have both since been surrounded by the love of a spiritual community unlike any I have ever truly experienced. I have been spoiled to have such a strong support system of friends and family to hold me up during the first three years of my illness. But I know now that it is bigger then just that. When your mortality is challenged all the other things complicating your life seem to disappear. I was afraid of what I didn't know. I have made a decision to get to know more and face that fear. I am only at the beginning of my relationship with God. What I do know is that I feel different now. I feel like I not only have my family and friends holding me up from the outside, but my heart is in the hands of someone even more powerful. I just had to find my faith. I had to dig deep and ask the hard questions. And what I have learned is that through Christ I can know God. God is the one thing I can know in both life and death. God has made it possible for me to not fear death. I am only learning about the many things that lead us to believe these truths. I have only seen the tip of the iceberg, but I am ready willing and able to understand now. I can physically feel my faith. It is a tangible thing that is out there. You just have to put aside your fears and trust that there is someone there to catch you when you fall.

I can say I have faith now. True faith. That my life will be saved no matter when or where my battle ends with this cancer. I have asked Christ into my heart and I know that my relationship with God can only grow from here and for that I am excited. I understand now what it means to have had Jesus make the ultimate sacrifice for us. To give his life and bear the burdens of man, just for us. That is how special we are; now we just need to realize that and live like it. Our friend Jeff- whose porch light opened my heart, will baptize me this weekend on Valentine's Day. Kelly, Josh, Brooke, Jennifer, Janet, Aimee, Robin, Kristin- and so many others have stood beside Aaron and I as we sought the answers to our questions. I am proud to say that I am no longer afraid. I have the best of both worlds. An amazing husband, family and friends to hold my hand and wipe my tears away and now a relationship with the one person who can bring us all back together in the end. Thank you to all of you that have had a hand in my spiritual growth. We owe you so much for love, patience and understanding. Aaron and I are growing together at our own paces and it's like we have a whole new topic to discuss. There are no limits- from evolution (which doesn't have to be a deal breaker by the way) to hope for the afterlife. What an amazing experience we have been missing out on!

I now have this powerful thing I can do and I do do which is prayer. I can truly say that I now pray for my life and to have a little more time to spend in this great life of mine. I pray for my medicine to overcome the cancer. I pray for a miracle and I hope you will too. Look at your own lives and ask yourself what you are afraid of and don't be afraid to face that fear. I did.

Much love from my full heart-

Jamie

Inspiring

73

THE LEGACY BOOK...

February 18, 2010

The Legacy Book...

For those of you that may have missed this letter on the www.lovingpink.com site... please see below.

Dear Friends,

We were all devastated to hear the news of Jamie's metastatic diagnosis. Let's pool our energy and emotion into something positive and celebrate the amazing woman Jamie is and the ways she has touched our lives. I will be putting together a Legacy Book for Jamie and her family. I'm not sure what form the book will take, i.e. scrapbook, photo book, memory box, etc., so I will just let the creative spirit take hold. I'm asking each of you to reflect on the time that you've spent with Jamie and create something to put in the Legacy Book. I will collect all the entries and find a way to present them in a way that will allow them to experience Jamie forever.

Here are some ideas of what to do, but do not let this list be a limit to your creativity.

* Write a letter to Jamie

* Write a letter to Kayden and/or Aaron

* Jot down memories and funny stories about your time together

* Send in pictures

* Draw a picture

* Send in a memento of your time together

* Take a video of yourself or send in a video of you and Jamie

* Make something to put in the book or box

* Write a poem

* Send a famous quote or story that you find embodies you, Jamie or how you are feeling right now

Each of you experience Jamie in your own way, and each of you is an individual. I'd like for your entry to be an expression of who you are as well as who Jamie is. Who we surround ourselves with is a reflection of who we are as people so don't be afraid to be you!

Please take some time in doing this and give it some thoughtful consideration. You are welcome to send in just a few lines or as many pages and memories as you'd like. This is a way for us to process and deal with the diagnosis as much as it will be a gift for Jamie and her family. She has shared her journey with us and now it's our turn to give back our part of the journey.

Any questions, feedback or finished entries can be sent to:

Liz Houston

ps. Thanks Liz for such a wonderful idea! Jamie

Spunky

74

LIVING IT LAWRENCE STYLE!

March 10, 2010

Living it Lawrence style!

What a hectic 2 weeks it has been since we moved into the new house! Sorry to be so out of touch but I can hardly keep up with it all! I will back up and fill you in on my medical details then the house. As of today I have had 5 rounds of Navilbean (chemo). Luckily my off week from my first cycle happened to fall on the week we moved. We had movers that came and packed up our house and moved us from KY to KS. It was a huge relief to not have to stress over the details. Then my parents flew in and drove Kayden and I back to KS in my car. We made a pit stop in Indianapolis and a visit with Dr. Schneider, my Indy oncologist. It was a very positive visit. He did an intense physical exam to see if we could pin point my back pain. There did not seem to be any areas that he could get a pain response from touching or manipulating my back/bones/hips. This is a good sign that the pain I am feeling would most likely be from my chemo rather then cancer spreading. I have started taking a oxycodone (percocet) in the last three weeks to help me deal with the daily aches and pains the chemo and cancer are causing. It has helped more then the Tylenol I was previously taking. So overall I had a pretty good off-week.

The closing went great and we were in the new house starting February 25th. The movers met us there and we had the semi unloaded by Friday morning. The boxes are a different story! My friends Kristin, Lisa, Julie and Aimee came from KC to help paint and unpack on Friday and Saturday. I also got to see my old friend Leigh who lives in Hawaii! It's been great to catch up with everyone! My parents, aunt and uncle and grandparents all came to help too. Sunday my brother and his girlfriend Heather and Aaron's parents joined us. It was a full house all weekend and I loved it!!

After some compromising Aaron agreed to let me paint Kayden's room and our master bathroom (the house is in great shape so it didn't really need painting). Guess what color I did in our bath? Well purple of course! I have to represent the wildcats in this town.... they sure are Jayhawk pushers!! Only kidding! Kayden keeps coming home with Jayhawk pictures and stickers. I think they are trying to lure her to the other side already! As far as Kayden's room goes... I have been researching some ideas (Rate My Space and Etsy.com) and was excited to make my vision a reality. I won't ruin it by telling you yet what we did. I have one last thing that should be completed this weekend hopefully so I will post before/after pics. Let's just say it is TOOO CUTE! I have had a ball with it and she loves it. We are slowly finding our way to the bottom of each box. The main living area is put away and organized. Aaron has been working away in the garage to get it just so. He and my dad spent the last week putting up shelving all along the top of our 11 ft. ceilings in the garage. It looks great and will provide the best storage we have ever had in any of our houses! I know he is excited to have a bigger garage again after our last house. The next project will be building a built in desk/cubby nook area in the hallway coming out of the garage entrance. Then we will move to the basement to finish it. I have a lot of purging to do in the basement as it currently holds all of our old attic storage stuff. Who knew we had collected soooo much stuff!!!!

Kadyen has started her preschool and loves it! We are adjusting a bit to school in the afternoon. She typically is exhausted afterwards and a bit grumpy the next day. She's not really napping anymore- even though she could probably use it. Hopefully, after another week or so we can get used to it and get into a more solid routine. She's been pretty defiant at home the past few days we are having to buckle down and put the rules back in place. We will get it figured out sooner or later. Aaron has had a full week at the new job at corporate office in Topeka. He doesn't seem to mind the 25 min. commute so far. He is able to be home more than when he was at the plant in BG so it is nice to have him around more! He is slowly adjusting to being back in the business casual attire instead of his previous jeans and Hill's polo :) I refused to be the good wife and do all of his ironing this time so the local dry cleaner has a new client! Sorry honey... not my forte!

It's been great to be back to KS so far. I have seen so many friends and family in the past two weeks! I have been feeling good enough most of the time to hang out and really enjoy their visits. I even get to see an old friend this afternoon that I haven't seen in over 5 years- Annie Dunbar (Dohl) and her three boys whom I've never met!! Yeah!

I started chemo here in Lawrence last Tuesday. It went very well. They have a really great staff and all of their chemo rooms are private. Much different from IU where it is a big room with lots of chairs. I got to sit down with Dr. Soule again and discuss our plan. We will continue the Navilbean, I had my second infusion in this cycle this Tuesday. I have one more next Tuesday and then we will do scans towards the end of my off week the following week. So far I seem to be tolerating the chemo well. I have had a queasy stomach at times but no actual sickness, no numbness in my fingers or toes. My counts have stayed ok so far this cycle, which means my immune system is not too compromised. I still have to be concerned about being around anyone who has had a fever in the past 2 days or been exposed to someone with a fever or infection. I am pretty anxious for this round of scans. It will tell us if the cancer has been stabilized or if the chemo has not stopped the progression of the cancer. They will look for any increase in size of the previous tumors or lesions. It's a burden to have that worry on my mind all of the time. I am trying to find a happy balance of living with the reality of my situation and not letting it drag me down in my day-to-day activities. Some days I stare at my super sized shampoo bottle and wonder if it will outlast me... other days I feel capable of making plans with someone a month out. I keep hearing myself say... well lets just wait and see what this next round of scans says. I can't seem to get past this next round of scans. I am so hung up on the thought of taking a chemo that is tougher on my body- which in turn means I don't get to be as active as I am lately. I feel like I have this hour glass in my life and I am counting down the days to being bed ridden and unable to be up and around. So- that is my focus for now. Not letting myself get so caught up in the scans and if the chemo is working or not. I find myself rubbing my tumor several times an hour... I need to stop. It's got to look odd to people around me that don't know my situation... me rubbing my breast constantly and all :) Aaron is constantly telling me to stop touching it. It's still hard and it feels like it changes every day. Some days it feels bigger some days smaller. Who knows? I need to stop wasting my energy on it. So if you see me rubbing it- swat me upside the head! I am going to let out the breath I have been holding for the past month and a half and try to live it up the next two weeks- take advantage of the times I am feeling good and be gentle with myself when I'm not. I am in search of my happy medium between situational reality and living realistically. I'll let you know when I am there.

It's been a long day and I've been pretty queasy and off today so I am going to sign off for now and hit the hay. Aaron is heading on a much needed boys trip this weekend so it's just us girls! We will be rooting for our Wildcats all weekend! We may live in Lawrence but we are all purple on the inside!!!

Much love from the new house (which already feels like home!)-

Jamie

Grace

75

THE POWER OF PERCEPTION

April 10, 2010

The power of perception

Some of you might be wondering why I used this title today. Perception is a funny word. If you look it up in the dictionary you will see that it means:

n. 1. The process, act, or faculty of perceiving.

2. The effect or product of perceiving.

3. Psychology

a. Recognition and interpretation of sensory stimuli based chiefly on memory.

b. The neurological processes by which such recognition and interpretation are effected.

4.a. Insight, intuition, or knowledge gained by perceiving.

b. The capacity for such insight.

Perception is described above as an internal process of the mind- but add a new piece of information to the mix and your mind has this funny way of opening doors to a new state of mind that includes the new information. Does it sound like I am talking greek to you yet? Trust me... I have thought a lot about this and the power of the mind over perceptions in the last few months. Let me explain it in an example. I walked into my doctor's appointment last November a healthy and happy individual. I had the insight to ask about the spot of skin on my breast that seemed new to me. I was given a piece of information later that week (that the spot was cancerous) and all of a sudden I was no longer healthy. Nothing else had changed from within my body. I was still the same Jamie I had been when I walked into that hospital- but I was armed with a new piece of information that told me I was sick again so naturally I was upset even though I felt no different. I was looking at it from a new state of mind, my perception had changed and I was no longer healthy.

The same can be said for my last two months I have been on the Navilbean (my chemotherapy). As you all know, I was very very sick. My cancer advanced at such a rapid pace over the holidays that I have never been so scared that I was going to lose this battle. Every pain I had, every twinge, headache, or bump left me stuck with a mind full of horrible thoughts. I truly feel like I was living with one foot out the door for a little while. It was such a sad and hopeless place to find myself. I pride myself on keeping a great attitude and being able to find the positive in most situations, but I was struggling to live with the reality that my life may end much sooner then I ever imagined possible. I found that I was constantly walking a tight rope of living and dying every day. I had to be realistic and yet still get out of bed and function from day to day. In the last month I could feel the tumor growing in my breast. I was constantly feeling it. Always taking notes in my head of all of the things I could feel as soon as I opened my eyes in the morning. I have had a lot of pain in my middle back and hips. It's hard to say if it is chemo related or possibly the cancer continuing to spread. I would wait to take my pain pills to make sure I knew what hurt and what didn't. You see, chemo is typically an all or nothing situation. It either works or it doesn't. It doesn't work in one spot and not another spot. So you can understand that when I can feel my breast tumor getting larger by the day then I come to perceive that my other pains must be cancer related. The more I thought about it the more I pulled the covers over my head. Last week I had my scans on Friday and Kayden and I spent the week in bed watching TV till noon every day. God Bless The Disney Channel. Scan-xiety is a term someone recently shared with me and I can't think of a better way to describe my funk I was in. I was truly afraid of what my scans were going to tell us.

I made it through the week, but not without the help of some very special people in my life both friends and family that let me be where I needed to be at the time and they helped lift me back out when I was ready. So many people prayed for us during our wait. It still continues to amaze me how far my prayer chain reaches. It is coast to coast and then some. I even have some old friends in Bowling Green that have started a Jamie Ministry. They meet each week to pray specifically for me and they send me cards and flowers. I feel so special. There is no other way to say it. My husband continues to stand beside me even though he is hurting as much as I am through this process. We are professional emotional roller coaster riders that is for sure. My parents are such pillars in my life too. They continue to hold me up as only a parent can. They love me in a way that I can only hope to emulate in my own relationship with Kayden. Aaron's parents have been so supportive even from Manhattan. Kitty drives down every week to spend a day with Kayden so I can go to chemo and then have some time to rest or run errands depending on how I am feeling. Phone calls and texts and emails and Facebook messages. Each one of you have played a part in how unbelievably supported I feel every day. Yes it was a rough week and yes I lost sight of my positive vow- but you know what? That's ok. It's what I needed at the time and having such a great support system I was able to be where I needed to be, safely.

On a fun note, we did family pictures last week thanks to some very giving people. My friend from college Kelli, helped arrange to have my hair cut and styled by a friend of hers- Stephanie Winkler at Rumors in Overland Park. She did an amazing job!!! It's always nice to see your potential when someone else does your hair :) Then I had my makeup done at Mario Tricoci. Another friend of Kelli's, Shannon Hey of Shannon Hey Photography had offered to do my family portraits at her studio in Shawnee. She was incredible! Even let the guys watch the game and did our pictures during commercials at times :) Shannon you get an A for patience! It was so fun to get dressed up and feel beautiful after such a stressful week. I can't even tell you how much better I felt that day- even though my Cats didn't come through with a win that afternoon :(That would have just been the icing on my cake! I can't wait to see the pictures when they are ready! I will for sure share with you all! Thank you to Kelli and Stephanie and Shannon for making this all possible!

We went to a new church on Sunday. We enjoyed it! I do miss my Living Hope Band and signing though! Aaron, my mom and I enjoyed watching Kayden slide right in with the other kids without a second thought as they paraded with palm tree leaves shouting Hosanna in honor of Palm Sunday. She even made a new friend that day that lives on our street! No surprise there in our small world we live in.

I got a call on Sunday night that topped off our wonderful weekend. Dr. Soule called to tell me that the scans showed the chemo was working in my organs, but that the breast tumor was indeed still growing. This is good news overall. Being me- I can't just get a good report card... there always has to be a but in there. So the decision at this point is that I am going to continue on Navilbean (chemo) today in fact I will be publishing this and leaving for the hospital. Then Dr. Thellman, a plastic surgeon here in town will surgically remove my breast tumor here next Thursday 4/8/10, not sure what time yet. We will not know how involved this surgery will be as the tumor is nestled in my reconstruction on the right side. It could be that it is a simple procedure and it could be that they have to remove the implant and if the chest wall is involved possibly ribs or more. I won't know which way they go till I wake up from the surgery. I will keep you updated as we find out more. Please pray for me to feel well physically after chemo today and till next week so I can prepare to be down and recovering from yet another surgery.

So now I bring you back to the matter of perception. I perceived that my tumor was growing in my breast and assumed that the cancer was growing everywhere based on the knowledge that chemo is all or nothing leaving me in a sad state of mind. Now after receiving new information my perception has changed and my state of mind had changed, as a person- I have not changed; these scans didn't physically do anything to me. The only thing different is that one little piece of news. I feel like I am a different person from one little piece of information. Funny how that perception thing works. I think I am going to stop "perceiving" so much and start living more. What a waste of time and energy it is to live according to what I "perceive" to be true. I'm back on my tightrope and I'm not looking down because it's full of could be's and what if's of scan-xiety. I'm done with all of that... well at least till the next time I have scans scheduled :)

Much love from my hopeful heart-

Jamie

ps. that's me and my grandpa Harry at the St. Patty's Day parade this year!

Spontaneous

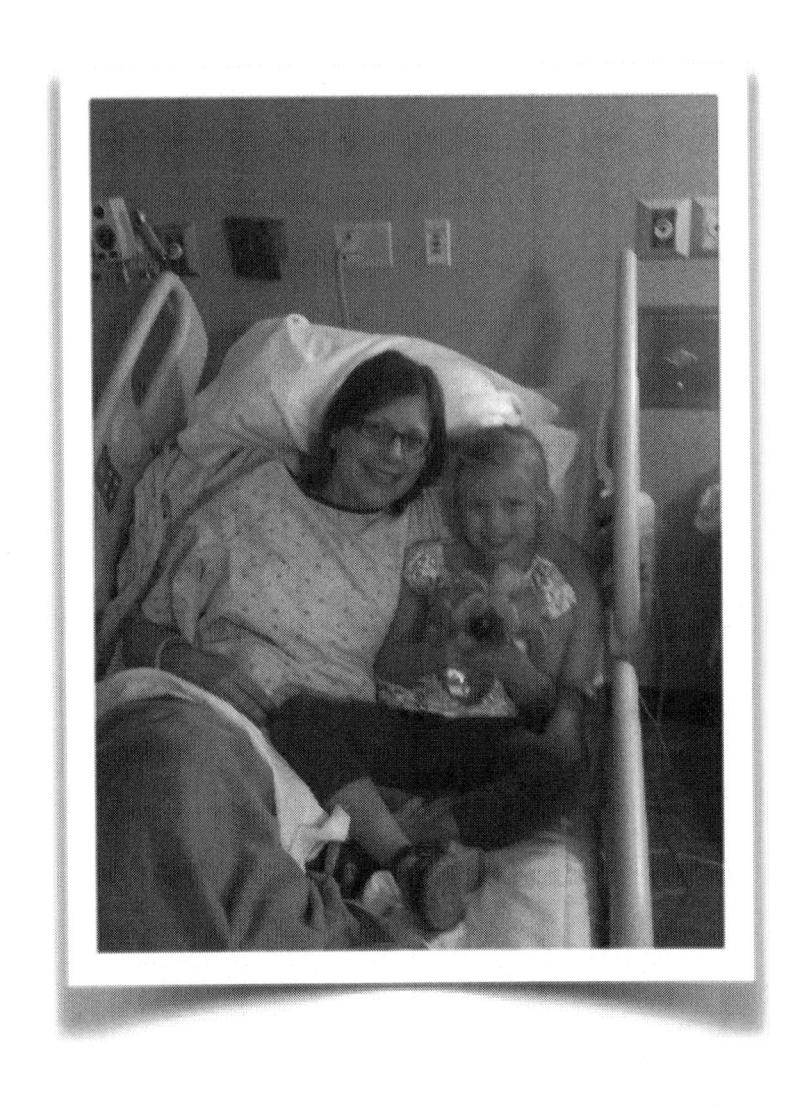

76
YET ANOTHER SURGERY UPDATE....

April 23, 2010

Yet another surgery update...

Well as usual- I am beginning with an apology for waiting so long to give my readers an update. I need to stop doing that! I am sitting here in my living room on this dreary day hoping that today is the day I find my inspiration and motivation to get to work! On this update, on organizing my house, getting my laundry done and put away, bills, exercising, meal planning (OK that one is more of a wish list)... but the rest is all stuff I have been procrastinating with a vengeance! Alright Alright... you don't care about my to do lists?! You want to hear about my surgery? Well, geesh! I guess I did make you wait almost two weeks. Many of you have heard through the grapevine that my surgery went very well! It was for once a best-case scenario, which we all know I don't get very often. My plastic surgeon Dr. Scott Thellman did the surgery with general surgeon Dr. Mark Prager standing by to assist. There was a lot of discussion in my pre-op appointments about whether the mass was involving: a. my muscle b. ribs/chest wall c. my skin. The general expectation was that we wouldn't know the extent of the damage until they got in there during surgery. So I went in that day not sure if I would even have a breast when I came out (worst case scenario). From my understanding the mass was located in between my latissimus dorsi muscle (remember it is wrapped around from my back to my breast area on the right side from my mastectomy/reconstruction July 2008) and the skin. If the mass had gotten into any of my ribs or chest wall it would have required a very major surgery to potentially remove the affected areas i.e.: ribs or even part of the chest wall. He told me if that was the case he would have probably sewn me back up and brought me back so we could discuss this further. The other thought was that we might have to remove my current implant if it had been compromised and put a temporary expander in to hold the place till we could go back in and get a new implant in place down the road. What we were hoping for was to do a simple lumpectomy where the tumor was removed and any surrounding tissue that was involved... which ended up being the case once they opened the area up! Yeah! The tumor was about the size of a golf ball and it did have surrounding tissue and skin that it had infected with its nasty cancer. I visualize is as a piece of fruit that looks nice on the inside and has a large pit. They remove the pit and all of the goo around, and cut out any other soft spots so the fruit is nice and unblemished afterwards. Your welcome for the visual =) Dr. Thellman took anything that looked troubling out (including some skin and other areas other than the mass itself) and then sent it off to the lab to be biopsied. He used my previous scar lines for his incision so I did not end up with new scars even. He was very pleased with the final product and my breast honestly does not even look all that much different now (other than some minor swelling) than it did before surgery! I expected it to be all deflated since the mass was so large, but it really isn't. It may cave in a bit down the road as it heals... but since it is on the outside edge it will be hid within my bra pretty easily. I stayed over in the hospital one night and was home around lunch-time the next day. I did come home with one jp drain and we all know how much I love those... but other than that my recovery was great! I was very mobile and my pain was very tolerable. I was out and at Kayden's soccer game two days after surgery. He took my drain out the following Friday. I also met with Dr. Soule my oncologist here in Lawrence that same Friday and we discussed the lab results of the mass. The surgeon removed all of the visible cancer, but there is still microscopic cancer cells that showed up in the lab results. Since I have cancer in other places in my body they did not do the surgery with hopes of getting ALL of the cancer out of my breast so don't get hung up on this detail. We just hope that now that it is just tiny miniscule cells they will respond to the chemo better then the large mass did. Interesting enough... the results showed that the cancer was triple negative. Meaning that it was ER-/PR- and Her2-. This is different then my original cancer had ever tested. I have up to this point been ER+/PR+ and Her2-. Dr. Soule was going to do some research and see what the actual percentages of my previous tests were so we could see if there was a dramatic change in the make up of the cancer or not. This is a lot of mumbo jumbo to most of you but it explains a lot to others so I wanted to include the info. The reason for knowing and understanding the genetic make up of cancer cells is because it helps you better choose the drugs to use for your treatment. Certain drugs work better for certain types of cancer. Up till recently my cancer was fed by Estrogen (the ER portion of my ER/PR rating) PR stands for Progesterone. Being ER+ means your cancer uses estrogen to grow, therefore we used Estrogen blocking drugs to try to starve my cancer and keep it from growing. Now that it is not acting like it is fed on Estrogen (ER-) then we want to stop focusing on Estrogen blocking drugs and move on to another type of drug. The ultimate decision is that I continue taking the chemo I have been on since February this year, Navilbine. I will continue getting chemo once a week on Tuesday's, and then after three weeks of chemo I get a week off. I refer to this as my 3 on 1 off schedule. I had a round of it just this last Tuesday in fact and I've been feeling pretty good the rest of this week. I also did a round of my Zometa (bone builder) a week ago today. I seem to be super sensitive to it for some reason and ended up having a rough day last Saturday with fatigue and nausea being the main culprits. But that's ok- it is what it is and I now know that it's going to probably give me some trouble the day after I get it, at least I can plan accordingly in the future.

Now as we move into week two of chemo this month I try to take advantage of the time I am feeling good which is more often then not at the beginning of the cycle. As it builds up in my body the fatigue increases and the nausea or motion sickness as I call it increases. But then in my off week it gets better and we start it all over again. I have to learn how to manage my time and Kayden so I can maximize the ups and lay low for the ick times. Thanks to everyone for their continued prayers and well wishes as we got through my latest surgery. So glad it is over!!

So we continue on in the Pursley household with soccer and play dates and our everyday grind. Guess you could say we are getting back to boring! We love boring around here. I know this was mostly just surgery talk so I will try to do another update soon. I am also going to be working on the www.lovingpink.com site so look for changes soon including the Merchandise Page, which is a work in progress. It is up but not all of the items are listed yet... they are working on it as I type. So give them till next week before you put your orders in! You don't want to miss the cool Team Jamie bracelets we got!

Much love from my happy boob-

Jamie

Playful

77

ANOTHER BUMP IN THE ROAD...

May 28, 2010

Another bump in the road..

As most of you probably now know, I had a PET CT scan done earlier this week. My tumor marker (click for a more in depth description) from the previous week had gone from 301 to 679. In layman's terms... they draw some blood and are able to measure certain proteins and other things in the blood for particular cancer activity. It comes back with a number, which is referred to your tumor marker. The lower the number the less cancer activity there is in the body, typically. I had originally started close to 400 back in early March and then after a month of the Navelbine it dropped to 301. Then as you remember I was off of chemo for 3-4 weeks for my surgery to remove the breast tumor that wasn't responding to my chemo. Then I got 3 more doses of chemo before they checked my tumor marker again. The jump in the tumor marker numbers is a red flag that there is some type of activity that needs to be addressed. So we did the PET/CT scan this past Tuesday. In addition to the tumor marker jump I had also noticed that my right breast was red and inflamed over the weekend. It was hot to the touch and somewhat uncomfortable. I called my dr. and she recommended I call my plastic surgeon to make sure we weren't dealing with an infection from surgery. He started me on an antibiotic and I went in Monday morning for him to take a look. He took a biopsy of the skin to check for infection and/or cancer cells. We found out on Wednesday afternoon that the biopsy was positive for cancer cells. The cancer had spread to my skin and was externally visible. It looks like I have a burn without blisters. I was also told that my PET/CT scan showed progression in my cancer. It had new cancer lesions (spots) in my liver, lymph nodes and multiple areas with new bone degeneration due to cancer (mainly in my right pelvis and hip areas). Not the news we were looking for. I had honestly hoped that the rest of the body was doing well and it was still just my breast that was causing problems. Then at least we could surgically remove the entire breast and dispose of the problem area. But that wasn't the case. It was obvious that the Navelbine was no longer doing its job. Insert sad face here.

I have had such an aversion to starting a different chemo. I have just had such good luck with Navelbine. It has been a very tolerable chemo that allowed me to keep my hair and my busy schedule both. What more can a cancer patient ask for? The new chemo regimen I will be starting will be called Gemcitabine and Carboplatin. GemCarbo for short. It is actually two drugs administered in conjunction with one another. Both are given on day 1 of the cycle. Then Gemcitabine is given again on day 8. There is an off week and then the cycle starts over again. The main side effects are low blood counts, hair loss, fatigue, nausea, neuropathy (tingling in hands and feet). Fun Fun. It is not going to be quite as tolerable as what I've been on unfortunately. It's hard to tell how I will tolerate the drugs because every one is different in how they metabolize the drug and how they react to it. I'm sitting here twirling a piece of my hair as I think about how long it took for me to grow my hair back to where it is now. 3 long years. I have about another month of it and it will be time to say goodbye hair hello baldy! I actually don't mind being bald- it's nice and easy. It's the growing back that is the hard part! I'm not typically a big wig wearer, especially in the summer. I will be more of a scarf, hat, bandanna girl. I will be on this chemo indefinitely for now so there isn't any chance it will grow back anytime soon. I remember last time I was bald it was during the time when Brittany Spears shaved her own head. I was in Wendy's one day and a little boy came in and saw me and ran outside yelling that Brittany Spears was in the restaurant. Now if that doesn't bring a smile to your face then you need to lighten up! True story! I'll make bald beautiful. I am not worried one bit. I hope that Kayden is able to understand the situation. We will be talking to her a lot in the next month to prepare her for the changes in our household. Enforcing hand washing and being very careful about our exposure to germs. Ugh. No fun! I'm prepared and ready to begin this next round of my battle. I'll be honest I am getting a bit weary of the battle, hopefully this chemo will be the answer to stopping this cancer in its tracks.

Kayden starts at Raintree Montessori here in Lawrence next week. She is so excited! She calls it her pool school because they swim twice a day in the summer! How fun is that?! She will be going full time and I can pull her out when I am feeling good so we can spend time together. I am very thankful we found this school and that we are able to send her there. It will be an awesome experience for her and a well needed break from my daily duties as I work on healing myself. Apparently it needs to be a full time job for a while. We are doing very well as a family in absorbing this new news. It is disappointing of course but we always knew it was a possibility. We are thankful for the time we had with the Navelbine and it's easy side effects. I started seeing a counselor to help me (and Aaron) work through feelings as my health continues to spiral in and out. It is going to be a big help to have an outside party to talk to.

I love you all so much. You continually amaze me with your support and cheers of Team Jamie! It is so comforting being here in my home state surrounded by my family and friends. I miss my KY crew dearly but home is where the heart feels best.

Many of you have asked me about the t-shirts. The merchandise page on my www.lovingpink.com site is now up and working. You can order your Team Jamie shirts there. We pre-ordered them so as the more popular ones run out we are re-ordering as quickly as we can.

I am signing off now because I have an amazing weekend planned with some wonderful Pi Beta Phi sorority sisters this weekend in Kansas City. We are whooping it up before I start chemo next Wednesday.

Much love from my hair, and me

Jamie

Amazing

78

SIDE EFFECTS....UGH

July 12, 2010

Side effects...ugh

Well, procrastination has gotten a hold of me this last month. I have been sitting around more then normal and still haven't done an update to let you all know how the GemCarbo is treating me. That's just not fair now is it??

I received both Gemcitabine and Carboplatin (they are given one after the other through my port) on Wednesday, June 2nd. That was considered Day 1 of my first "cycle" of chemo. Then on Day 8 (or the following Wednesday) I received only the Gemcitabine . Then on Day 15 (the following Wednesday) I had what was considered my off week from chemo which was the end of my first "cycle" . Overall the side effects were more bearable than I had anticipated. I had a lot of fatigue during the day, as well as what I call motion sickness which is not necessarily being nauseous, but fast movements and lights would make my stomach queasy. It was hard to watch a fast paced show on tv or sit in the car in the evening with headlights coming at you. I was able to keep the majority of these effects under control with nausea meds and lots of rest. I wasn't super sore or feeling a lot of pain anywhere at this point in the month. After my first cycle of the new chemos, I got good news that my tumor marker had come down 30 points from the week we had started the chemo! It's not a lot but it is the right direction so we celebrated that small victory!

After my big week off from chemo (which I felt really good for by the way) I went in to do my standard blood draw on Monday before my chemo. I got a call that afternoon that my ANC counts (click on it for a description) were too low to administer the chemo. They needed to be between 1000-1500 and mine were in the 600 range. My immune system was just not recovered enough to be hit with another dose of the chemo. GRRRRRR...... part of a chemotherapy drug's job is to break down the body's systems in order to do it's intended job of killing the fast growing cancer cells. Unfortunately, my body has proven over time to be pretty sensitive to the lowered immune system and it takes me awhile to recover and be back at a level where I can safely get the chemo again. I ended up with two extra weeks off due to low counts. I was super frustrated but tried to embrace the extra time off and feeling fairly side effect free. I was able to have a great 4th of July with friends at the lake as we always do. Too bad the rain decided to stick around or I might actually have that tan I was hoping for!

Thankfully, there is a shot that I am now self administering that is able to synthetically help give my bone marrow a boost and get those white blood cells pumping through my body. It's called Nuepogen and I get it for 5 days after my first week of chemo and then the following week I get it for 4 days following my second dose of chemo in the cycle. The main side effect has been a massive headache. It starts between my temples and then goes up to about the top of my head. I finally found an over the counter migraine pill that seems to give me some relief. I also get pretty sore in my upper shoulder and neck area from these shots. But over all they are doing their job and I was able to finally receive chemo this past Tuesday! I was ready. I was starting to see some redness return to the skin on my right breast, it was getting hot to the touch and itchy. All signs that the caner is rearing its ugly head again on my skin. I also began to have some hip aches on my right side over my three weeks off. Never a good sign when the cancer seems to be able to creep back into my bones and body in only a three week window. My tumor marker jumped from 660 to 840 just after having the two extra weeks off from the chemo due to low counts. I can't tell you how frustrated I get with this song and dance. It's like two steps forward ten steps back. Enough of that complaining. Needless to say, I'm very glad that I am back on the chemo and hopefully will not have such highs and lows in how I am feeling. The longer I am on a particular chemo the better I am able to tinker with my pain and nausea meds to try to stay on top of any side effects. It can be a full time job. Good days = lots of activity and bad days = no activity. It's not hard to figure out. I just have to listen to my body. I just wish it would coincide properly with my social calendar and the things I would like to take part in. The hardest part is probably having everyone see me in such fluctuation of how I am feeling. It feels like everyone's plans always hinge on how I am feeling, which I truly appreciate, but I can only imagine how annoying that must be over time. Poor Aaron is constantly trying to guesstimate my state of health so we can make plans. I try really hard not to let it seep into our lives any more than it has too. Just because I am having an off day it doesn't mean everyone around me has to be off too. I'm still trying to convince Aaron that it is ok to leave me be on the bad days and take Kayden and live life! He's not so good at leaving me behind :) I can only imagine it's one of those danged if you do danged if you don't instincts he must feel when it comes up. Ha Ha. I keep telling him GO. Have fun! I would rather be miserable in peace honestly! He is so good about picking up where I have to drop things sometimes, whether it's with Kayden, or the dishes or whatever task it may be... he does it without complaint. I can't tell you how lucky I am to have him by my side through all of this. It truly does make it easier for me to know that he is there to lean on.

On a positive note, my hair seems to be hanging in there even after the third dose of chemo last week. I don't want to get too excited yet... I try to expect the worst so I won't be disappointed on matters of cancer. I have been preparing Kayden for over a month now telling her that my medicine will cause all of my hair to "get out" as she calls it. Now that it's been over a month she has a lot of questions as to "why" and "when" the medicine will work? Not an easy question to answer and she requires more then just simple answers of course. It's funny because people don't necessarily want to ask me if they talk to me via phone, but you can tell they are wondering. Then when I see them they are surprised that I have a full head of hair! I like to tell people that I promise not to let it get all creepy thin like on the horror movies, or start my own comb over look! I will definitely shave it way before that!!! Although it would be kind of fun if halloween was around the corner :) Who knows if it is here to stay or if this current cycle of chemo will be the end of it... I continue to wait with baited breath and I try not to worry about it all that much. It is definitely possible that since I naturally have thick hair and a lot of it that it could just thin and I might just dodge this bald bullet.... everyone knock on some wood now. I will keep you posted!

It's taken me all weekend to get this update finished so I hope it doesn't jump all over the place as you read it! Today is a "good" day for me and I have spent it weeding our jungle, I mean landscaping this morning. I have to go in to get my blood draw at 3:30 to make sure my counts are high enough to get chemo tomorrow. If my Nuepogen shots are doing their job then there should be no problem. Aaron and I are going to have a little date night tonight. I'm making him go see the new Twilight movie. Fun Fun!

Much love from me to you on a "good" day-

Jamie

Advocate

79

RACE FOR THE CURE KANSAS CITY

July 12, 2010

Race for the Cure Kansas City

As you may already know the Kansas City - Susan G. Komen Race for the Cure is coming up on Sunday, August 8th, 2010 at 7:30am. This 5K race is something I have participated in no matter where we were living. We try not to inundate people with requests to support our cause, so this race is our personal request for this year. I've done both the Indianapolis, IN and Nashville, TN one, but my favorite race has always been the Kansas City one! My friends have had a Team Jamie for the past 3 years and it continues to grow every year! I want to invite you all to participate as we raise funds to go towards critical drug research that may just help save my life some day!

If you would like to donate to Team Jamie or walk/run as a part of Team Jamie please sign up soon! The deadline is July 25th at 7:00pm.

Click here to participate or make a donation for Team Jamie!

You can sign up to participate in the race from this site or make a donation towards our Team Fundraising goal of $2000 which I hope we blow past! The registration fee is $25 to participate and you do not have to actively fundraise if you don't feel comfortable doing so. I am just excited to have everyone there the day of the race. It is a very fun and exciting event that I would love to share with all of my support crew. As a team we will wear our Team Jamie shirts that can be obtained from my merchandise page on the www.lovingpink.com site. I am working now to have tank tops available... no promises at this point. I will let you know! So lace up your shoes or get out your checkbooks! It's time to get together and Race for the Cure together!

Thanks as always for your continued support in our fight against breast cancer! I can't wait till race day!

Jamie

Bubbly

80

TIME TO GET MOVING....

August 20, 2010

Time to get moving...

So much to cover in this update! We had an AWESOME day at the Komen Race for the Cure in Kansas City on August 8th. There were 45+ people signed up to walk/run in my honor. Talk about a humbling experience! I was able to have some Team Jamie tank tops and dry fit muscle tee's made up just in time for the race thanks to my friend Carrie Peterson at Branding Stop in Lenexa. Our team captain Kelli (Sweeney) Alldredge and I stayed up Saturday night putting everyone's race numbers together with their race shirts and tank tops. It was an early morning for all as we met away from downtown and attempted to car pool. It was quite a feat to try to keep such a big group in one place headed in one direction so we could start the race together. I definitely learned a few tricks we can use to make next year even better. Like a Team Jamie sign we can hold up so you can see over the crowd of 30,000 people's heads! I was walking around with my camera held up in the air trying to get everyone together. Fun Fun! It was so cool to see everyone in their shirts and I felt so loved and supported. I can't even begin to put it in words. It is an event I look forward to every year and I am so proud to have such an amazing support system to be there for me! Our team alone was able to raise over $4000 between our donations and our swim party we had afterwards!! I added the new shirts to the merchandise page on my www.lovingpink.com site and also added some pictures of the event. Thanks again to everyone who participated and contributed to such a successful day!

As far as health goes. I have been doing really well this past month. I continue to receive the Gem/Carbo combination chemotherapy, as well as Zometa (my monthly bone builder). Since I last updated you all I have been entered into a clinical trial/compassionate use trial for a drug called BSI-201. This drug is in the process of being approved by the FDA. In the interim they will be offering what is referred to as a compassionate use of the drug to people who qualify for it. I fall in to that category. I have been working with the Kansas City Cancer Clinic to be enrolled in the process. The good news is that this drug would be done along side the drugs I am already doing. My name is now in a drawing of other eligible people hoping to get in the trial as well. They do a lottery drawing every Thursday to pick one name out to start the drug. This way it is ultimately fair for all of us in the way we are chosen to get the drug. I have not been chosen the past two weeks unfortunately, but I know that it will happen eventually! Then I will be able to add on a new arm to my current treatment in hopes to continue to beat back this cancer. Once I am chosen I will move all of my treatments to the Kansas City Cancer Clinic as that is where the trial is available. My most current tumor marker was down almost 100 points at 525 and continues to drop. For those of you that need a refresher- the tumor marker measures how well my cancer is reacting to the chemo. This is all good news!

Every since the Komen race I've been really trying to focus on getting more active, physically. If that many people can get up and walk in my honor that's the least I can do in return. So I have committed to working out with my friend Kelli at a 68's Gym in Overland Park. She is an awesome personal trainer and has been able to help me make the most of my time in the gym based on how I am feeling that day. Some days are better then others... but so far I have two full weeks under my belt and I am feeling better because of it! I can't wait to not be winded from a simple set of stairs. It is crazy how quickly your muscle tone can disappear with a few months of inactivity. Just because I have pain from my cancer/chemo... I am learning I can't just stay seated. It is not good for the body/mind or waist size! So I'm on a mission to get moving and hopefully maybe even get back out on the tennis court this summer! Especially since we hear about my pelvic fracture healing! All things to look forward to! In the meantime, we are still loving Lawrence. We have spent lots of time on the lake this summer. I was even up on the wakeboard a few weeks ago. I honestly never thought I was going to be able to do that again. It was quite a feeling to conquer yet another task I had put in the past. I sure like proving that things can still be done by this cancer girl!

I am sitting here in the hospital today getting a quick, well it's actually a long, blood transfusion. My hemoglobin count was low for the second week in a row- 8.6. We decided to do a transfusion to help me feel less fatigued and get some more oxygenated cells working in my body. It's a process we may need to do every few months as my body is taking extra long to recover from the effects of chemo. No worries... it's merely something we are being proactive about and I would love any extra energy I can get! I'm on my second pint of good ole B-blood and will be done by late afternoon. Aaron and I are attending a fabulous event tomorrow evening in Kansas City called "In Living Pink" it is a Galla for young survivors of breast cancer. We are excited to get dressed up and have a fun night out! I will be sure to take pics to share! Hope all is well with everyone as they get started with school and full fall schedules! We start soccer for Kayden on Saturday! I can't wait! Hopefully I can hold my tongue this season a little more on the sidelines. 4 year old soccer is brutal to watch sometimes! Talk to you soon!

Much love from my transfusion chair!

Jamie

Transcendental

81

LOVING OUR "NORMAL" LIFE!!

September 17, 2010

Loving our "normal" life!!

As I open my program to do this update I realize that my last update never published. Oops! So you are going to get a two for one today! I think that for some reason when I try to publish while I'm at the hospital it doesn't work, so I have to remember to do it when I get home. That's asking a lot you know! I'm sitting here in the waiting room of the oncology center at LMH (Lawrence Memorial Hospital) waiting to go back to my own special room for my chemo infusion this week. I usually have chemo on Wednesdays but last week my platelets were too low to do chemo as scheduled on Wednesday. I had to wait a couple of days in hopes that my body would recover and I was able to get my gem/carbo on Friday finally. That was week one of my three-week cycle, which in turn means I had to get chemo on Friday this week. Fun Fun. Nothing like a round of chemo to kick off the weekend! I am also getting my monthly round of Zometa (bone builder), which I am typically kind of sensitive to. We will see....

Last week my tumor markers jumped up almost 40 points unfortunately. Not necessarily a good sign, but it can also mean a lot of things. I am hoping that it is just because I had such a great time over Labor Day weekend at the lake. We will wait and see if the upward trend continues, I will keep you updated, as we know more. I also found out that once again I had not been picked for the Parp trial lottery drawing. It's been just over 7 weeks, and I have been waiting patiently hoping it will be my turn soon. As long as everything is going well with my gem/carbo combo then I am not too stressed about being drawn, but as soon as there is a hint of there being a problem then all of a sudden I am itching to get started. I'm sure you can understand my mild concern! It's easy to let the doubt creep in at every little thing. Working on keeping a lid on that till we get more information.

I've been able to stick with my twice a week trips to Kansas City to do my workouts with Kelli! I have truly seen a difference in how I feel after each workout, and the slow change in my endurance, balance and strength. It's a painstakingly slow process compared to how I used to be able to workout... but Kelli has been a great cheerleader and helped me listen to my body and adjust my workout according to my level of fatigue/nausea and everything else that my body throws at us. I actually find myself enjoying my drive and the social aspect of meeting her other clients. I leave there feeling refreshed and like I accomplished something. A nice change from finding myself inactive and unproductive at home. So I am going to definitely keep with it and hopefully will continue to see positive physical results in the days to come!

Chemo was a success. I was able to finish both the Gemcitabine and the Zometa. So now I am headed to go pick Kayden up at school. We have soccer tomorrow morning and a fairly laid back weekend thankfully! Next week will be my off week for chemo which always brings a whirlwind of activity! I am headed to GA late next week to spend the weekend with Aaron's sister for her birthday. Sure looking forward to my ladies weekend of shopping and hanging out! Kayden is going to be maaaadddd when she finds out I am going to see Aunt Jen without her. She gets to go with Grandma and Papa later in November so she will get her chance!

I used a picture of myself and two other young survivors at the recent Topeka Race Against Breast Cancer. They are my "cancer girls". Carrie is in the middle and Leslie on the far right. We are all treated by my same doctor in Lawrence and we have become quick friends and are able to enjoy a monthly lunch where we catch up and compare notes :) So fun to have such great friends in a similar boat as I am. On another note I am also excited about another trip I recently booked for me to go to San Diego to be there during the big 3-Day Komen Race for the Cure my friends are taking part in! I am just going as a bystander to cheer them all on! Very excited for this opportunity to see my Team in action! Thanks so much Amy for my ticket to come and be a part of the action! I hope that I am not jinxing myself by making all of these travel arrangements for the next few months. My doctor encouraged me to make plans and travel especially as well as I have been feeling so that's what I'm doing! Cross your fingers that it all works out!

Now that October is almost here... I am looking forward to a month of Pink for breast cancer awareness! I have several fun events I am associated with coming up in the next month. I will post information and links for them this week, so be sure to check back! Better get back to my ever demanding 4 year old. She apparently cannot function without my help on ANYTHING right now!

Much love from a happy me to hopefully a happy you!

Jamie

Gleeful

82

COSTUMES FOR THE CURE!

September 20, 2010

Costumes for the Cure!

My friend is hosting a fun Fall photography session for kids in their Halloween costumes! There is a minimum $25 donation and all of that money goes to the Komen 3-Day Race for the Cure and you get all the images from your session! Pass on the word!

Shannon Hey Photography

Engaging

83

HANGING ON FOR THE RIDE...

September 28, 2010

Hanging on for the ride...

For several years now I have been a prisoner to my diagnosis. Pretty much all decisions are made based with one thing in mind, my cancer. As hard as I try I cannot leave that tad detail behind me no matter what I do. I can embrace it or I can wallow in it. Of course there is always the possibility that I may do a little of both when necessary. It is smooth sailing when life is good and it is a rocky road when things are not- just like your life. My roller coaster is just way more prone to derailment then most. Just a couple of weeks ago as I spent a weekend in GA with Jen, We were enjoying our weekend and shopping to our hearts content when I look down and see a large patch of what look like blood blisters on my leg above my right knee. Shreeeeeechhhh (that's the sound of my fun train coming to a halt)... what the heck is that?? I did a quick full body inspection and found several different areas of similar spots. They did not itch, they weren't raised and they didn't blanch when you pressed on them. All questions I asked to the WebMD page I immediately goggled, which by the way can be your worst enemy when trying to self diagnose. Looks like petechiae (pe-te-ke-a) according to the site. I texted my doctor and pondered on if it was a life or death issue, eventually deciding it was not... and dealt with it when I got home. It ended up that my platelets were very low, and I needed a bag of someone else's platelets infused into my body to help me get mine back up. So as soon as I got home I headed to the hospital and got hooked up to a bag of platelets. It didn't take near as long as getting blood takes. Not bad at all, and it did the trick. My platelet counts jumped back up in a couple of days. I also ended up getting blood later that week because my hemoglobin levels were low again. So needless to say I was having a low week all around and was hooked up to two bags of the good stuff- but all for good reason. I felt better for it and hopefully I won't have to do either again for a while.

I talked with my doctor about why this keeps happening, my counts taking so long to rebound. She explained that my body is tired after all of the chemo. The more tired it is... the longer it takes for them to recover. If we need to do these infusions in the future to help me limp along then we will. There is no medical reason I can't get infusions other then the fact that I am exposed to having a potential reaction to the stuff being infused (there is a bag of whatever hooked up to a needle that is inserted into my port for those of you that don't know what infused means). There is always that potential for a reaction when a foreign substance is introduced into the body, even blood that's the same type as mine. But that is not so bad considering how dangerous it is for me to hover in the low counts – which means that I am susceptible for infection. Ideally the most important thing is keeping me on the chemo, but we can't sacrifice my overall health in the end. So it is kind of a dance we will be doing to keep me healthy enough to do chemo if at all possible. I know all of this talk of low counts and staying healthy might make you think I am sickly. But truly that is not the case. I get tired and have down days... but to look at me you wouldn't know I was sick. I tell people that my 100% is more like your 75%. So we continue on with my same chemo regimen and do the infusions as necessary. It kind of sucks because I am always worried about where my counts are at, but there isn't much I can do unfortunately other then listen to my body and look for signs like my blood spots that alert me that something is going on. Welcome to my roller coaster =)

On another note I am still in the lottery for the compassionate use drug, the Parp Inhibitor Trial I talked about earlier this summer. There are different sites nationwide like the Kansas City one I am a candidate at. They each have their own pool of candidates. There is only enough drug being produced currently to add one person a week to the trail. So the name being selected each Thursday is drawn from the collective pool of all of us candidates. It's frustrating, but I continue to wait in hopes that my name will be drawn and I can add this new drug to my current regimen. Hard to tell if it is going to be that one thing that keeps my cancer at bay, but we won't know till I try it. I'd like to think that every cancer has a drug out there that can hold back the spread of the disease long term... rather then on a week to week basis as we are doing currently. Stabilizing is always good and I'm not complaining, but I would rather eradicate this disease if I got my choice!

As we march on into fall with our busy schedules and the holidays looming, I can't help but take a minute to appreciate where I am. I mean truly, here I was worried about being around to finish my gigantic bottle of shampoo earlier this year. I have managed to squeak by another season and am still able to say that I am in pretty good health, overall. I wish I could look into my crystal ball or be able to see the sands of my own hourglass. But we cannot and should not know this type of information. There is a reason we don't know. The weight of that knowledge is too much to bear, trust me, Aaron and I have witnessed that first hand. I need to not wallow or hover in my own mortality. No one should, we need to only look to the future and do everything in our power to make it a good ride. I keep trying to remember this when I begin to feel frustrated or down or overwhelmed by my obstacles. I continue to ride my roller coaster of emotions and put one foot in front of the other. I am thankful that I have what I have and I don't want the upcoming busy time of the year to cause me to lose sight of that. So slow down for just a minute and look around. We could all use a pause button every once in awhile, don't you think?

Much love-

Jamie

Love

84

HAPPY ANNIVERSARY TO ME...

October 19, 2010

Happy Anniversary to me...

I'm laying here tonight on the eve of my diagnosis- 4 years ago. That's right... 4 years ago (10/20/06) I was originally diagnosed with breast cancer. I have to laugh that I did a whole posting earlier today and didn't even mention that little tid bit. It's one of those dates you kind of want to forget... but I can't forget it. It needs to be a celebration of what I have overcome. Aaron even said "wow can you believe it was only 4 years ago?" Tell me about it! We sure have packed a lot into the last 4 years. Never a dull moment in our household.

I think about all of the other survivors I have met over the last 4 years. Other women, most of them young like myself, that are battling the same fight I am. So many stories that are all so different, but have the same common denominator. One of the first friends I made on this journey passed away this past February. I think about her often as she was a mother, who found her lump while breast feeding. She was metastatic when I met her in 2006. She and her husband were very helpful to us as we stumbled around at IU figuring out the ropes of chemo and the long days at the hospital. They both offered a great voice of reason for Aaron and I as we dealt with my metastatic diagnosis last November. It was a very hard blow to see her lose her fight to breast cancer at the age of 39. Tomorrow would have been her 40th birthday. As I caught her husband's latest update on his blog tonight I noticed that he had some new photos posted. I was extremely surprised to see that it was new family pictures and there was another woman in the photos. I realized after looking at his facebook status that he was engaged. In keeping to my honestly with you all... I was shocked. In my mind I couldn't believe that he had already moved on... and before I could voice that Aaron asked me why I was upset?? I knew I was being super sensitive.. but I just couldn't stop the tears. Here I am, not even sure of what their situation is or in any place to judge it... and I couldn't stop crying for my friend. In truth, it wasn't even that he was re-marrying, it was that in my mind he should still be missing her and not ready to move on. But who am I to decide what is ok and not ok for those that are left behind after a spouse dies? I feel so judgmental and horrible for my reaction to his happiness. It just hit so close to home with some of my inner most fears and feelings about dying. What is to become of our happy little family we have? How are they going to go on without me? But that's the thing about life... it moves on with or without you. I can't expect for him to wallow in his grief any more then I would want my loved ones to. Why wouldn't I want Aaron to be able to find love again and live a happy life once I am gone? How selfish am I that I think there is some acceptable amount of time that should pass before he gets to be happy again? I feel bad now because I know it is something that Aaron has probably wondered about, and now here I am making him feel like it is not ok to move on eventually. It's such a horrible thing to think about - but because of my cancer it is our reality. People die every day and leave loved ones behind. There is no handbook to how to grieve and we all do it differently. So as I think back to my friend and everything she taught me, I realize that she continues to help me even after she has passed. I know in my heart that she would have only wanted for her family to be happy again. I can say that I am grateful he has been able to bring that back into their lives, they all deserve it. I can only hope that if I am gone some day that my little family will be able to move on in their life and find happiness again. No matter how long it may or may not take.

I guess I was inspired to write about this as weird as it may seem. I just thought I would share. Two postings in one day must be a record, eh?!

Much Love-

Jamie

Biographer

85

GO FIGURE....

October 27, 2010

Go figure...

So today is another day I get to feel inspired to write. Unfortunately, it is fueled by frustration. I'm sitting here listening to the song that plays on my lovingpink site. It's called Hope (by Addison Road).

"Everything rides on hope now, Everything rides on faith somehow. So when the world has broken me down... your love sets me free."

There are times when all I can do is give it to God. Today is one of those days. I found out this morning that my tumor markers have made another big jump, over 150 points putting me back around 750. This is a pretty good sign that the cancer is out maneuvering the chemo again. I started this last chemo regimen on June 2nd, 2010. Assuming that we will move on to a new drug now, that means we got a mere 5 months out of this treatment. Dr. Soule uses tumor markers as only a guideline to what is going on in my body. We will be scheduling scans on Friday or Monday to get proof that the disease is progressing. Cancer can be a tricky beast, mine is no exception. As my previous oncologist said it is much like a high stakes game of chess. We attempt to block and out-maneuver the disease and it strives to push past all of our moves to get control of my body. Its only desire is to multiply and grow. It is going to essentially evolve however it needs to in order to be able to do this. We have to be one step ahead if at all possible.

We will continue to try drug regimens until we hopefully find that one key that can contain this beast inside me. My hope would be to get more then 5 months out of each drug but that's not always the case as we have seen. Some people find drugs that hold their cancer back for years before they have to move on to try new treatments. The faster we move through the drugs the closer we are to the bottom of the bag. At some point we will come to where we have no more drugs to try. That is a cliff I never want to be standing on. We can only hope that research continues to bring new drugs to the table and that we can stay ahead of my beast so I can continue the quality of life that I have now for as long as possible. It's scary to not know what to expect in the next week. I really hate this uncertain period we always deal with during scans and deciding our next move. Bring on the scan-xiety! It's hard not to fall back into my shadowy hole of what ifs. But this is all a part of the dance and I need to learn to deal with it so I don't find myself depressed and withdrawn. So I am going to stay busy and hope for the best at this point.

As I said at the beginning... give it to God. It's time I leaned a little more and struggled a little less.

I will keep you updated on scan results and what's next. I know you all worry about me when I get news like this... but please don't worry. It helps me lots to just sit here and write about it. I have a feeling I will have an extremely organized iTunes or kitchen cabinets or something. All are external things I can control when I personally feel out of control on the inside. Good therapy and it's free =) Thanks for letting me vent. Be in touch soon.

Much love from my frustrated heart,

Jamie

Update:

Funny thing happened after I did this posting this morning. I got a call saying my name had been drawn for the Parp Inhibitor trial. Well... that sure makes things a little more complicated. We are going to move forward with my scans on Friday and then discuss the results and make a collective call from there as to whether or not I am still eligible for the trial (may not be if the disease has progressed), and if that is the best route for me or if maybe I should start a new chemo. I'm not going to hang a lot of hopes on this new opportunity, but I'm glad to have another option. Only time will tell...

Journalist

86
RESULTS....

October 29, 2010

Results....

I wanted to fill you all in on my scan results since everyone has been so supportive today while I waited. I won't lie... I hate waiting. It makes me annoyed and agitated and I tend to want to hang by myself and not talk, so I apologize to anyone I haven't called back or responded to text wise. It's just been one of those days.

I was able to actually sit down with Dr. Soule (my oncologist) and go over the CT results this afternoon. The last CT I had done on 8/3/10, so we are comparing today's films to the previous ones. Here is a generalized gist of the results:

There has been disease progression- not super surprised after my tumor markers shot up like they did. Some people have asked what I mean by progression so I thought I would clarify that term so you can better understand the following information: Progression means that there is either growth of an existing lesion (spots of cancer) or new lesions when comparing that area to the previous scan in the same area. That being said, there are a couple of lymph nodes in my left armpit that have gotten bigger. I actually woke up this morning with an ache in my armpit. It ached all day today, don't know if it was because I was touching it more or because I was thinking about it more or what. Obviously if it is bigger then that explains the ache to some extent. There are also signs of disease progression in my lower back/tailbone area, specifically L1 to L4 vertebras. I have had some minor pain there that I attributed to just sleeping wrong or from working out. It hasn't been bad enough to take more than aspirin yet. It also showed that my right and left hip both have gotten worse. The biggest change is that there are new lesions in my liver and the one in the dome of the liver has gone from 1.8 x 1.3 cm to 3.0 x 3.3 cm. This is a lot of medical mumbo jumbo for most people... but the bottom line is that the chemo seems to be slowly not able to hold back the cancer as much as we has hoped. None of the above progression is life threatening, not at this point at least. It is very concerning, I won't lie. It's not good that the chemo is already starting to fail, but we still have some options so that is what we are going to focus on.

I basically have two options that we talked through this afternoon.

Option #1- Take part in the trial and continue on with my current drugs, but add in the parp inhibitor to see if it makes a difference.

Option #2- Forget the trial and start on a new chemotherapy all together. The next drug I would do is Ixabepilone in conjunction with Avastin (which I did in a previous trial back in 2007).

For the sake of having this opportunity to do the trial we have decided to go with the first option. I don't want to move forward with a new chemo and look back and wonder if the parp inhibitor could have been the key to my treatment. It seems almost too perfect that I was finally picked after waiting all summer, just when I needed it most, maybe it was meant to be? I'd like to think so. Either way, I am taking the chance. We still need to work out the logistics with the Kansas City Cancer Clinic (KCCC) where I will receive all of my drugs once I start the trial. My hope is that we are able to start as soon as Monday or Tuesday next week, but until we are able to talk with the Dr. in charge there we won't know details on when I start.

I'm exhausted and will fill you all in more on Monday after we have had a chance to discuss the final details of my schedule with KCCC. Aaron, Kayden and I appreciate your support and positive thoughts, vibes and prayers or what ever you have sent our way. I feel the LOVE! I am anxious and am trying not to hang a lot of hope on any one thing at this point. I just want to get started so I can again begin to rid my body of this disease once more. One step at a time. That's all we can do.

Much love and hope,

Jamie

Blogger

87
WOO WOO WOO…..

November 5, 2010

Woo Woo Woo....

Lucky me... this is how my morning started today. On my way to Kansas City to get started on my new drug! Guess I was a little too eager to get there...riiiiiigggghhhhht. Truth be told- I was really running late as usual and took a shortcut that had a 30 mph speed limit in which I was driving 46 mph when he pulled me over. He was very nice but I could tell he wasn't going to be quick to give me a warning, so I did it. I pulled the cancer card. I don't do that very often but I was shameless this morning, explained I was on my way to my first day of a new chemo at a new place in KC. Luck was on my side. He wrote me a warning and very nicely explained that my ticket could have cost $174. Ouch! That is an expensive mistake he said. No kidding! Aaron would have throttled me! So with tears in my eyes I drove away hoping this was a sign that my luck was taking a turn for the better. It's gonna be a good day for me on the cancer front. Yep it is. Getting the good stuff again and kicking cancer in the arse. That's my plan for the day.

So for those of you that have not been caught up on this weeks events since my scan results, I got final word on Wednesday that I was going to be able to start the new trial drug. I was pretty insistent that I start my chemo back up as soon as possible (I've been off for almost 4 weeks now with all of the waiting) so they jumped through hoops and were able to get me on the schedule for first thing today, Friday. I am excited and hopeful that this trial will offer opportunity for me to stay on the Gem/Carbo regimen for as long as possible. For the sake of an easy explanation here is how my chemo schedule will work now:

Day 1- Gem/Carbop and also the Parp Inhibitor (actual drug name is BSI-201) 3-4 hours in the chemo chair.

Day 8- Parp Inhibitor- 1 hr in chemo chair.

Day 11- Gem/Carbop and also the Parp Inhibitor (actual drug name is BSI-201) 3-4 hours in the chemo chair.

Day 15- Parp Inhibitor- 1 hr in chemo chair.

All will be done at the Kansas City Cancer Clinic (from here on out I will call it KC3), all done intravenously through my port. Same side effects I've been dealing with all summer- mainly fatigue and slight nausea. The Parp Inhibitor does not add any additional side effects supposedly. The jury is still out on that. I am currently hooked up and getting my first dose of the new drug now. I can only hope with every fiber of my being that this will buy us lots more time, and I promise I will be grateful for every minute of it! Cross your fingers, cross your toes, whatever you can do to keep the good luck coming our way. I can use it! As always I so appreciate your support and love and cards and messages. My support system is the best! I wish I could loan you out sometime for someone that isn't so lucky as I am. I'll keep you updated as to how this first week goes with the new drug!

Much love from my new seat at KC3-

Jamie

Grateful

88

ANOTHER DAY, ANOTHER DECISION....

December 18, 2010

Another day, another decision...

I left off last time by telling you that I had been accepted into the trial and had started my first cycle (3 weeks) of the trial drug, the parp inhibitor. We went into that trial knowing there was a slim chance that my body was already rejecting the gemcitabine and carboplatin (chemos that are used in conjunction with parp inhibitor), as my tumor markers had began to creep up in the weeks prior to me being drawn for the trial. We made the decision to go for it in hopes that adding the new drug might make the difference. I was feeling pretty good overall, tired as usual but that's nothing new. My second cycle was unfortunately disrupted by a trip Aaron and I, my parents and another couple had planned to Bora Bora starting Nov. 30th. The doctors were very understanding that this trip was very important to us and they worked with us to make sure I was able to make it. Right before the trip we did a tumor marker to see how the first cycle had done... it came back with a huge increase- went from 850 up to 1800. Not good. It was frustrating news to carry with us onto the trip, but we didn't have much of a choice. Even if we stayed and skipped the trip it wouldn't ensure that another cycle of chemo would bring that number back down. Aaron and I made the decision to go and enjoy ourselves and come back refreshed and ready to make whatever changes were necessary with my treatment path.

So we jumped on the plane and enjoyed our trip (I will do a separate update on that since there is so much to share). It was an amazing time, we were able to relax and really have a good time together. We got back into KS on Dec. 7th. As soon as we touched down in Kansas City bleary eyed from 24 hours of travel- I started having chest pains on my left side before we even got off the plane. I immediately went to the worst case scenario... blood clot. I was in a lot of pain and started to get pretty worried after it didn't get better from pain pills. I talked to my oncologist in Lawrence and we both agreed I should go ahead and go to the ER to get the pain checked out. We rolled into Lawrence around 7:00pm and I gave Kayden a big birthday hug, heard all about what she did while we were on vacation (traveled with Aaron's parents), I showered and was at the ER by 8:30pm. To make a long story short it was quite a mess at the ER between my port not wanting to work, and the immense amount of medical history they had to shuffle through to figure my case out. Finally after quite a bit of back and forth they admitted me to the hospital at about 2:30am with a diagnosis of pulmonary embolism. Not good at all... I was extremely concerned and still in pain. They started me on blood thinners right away to try to keep the PE from moving anywhere else in the body. It can be fatal if it were to travel to the heart or lungs or brain. Scary stuff. My oncologist, Dr. Sherri Soule, stopped by and we talked about the situation. She was very concerned as well and wanted to go back and look over the scans they had done the previous night in the ER. In the end she asked for a CT scan to be done to get a better look at my chest and the PE. I got that test done around lunch time on Wednesday. By 1:30pm they had called me to tell me that I did not have a pulmonary embolism, wheeewww! It was actually early signs of pneumonia in my left lung, there are many nerves in the lungs and that was what was causing the pain. The pneumonia is able to be treated with a heavy dose of antibiotics. A much better option then the daily shots I would have been doing to thin my blood for a PE. Needless to say I believe there were more than a few prayers answered in my case. I was able to leave the hospital and be home for dinner Wednesday night. I started my meds that night and had to take them for 7 days. The pain got better each day which was a relief. I did have some after effects of the pneumonia being that I was short of breath and pretty wiped out for a couple of days after I left the hospital. I had Thursday and Friday to prepare for Kayden's big birthday party we were hosting at our house Saturday morning, which was also the same day as my 35th birthday. Needless to say it has been a whirlwind since we've been back.

The birthday party was a blast! The theme was pancakes and pajamas this year and they all came at 9am. It was absolute chaos with each kid picking their own toppings and helping us cook the pancakes. We had strawberries, blueberries, bananas, chocolate chips and more. It was quite the spread! I can honestly say that this is the LAST year we are doing the party at our house. These kids are just getting too big to have running around and bouncing off one another. She was all smiles as she opened her gifts and had a great time for sure! Thankfully I had my sister-in-law to be, Heather, there as well as my awesome friends at the party that jumped in to help me out when I ran out of steam, which I did. It took all weekend for me to recover but it was more than worth it! I spent the rest of Saturday relaxing and enjoying my birthday. Kayden had a slumber party that night so Aaron and I went out for sushi and then cuddled up with a redbox movie. A perfect 35th birthday!

We had to get back to business once Monday rolled around. I got word that my tumor marker had gone up another 1000 points, which ended up at 2800. I was so frustrated at this point. It was more than obvious that the trial drug in Kansas City was not doing anything for me at this time. I was sad to withdraw, but both Aaron and I realized that it was time to move on to a new drug. And that is what we have done. Along with my previous oncologist in Indianapolis and Dr. Soule in Lawrence we decided to use Halaven which is a drug that was recently released by the FDA in November. I spent this week doing new baseline scans such as a CT scan, an EKG to check my heart, and we also did some x-rays of my mid back, lower spine and hips and pelvis. These tests all just give us a snapshot of my body prior to starting this new drug. That way once we get a cycle or two under my belt then we can see exactly where the changes are at. The scan results showed that liver, lungs and bones all showed signs of progression. This information just reinforces the fact that we needed to change drugs. I tried not to get down about all of that crappy news and instead just focus on this new opportunity to come back to Lawrence for my treatments and start the new drug regimen. I got my first dose under my belt this past Thursday. So far so good.... not a lot of side effects. I'll keep you posted. My next dose will be this Thursday and then I will have an off week. The side effects are very similar to my previous chemos and I hope to continue to keep my hair (hopefully I didn't just jinx myself).

Sorry this posting is purely informative but I had so much information to share with you. I promise to work on getting you caught up on all of the fun stuff we have had going on as well! I hope you are all enjoying the holiday season and have plans to spend time with your family and friends this next week! We love you all and wish you a very Merry Christmas!

Much love from my whirlwind-

Jamie

Gifted

89

HAPPY NEW YEAR!

January 7, 2011

Happy New Year!

Can you believe it is already 2011?? What are your resolutions? It's safe to say that the Pursley motto will be to find HEALTH in the New Year! It's been very busy around here the past month so I will try to hit on the highlights.

On Dec. 16th I started the new chemo Halaven. It's a quick process, 5 minutes at most. It's nice to not be there as long. The side effects have seemed pretty similar to all the others. The typical fatigue is my biggest complaint. I ended up having some signs of pneumonia show up on my right side and we did another round of antibiotics to get over that. We went into Christmas with light hearts and happy to be surrounded by family (and loving not having to do the 10 hour drive from Kentucky to get here!). Santa was very good to us this year. He must have overlooked all those time outs little miss found herself in =) She was very into leaving out the cookies and getting a note from Santa the next day. Between turning 5 and Christmas, Kayden has been VERY blessed this month! It takes us at least a month to undo all of the fanfare she has had. All in all it was a wonderful time and we are so absolutely lucky to be surrounded by our families and feeling their love!

At the last minute we made a decision to make the 10-hour drive (AGH!) back to Bowling Green to spend New Year's with our friends there. It was so worth the drive! =) We had not seen many of them since we moved in Feb. last year. It was great to catch up and see how much all of the kids had grown. Kayden was in heaven with her old gaggle of girls she used to run around with, oh- and Meyer of course! It truly filled my soul up with enough love to last me quite awhile. We were so glad it all worked out. I feel lucky to have been able to live there for 3 short years and have made such amazing friends. My life is definitely fuller having these people in my life.

Unfortunately, while in KY my hair started to fall out, more then just shedding. It started on New Year's Eve and progressively got worse. I'm sure both the Melda's and the Gable's will have to put some Drain-o in their drains thanks to me. It was a frustrating blow after making it a whole year on chemo and not losing it. I truly had started to take it for granted. I was surprised how much it affected me. I thought I had prepared myself better than that. I had a minor break down Sunday morning before we went to church because I could hardly make it look reasonable enough to leave the house. Everywhere I went I was leaving behind long strands of my hard earned hair. It was just not fair. To top it off I had noticed some red inflammation on my right breast again. Just like earlier this summer when the chemo wasn't working and the cancer showed up on my skin. It was disheartening to think that it was possible that this new chemo wasn't even working and it was going to take my hair as well. Argh.... here we go again. Sometimes it just feels like one thing after another. I would give anything to just be able to have a normal life again, to not have to constantly worry, or hurt, or struggle, or rise above. I'm tired. I'm tired. I'm tired. There I said it. I'm not some super human breast cancer poster girl. I'm just a girl struggling to live. Some days I feel like I just wasn't cut out for this, but know what? It doesn't matter. It's happening and there's nothing any of us can do about it. So I do what is necessary and march on. I get to do it bald... again. So we have rung in this New Year with high hopes that the next round of chemo will kick in and get to work. It's too soon to have to move on again. Not an option. My tumor markers are up again from 2800 to 7000. We made the decision to do another cycle and give this drug a chance to work before stopping. We also made the decision to add a hormone blocker called Faslodex into my regime. Just on the off chance we are missing something going on inside treating it as a triple negative cancer. I had my first dose yesterday of this cycle. I'll touch base in the next two weeks to let you know how it's going.

Much love from my comfy bed-

Jamie

ps: Be sure to check out the pictures! I've added many and have more coming.

Awesome

90

THE BOOK THAT CAPTURED MY HEART...

January 11, 2011

The book that captured my heart...

I sit here on this snowy day with Kayden engrossed in a Scooby Doo movie and Roxy holding down the blankets on the bed. I've been reading the recently released book by Nancy Brinker- the founder of Susan G. Komen (in honor of her deceased sister). It was given to me by Aaron's aunt Sunny who has a bookstore in Seattle. What an appropriate gift! Many thanks to Aunt Sunny!

As many of you know I went to San Diego in November to cheer on my very own Team Jamie in the Susan G. Komen 3- Day walk. I have a ton of pictures I am working on getting up so you can look at them, better late then never! My A-mazing friends raised $31K. Yep- you read that right! $31,000. Now that is impressive!! We hope to break $40K next year and add more team members to Team Jamie- San Diego. The whole race raised $10.6 million dollars. That is a lot of money going to such an important cause, and more importantly breast cancer research which we all know is what my life is depending on. So needless to say I am a true believer in the Susan G. Komen foundation and their fundraising. I am truly grateful for their hard work that gets us closer to eradicating the disease. So I was super excited to be able to read about how it all came about in the book about Susan Komen.

Right away it captured my heart and soul as I read it, peeking into the lives of another family ravaged by this disease. It has been tough to read at times because of the similarities to my own situation. The book has captured so many of the emotions that I have been through over the past four years. I have several times felt the urge to get a hi-lighter out and note the things that felt as if they came from my own heart... truly I couldn't have said it better myself. She talks about how hard it was to watch her sister battle for her life, to constantly struggle to hang on to the positive and hope and continue to speak of the future. It gives insight to what it is like to be a co-survivor. To feel powerless and out of control, racked with guilt and fear and contempt for the beast that is cancer. Pride and beauty, health and endurance... this is only the beginning of a list of things that cancer strips from your life. I find myself overwhelmed with a duty to maximize my life. I feel indebted to leave things behind that will in a sense allow me to continue on way past my physical existence. A journal, a song list, a recipe book, a how to raise Kayden manual, a reason for everyone to not forget me. What a burden this creates on my heart. How can I possibly think that all of these things will ever replace the memories and moments that I have created unknowingly in my life with each of you.

The things that I would love to do are just that... things. Don't get me wrong, I plan to still do some of those things. But I think I need to stop feeling like my legacy is those things. That makes the tasks seem way more manageable in my mind. I know this is kind of deep... but I guess I was feeling inspired to write and in staying true to that promise to share my journey with you that is what I did in this post.

Please don't confuse my mindset with giving up or being at the end or anything like that... it's just part of my cycle of emotions that I go through all the time.

Much love to you all-

Jamie

Shopper

91

TIME FOR THE HAIR TO GO...

January 13, 2011

Time for the hair to go...

I have made it almost an entire year on 3 different chemotherapies without losing my hair; unfortunately it started falling out on New Year's Eve. Boo. It was 2006 the last time I lost my hair. It has taken a long time for me to have it back to where I love it, but unfortunately it wasn't in the cards for me to keep it with this latest chemo. After several days of this massive hair loss it was obvious that it was time to shave it. I had a couple of bummer days where I kind of grieved the loss, but once it was time, I was ok with it and able to move on. On the bright side, there are a lot of perks to not having hair!

Aaron and Kayden helped me do the task this past Wednesday. Kayden was so sweet holding my hand and patting my back, even wiping my tears at one point. Aaron manned the clippers and we attacked the task at hand. I had a friend, Chris Deffenbaugh, video it and I will share that video once he edits it and gets it back to me. Not really wanting to dwell on it at this point. I've dug out my old hats, bandanas and scarves. I even went to check out a place in Kansas City yesterday to see if I could find a wig. It was a great experience! I loved Tina the owner of Wigged Out and had lots of variety in styles. My friend Kelli came to help me decide what looked good. I was excited to find one I really liked. I'm not promising that I will wear it all the time because it is definitely something to get used to, but it is great to have this option to play with and shake things up when I want to! Hopefully you will like it too. I will post pictures soon! Better go for now- I have chemo today!

Much love from a professional baldy-

Jamie

Powerful

92

ACTIVATE TEAM JAMIE PRAYER CHAIN

February 2, 2011

Activate Team Jamie Prayer Chain

I am so blessed to have all of you out there following my journey and sending prayers my way. I would like to use that power of prayer to help out someone else.

Recently I found out that one of Kayden's favorite classmate's is having brain surgery for her epilepsy. She is 3 almost 4 years old. Her name is Sydney. She has already had one surgery just before she was 2.

They will have to shave Sydney's head unfortunately. Hopefully now that all of the children in her class have seen my bald head around it won't be such a surprise when she finally is able to get back to class. Plus Kayden will be a great liaison to help the other kids understand it better. I really wanted to do anything I could to help so I commissioned my friend Sue, whose husband is currently going through brain cancer treatment, to make some pint sized hats. She is an avid sewer and jumped at the chance to help and was able to make 4 hats (including one that had a tiara crocheted into it!) for her in a very short time frame. Thanks again Sue! I included her hats in a little care package we made for her and we were able to see them Sunday so Kayden could give her a hug goodbye.

The surgery is scheduled for tomorrow morning, Feb. 3rd, in Cleveland, OH (there is a speciality doctor there). Her mom and her flew up Monday while her father stayed behind to get their oldest daughter settled while they are gone. He is now working to get there with all this weather. First of all I'd like to request prayers for his safety as he gets to OH in time for the surgery. Second, I request prayers for Sydney's safety, a successful surgery, a speedy recovery, as well as the ability to understand what is happening to her as she goes through this. Lastly, I want to request prayers for strength and comfort for her family during this scary time.

I know you guys and I know what you can do with your prayers! So please help me with these specific requests.

I am doing well and have had one round of the new chemo so far. It's a tough one, leaving me queasy and sleepy. It feels like it's definitely doing something so far! Let's keep our fingers crossed! I will post again soon!

Much love from our little igloo-

Jamie

Missed

93

THE FUN STUFF....

February 25, 2011

The fun stuff....

I have a lot of positive things that have happened that I would like to dedicate time on my blog to but unfortunately I can only brush over these as I have other information I need to share in the following post.

Last Saturday I had the opportunity to participate as honorary coach for the Kansas Jayhawks Ladies Pink Zone game against the Missouri Tigers. It is such a small world. It turns out that a couple, The Capps, we were friends with in Bowling Green, have family in Eudora. They introduced my story to Katie Capps (seen in the pic above) here in KS and she had been following my journey. Katie also works on the staff of the Ladies basketball game and offered me up as a potential coach for their annual basketball game honoring breast cancer. We got to sit behind the bench, go into the locker room with the team before and after... and we got to see an awesome game that went into OT with a win for the Jayhawks. It was such an awesome opportunity and I can't thank Katie, the team and its coaching staff enough for the chance for my family to enjoy the excitement! In addition to the fun I was also nominated to receive two free airline tickets from Allegiant Airlines for Aaron and I to use to go to Phoenix, Vegas or LA. I was so surprised/excited to have that gift given to us. To those that are wondering... yes these Wildcats did wear the KU attire and no we didn't sneak in any purple =) I was proud to wear a pink shirt with a Jayhawk on it! Aaron borrowed a shirt, ha ha! Kayden on the other hand wore a pink dress and black tights with purple leopard spots on it. I swear she dressed herself in those tights!

I also had the opportunity to take part in the third annual Rally for the Cure tennis event at the Wood Valley Racquet Club in Topeka. It's an event my mom has been involved in since its inception. It has grown steadily each year and I was excited to help with getting the word out on this year's event. I got to do a spot on a local TV show (Ralph Hipp @ 4pm on WIBW), and the Topeka Capital Journal also interviewed me. It was a lot of fun!

The only downside is that I wasn't able to take part in the tennis playing itself. =(I miss playing a lot. I will be posting pictures of both events as soon as possible.

One last piece I wanted to share since I know many of you have been following and praying for our sweet Sydney, Kayden's friend that recently had brain surgery for her epilepsy. She was released from the hospital and they flew home today! She still has a long road to recover before she will return to school but I am sure it will be very helpful for the whole family to be back in the comfort of their home! Those prayers helped and I hope you continue them as she continues to heal and learn to live with things that have changed for her.

You have to forgive me for doing two posts again but I don't want things to get too long and it is easier for me when I get behind on posting to do it this way. I will sign off from this and move on to my next posting.

Much love,

Jamie

"i feel indebted to leave things behind that will in a sense allow me to continue on way past my physical existence:

94

THIS IS A HARD ONE....

February 26, 2011

This is a hard one...

Well... I know this is the posting that most of you were probably expecting to read this morning after all of the postings on Facebook and word of mouth over the last 24 hours. Unfortunately, there has been a change in my health over the past three days. I will do my best to explain things without getting too detailed. I plead that if you have questions you can email myself or Aaron and we will do our best to answer them health wise.

Wednesday morning I woke up and felt very discombobulated for lack of a better word. I was stumbling a bit right when I got out of bed, but it seemed to get better as I got ready for my appointment to get my labs drawn that morning. I was hoping to start moving my chemo days closer to the beginning of the week so my crappy days weren't interfering with my weekends and spending time with Aaron and Kayden. While I was at the hospital I told them about my stumbling and they decided to do a head MRI to make sure that nothing had possibly gotten into the brain. We held our breath and thankfully that scan came back normal. My labs also showed that day that my blood counts were not quite where we needed them to be to get chemo so I made an appointment to go back Thursday morning.

Thursday morning when I went back in my labs were drawn and showed an increase in my liver enzymes and my Bilirubin levels. Both of these are indicators of liver function. Both levels had increased from the previous day's labs. I have been feeling pretty bloated and full lately but had shrugged it off to the shrinking of my stomach, as I hadn't been eating much, so when I did I was quick to feel full. Dr. Soule made the decision to do a chest and abdomen CT scan to get a better look of what was going on in with my liver. We had to wait overnight to get the results and she called Friday morning on her way to work. I so appreciate how she is willing to make conference calls with Aaron and I so we are getting the same info and can ask questions on the spot, it helps getting news so much. The results showed that my tumors on my liver had actually caused the liver to become compromised (not function properly). The liver has actually begun to push up into my rib cage and against my lungs. There is a small pocket of air in one lobe as well as an area that has become collapsed and caused me to become short of breath... another symptom I have had but contributed it to being out of shape from this last chemo. Aaron took the day off to come in and meet with Dr. Soule at the office yesterday to discuss what our options were. At this time the liver is our top priority and we need it to subside and begin to function properly because it can affect so many other things in the body. There is a slim chance that the previous chemo could have caused the liver to go down this path. We can only know with time at this point. The further out we get from that chemo my liver function could get better. We also made the choice to start yet another chemo in hopes that it will assist in the process of rectifying the situation. We are on a time clock. My body and bone marrow are so tired from everything we have put it through. It's hard to tell how things will go with this new chemo. I will get it once a week for three weeks and then I will have an off week.

A long time ago I asked that Shari (my doctor) let me know when I needed to worry. Yesterday she said those words to me. I can't tell you how much those words cut through my cloud of reality that I have been coasting on for the last year. It's scary, it's incomprehensible, it's immobilizing. I asked if I needed to call hospice yet and her answer was no. We are still fighting this with all we have. We will have to take it one week at a time as we draw labs on Fridays and hope the liver tests get better, not to mention continuing to get my chemo doses. That is our best-case scenario. We are praying for the health of my liver to be returned. Unfortunately we can't do anything else to make this happen. No surgery, no transplant, and radiation is not an option. So I am staying strong and putting a whole lot of faith in the fact that my time is not done here. I feel that He is here and comforting my fears, but it's not my time to go. He has to know that.

As you can probably imagine, Aaron, my family and myself continue to absorb this quick turn of events and emotions are all over the place. I know this leaves so many of you feeling helpless and I don't have all the answers, but I want you to know how much I love and appreciate each and everyone of you. I would like to list one of my best friends as a contact to help keep some of the phone calls and emails down a bit on our end. We are going to work on some plans that may help with offers for meals and possible visits or other things that may come up easier to organize. Here is her information:

Robin Wilson-

If you have medical questions or want to just drop a note please send to Aaron's email or mine.

I may not be able to respond to everyone but know that I read each message. It was a long restless night and I still have things here at home that I am taking care of, so I will have to sign off for now. I promise to keep in touch and please remember to pray for my liver's health and comfort for Aaron, Kayden, my family and of course myself.

Much love to you all,

Jamie

EPILOGUE

After a valiant fight with breast cancer, Jamie was welcomed into Heaven on March 29, 2011. Her words continue to stay with those of us who knew and loved her, and we hope they have been an inspiration to you as well.

To view pictures and read Jamie's blog online, visit www.lovingpink.com. Thank you for sharing in Jamie's story of belief, love, and hope.

All proceeds of this book will benefit Jamie's Wish Foundation, www.jamieswish.org. Keep reading to learn more about the origin of this amazing organization.

About Jamie's Wish Foundation

Throughout her cancer journey, Jamie spent many hours receiving chemotherapy in the infusion rooms in the Oncology & Hematology Center at Lawrence Memorial Hospital in Lawrence, KS. While she was facing her own difficult battle, she couldn't stop thinking of the people who would come after her and spend so much time in the same infusion rooms where she had been treated the last year of her life. Jamie wanted the 15 private infusion rooms to be a more comfortable and soothing space for patients as well as their friends and family. This was a perfect reflection of her selfless attitude in life.

Just before Jamie passed away, she shared a wish with several of her closest friends. Her last wish was to renovate the 15 private infusion rooms at LMH. It was extremely important to her. Jamie's friends gathered together on the eve of her passing and vowed to her that they would fulfill her dying wish.

Those friends created a foundation titled Jamie's Wish immediately after her death. Almost a year to the day of her passing, Jamie's wish came true. Thanks to the generous support of the Lawrence, KS community, as well as donations from individuals and organizations around the country, the organization raised nearly $150,000 to bring Jamie's wish to life! The renovation included 15 new infusion chairs for the patients, new guest seating in each room, new flooring, new paint, new flat screen TV's, and new countertops to create a true comfortable environment based on Jamie's vision.

Jamie's friends that started Jamie's Wish realized that there are many oncology infusion centers that need renovation to create a peaceful place for patients to receive treatment. Jamie's Wish was formally turned into Jamie's Wish Foundation in the summer of 2016 and has become a 501©3 non-profit organization. The foundation is managed by an all-volunteer staff who continue to move Jamie's last wish of renovating oncology infusion centers forward. They have recently started working on the next patient-driven project, which will include renovating the infusion room at the University of Kansas Cancer Center North in Kansas City, MO. To learn more about this project, and to be a part of continuing to shine Jamie's light, please visit www.jamieswish.org.

Made in the USA
Middletown, DE
05 August 2017